MEN, MONEY, AND MAGIC

Books by Jeffrey Potter
DISASTER BY OIL

For Children
ELEPHANT BRIDGE
ROBIN IS A BEAR

MEN, MONEY & MAGIC

The story of
Dorothy Schiff

by

Jeffrey Potter

Coward, McCann & Geoghegan, Inc. New York

Second Impression

Copyright © 1976 by Jeffrey Potter

SBN: 698–10666–0

Library of Congress Cataloging in Publication Data

Potter, Jeffrey.
  Men, money and magic: the story of Dorothy Schiff.

  Includes index.
1. Schiff, Dorothy.   I.   Title.
PN4874.S33P6   070.5′092′4[B]   74–30608

PRINTED IN THE UNITED STATES OF AMERICA

Editor's Note

The form which this biography of Dorothy Schiff has taken requires a word of explanation. The reader will note that the narrative is carried sometimes by the author, Jeffrey Potter, and sometimes by the subject of the biography, Dorothy Schiff, speaking in her own voice. These extraordinary direct statements—a kind of oral history—supplement memos and other notes and diaries from Dorothy Schiff's personal and professional files which were made available to the author. The author selected and edited these rich materials, and Dorothy Schiff retained only the privilege of checking them for accuracy.

The result of this collaboration between author and subject is a portrait of a woman of our time which has taken its own form, one which permits the reader a more intimate view of the subject than is usually possible in a biography of a living person.

DOROTHY SCHIFF
Publisher

March 11, 1903 Born, daughter of Mortimer L. and Adele
              A. (Neustadt) Schiff

1923   Married Richard B. W. Hall
              Two children: Mortimer W. and Adele T.

1932   Married George Backer
              One child: Sarah Ann

1939–1942   Director, vice-president, and treasurer
              New York *Post*

1942   President and publisher, New York *Post*

1943   Owner and publisher, New York *Post*

1943   Married Theodore Olin Thackrey

1953   Married Rudolf Sonneborn

I

"Marriage was the only escape in those days, since you couldn't take an apartment on your own at eighteen. That was all I cared about, getting away from things."

An austere block-long building without name or trademark stands on Manhattan's South Street, between the Williamsburg and Brooklyn bridges. Although a number, 210, is over the busy revolving door, the roof of this structure bears no advertising, its flagpoles carry no banners, and the gray uniformed guards scarcely invite inquiries. Its identity is established by the New York *Post* delivery trucks crowding the loading bays around the corner. The owner, publisher and editor in chief of the newspaper is Mrs. Dorothy Schiff, who has been called "the most powerful woman in New York," an accolade she rejects.

"Influence, not power is what interests me," she says.

This mercurial lady, born to a line which has been traced back to King Solomon, is an original; her success, which amazes many and outrages some, merely bemuses her. A mother, grandmother and great-grandmother, she has attracted four husbands, the attentions of even more admirers and, at seventy-two, turns on men half her age. Reared in a luxury tainted by exclusion and rejection and so overprotected that a chaperone was always in attendance and public conveyances were forbidden until she was of college age, yet she has become a recognized leader of the liberal tradition in the East.

She is as at home with heads of state as with financial movers and shakers; she is an effective opinion maker, creator and breaker of hopeful candidates for office and daring political strategist; she is a cautious editor but adventurous publisher, self-assured executive but insecure hostess, superb seller of advertising space but loather of self-promotion; she is a conservative investor and careful spender; and, though one of the world's few unsalaried top executives, she owns and controls all the stock in her company.

In spite of all this, she is no stranger to depression, loneliness and anxiety, and she sees herself not as a heroine, but as an outsider fated to end up a failure. She is subject to acrophobia, claustrophobia and fear of conveyances, and in shyness, she will tighten her grasp on an escort's arm when entering crowded rooms.

Some say the better they know Dorothy Schiff the more "whys" there are. Why does she conceal her largess and concern for others with such modesty? Why proclaim all she ever wanted was a man to work for and live forever with (and then dismiss so many)? Why is she so dependent on routine that holidays are dreaded as an interruption?

There is something a little fragile about this slender, chic lady with the carefully upswept silver hair, fine-boned features and eyes that are of a blue that can be very blue indeed. The accumulation of her years becomes her, emphasizing the cool manner, graceful carriage and elegant simplicity of dress. Although she is always being given the names of *hauts couturiers,* her things are mostly ready-made ("it's not the money, but the time"); this her size 10 figure makes easy.

Her working costume is apt to consist of blouse, slacks and open-toed sandals, the shoes she much prefers. Asked why slacks are such a mainstay both at home and the office, she replies that they are comfortable and, in view of her habit of sitting with one leg tucked under her, practical. There is a drawback, she admits; they hide one of her particular assets.

"Serge [Colonel, formerly Prince Obolensky] said I had the 'finest gams' in New York. In fact, he still does. As a recognized connoisseur and the way he gets around at eighty-odd, he should know."

The memory brings a laugh. A somewhat distant smile is common enough with her, but laughter doesn't happen often. The eyes, widening with pleasure, take on a look the late Herbert Bayard Swope (the New York *World* editor) described as Coptic.

This is a word she prefers to Byzantine, which she associates with slyness.

It is hard to believe her accumulation of years and harder that of names. These are, in order of seniority: Dorothy Schiff, Hall, Backer, Thackrey, Sonneborn and, again, Schiff, making her a veritable Schiff of Schiffs. Formally, she is addressed as Mrs., a decision reached by her sole sibling, John M. Schiff, a general partner and the guiding light of the family bankinghouse, Kuhn (pronounced coon by old-timers), Loeb & Co. John, who is seventeen months younger than Dorothy and who serves as her conscience and benchmark, felt that a "Miss" would be inadequate in view of her three children. Occasionally, she gets a "Miss" anyway, and without objection by her, but she draws the line at Ms. ("it sounds awful, looks funny and just shouldn't be").

Husbands No. 1 and No.4—Richard B. W. Hall and Rudolf G. Sonneborn—called her Dorothy, while the middle mates— George Backer and Theodore O. Thackrey—favored Dolly. Admirers varied, too: Serge Obolensky called her Dolly, as did the Vicomte Sebastien Foy, but President Franklin D. Roosevelt, Lord Beaverbrook and Leslie Hore-Belisha opted for Dorothy. School friends used either Dottie or Schiffy; her children say Mamma (accented on the second syllable) or Mother; the grandchildren, Goggy; brother John, Dolly; and his very proper Scots butler, Mrs. Dorothy. Social intimates mostly call her Dolly, as do some who would like to be so thought (and by so doing never gain such status). Then there are those who, out of insecurity or reserve, prefer the use of Dorothy, as do the ones who try for objectivity.

"The trouble with being known by more than one name," Dorothy says, "is that when you sign a letter, you have to remember whom it's for."

So identified is she with the *Post* she has been addressed as Mrs. Post. Its building, where she is known as "the Publisher" and addressed as Mrs. Schiff (with two exceptions, who are on a Dolly basis), used to be the home of the *Journal-American*. The *Post* moved there from 75 West Street in March, 1970, and the building's anonymity reflects the Schiff antipathy to publicity (a family member is mentioned in the paper only with her permission), together with the hope that if disgruntled readers don't know it's the paper's home, they won't lay siege to it.

The *Post* is the country's oldest continuously published daily, having been founded by Alexander Hamilton in 1801. It is also the country's largest selling paper at its price in the afternoon field and the only afternoon paper in New York. A clue to the paper's success lies in Dorothy's commitment to it, which is expressed in an inviolate routine.

The latter begins with an 8 A.M. awakening for coffee and milk (no sugar) and dog food for her diminutive Yorkshire, Suzy Q. The apartment is in the hands of Aery Lawson, a personable, composed and highly efficient cook-housekeeper, whose husband, Everette, takes care of heavier duties, in addition to acting as Dorothy's driver. The Lawsons came to her through their ad in a help wanted column in 1960.

"I like doing things for myself," Dorothy explains, "but the children worry. Besides, I'm no good at it."

With Dorothy's coffee comes the New York *Times* (the bulldog edition of the *Daily News* having been delivered the night before, together with the last edition of the *Post* known as the Final), then perhaps a few business calls via direct line from the office. She may also make a couple of calls to family members. Unless she goes to her hairdresser for a thrice-weekly combing, by a little after ten in good weather she is walking a few blocks, to be met by Everette on a convenient corner. He has with him her black dispatch case and the *Post*'s first edition, called the Late City.

The motor of her Cadillac—not a limousine, but a Fleetwood four-door sedan with white top and upholstery—is idling, and the radio is tuned to a news station. Its license plates bear the letters NYP, which permit her unofficial parking privileges and equally unofficial police cooperation, and the number is high enough so that Dorothy can't remember what it is. She won't have a phone in the car, nor does she like a window separating front and rear seats. As a conscientious backseat driver she doesn't like being out of touch.

The trip downtown is driven with little conversation and as fast as traffic and NYP plates permit. On arrival the no-parking zone at the main entrance is vacant, the revolving door is in motion. The elevator is rung for, and into this she steps with Suzy, followed by Everette with dispatch case and subdued greeting of guards. Everette cuts out the elevator's automatic controls to ensure there are no stops or intrusions, but Dorothy is always a little anxious; she does not like elevators. Among the lunches she has turned down to avoid their use was one for the mayor of Moscow on a fortieth floor.

On the sixth floor she is greeted by a receptionist sitting beneath the portrait of an early *Post* editor, William Coleman. A buzzer releases the lock on a door opening on a hall in which are hung portraits of Alexander Hamilton and William Cullen Bryant. At one side is the personnel department with its conference room, where labor negotiations are conducted, and on the right wall is the door to the publisher's suite. Near it hangs a copy by the artist Harrington Mann of a large portrait of Dorothy's paternal grandfather, Jacob H. Schiff, who was an investment banker, philanthropist and the foremost Jewish leader in the United States. The original portrait graces the offices of Kuhn, Loeb. It shows Jacob with his goateed chin resting on a ringed hand and wearing starched cuffs, stiff collar, white-edged waistcoat and diamond stickpin. The light-blue eyes have a quizzical look.

The publisher's suite includes offices for two secretaries and a large one intended for an associate publisher. This space has become a sort of trophy room in which are hung awards presented to the *Post*, together with those honoring Dorothy. Photographs of her in the company of notables from U.S. Presidents to labor negotiators crowd the walls, and there is one curiosity which has unnerved many a visitor. This is a life-size papier-mâché figure of Alexander Hamilton in period costume with wig, engaged in writing with a quill pen on the wing of an early editor's chair. He looks pensive, as well he might after all these years.

Access to the publisher's office is through double doors from a foyer. The room is oval, about forty feet long by twenty feet wide, and is painted white. The trim, doors, shelving and carpet are green, concealed lighting in the high ceiling produces a subdued glow, and six tall windows look out on the river and the Brooklyn shore. The feeling is one of spaciousness, dignity and power.

An eighteenth-century English partner's desk, double-sided and with a flat top, dominates the scene at the end of the room. Lady Colefax, a London decorator and hostess of note, found this and other antiques for Dorothy's former Georgian country house. Behind the desk is a breakfront filled with favorite books.

Dorothy Schiff in her office at the Post, *in 1968.*

A pair of leather chairs stand on either side. A round luncheon table with four chairs is near the windows halfway along the room; across from it on the inner wall are a bar and bookcases with closets at each end. Dominating the wall opposite the breakfront is a contemporary French painting by Noyer of a nude lady in her boudoir. Beneath it is a long sofa with coffee table, flanked by pairs of upholstered armchairs in the same green as the curtains. A door to the right of the breakfront opens onto a dressing room-lavatory, and double doors at the other end lead to a foyer with boardroom and well-equipped kitchen.

The suite is not as grand as the one in the old office on West Street and lacks the executive elevator provided in the plans; this would have cost $100,000, which, together with the salary of additional guards, was enough to persuade Dorothy to do without. As it is, the five elevators in the building are a lot for one who doesn't trust them.

The office routine begins with the acknowledgment of greetings from her administrative assistant, Jean Gillette, and a secretary. The metamorphosis from East Side matron to publisher and editor in chief is complete as she sits in a capacious swivel chair behind the partner's desk, a cigarette in its holder firmly clenched by her teeth. Dorothy's voice, a little lacking in timbre, becomes crisp at the office. She expresses herself with an economy of words, and while her manner may seem distant, even rude to some, it is based on the belief that the best communication is a clear one. And clarity is vital in running a highly complicated business with 1,300 employees, many of whom see themselves as creative types and dislike noncreative orders.

The partner's desk has a three-circuit phone with direct line to the apartment and a three-position intercom (one of three such instruments in the room), and near it are the latest editions of the New York *Times, Daily News, Wall Street Journal* and *Post.* Next to them is a large folder with opened mail (those marked personal from a sender known to the publisher remain sealed), and alongside is a neatly typed list of telephone messages. The plethora of objects on the desk contrasts with its empty drawers.

"I used to think they'd be good for hiding things," she says, "but then the question was, what things? Besides, there are no keys."

After dealing with the mail, she usually consults with executive editor Paul Sann by phone or perhaps makes a headline decision with managing editor Robert Spitzler, after which outside calls are made and received. The newspapers at hand are read, and at twelve thirty editorial page editor James A. Wechsler calls about the next day's editorials and political affairs. During this call, which can run fifteen or twenty minutes, Dorothy mainly listens; if she disagrees, she does so tactfully, often by asking a question. Her instructions to executives are low-key, as she switches between the sometimes conflicting roles of publisher and editor in chief. It's a taut wire that this lady walks on such occasions.

Dorothy lunches at one, usually alone, and her menu is unvarying—a glass of Clamato juice (chilled, no ice and never alcohol) and a bacon, lettuce and tomato sandwich toasted, a small amount of mayonnaise (pronounced my) on the side, and two cups of coffee from an insulated container, again milk but no sugar. When there is a guest, she may also invite two staff members, as she finds three at table awkward.

Just before 2 P.M. routine takes over, and the next hour is occupied with executive conferences, usually with general manager Byron Greenberg and more often by phone than in person. Topics are roughly one-third personnel and labor relations, another third advertising and circulation, and the balance finance and planning. Another hour is taken up with dictation and further outside calls, and by four thirty, when the pressure is off the city room, she is often in phone conference with the managing editor. By five Dorothy's office day is about over (the dispatch case accompanies her home, where her reading is done), unless there is a special meeting, such as a postmortem on the handling of a news story.

The drive home with Suzy is likely to be more conversational than the one in the morning, and Everette gets a chance to voice an opinion or two. But in spite of his accident-free years, Dorothy is an uneasy passenger and is quick to warn of impending danger. The apartment is reached in time for evening TV news programs, during which she does her needlepoint and may sip water and white wine. Often, a solitary supper of cheeseburger and green salad follows; on the two evenings out she averages each week, she is home early. After supper, there are TV hours of cultural or political interest and reading with an eye to *Post* serialization. By about midnight Dorothy and Suzy are in their queen-size bed, with a mild pill for the former and a puppy biscuit for the latter.

Dorothy always sleeps on her right side to make it easier for her heart. It explains, she says, why her coiffure is flatter on that side, and the custom stems from advice she read somewhere. She adds she hopes it *is* the right side. Probably, the night will be peaceful, but there is always anxiety that she may not be called in event of a news break or *Post* catastrophe.

"Sometimes, the paper is an octopus," Dorothy muses, "especially when circulation or advertising revenue is off. It's an all-devouring thing, and it's never satisfied."

On Saturdays she tries to sleep late and may mark her day off by having a daughter in for a simple lunch; she used to patronize a neighborhood restaurant, but that means leaving Suzy home. An afternoon nap is likely to follow, and in the evening the routine resembles that of weekdays. On Sunday there are the New York *Times* and *News* to work through and TV talk and interview shows, with notes to take. Jimmy Wechsler calls at 2 P.M., a shorter call when there is a televised football or baseball game. The weekend is almost over then, and what is left is spent in further reading on behalf of the paper and in planning the new week. By the time Dorothy goes to bed, she knows that the night side people are bringing life back to the *Post* building and that things are moving toward Monday's first edition.

As publisher Dorothy doesn't have direct financial compensation, nor are there dividends or bonuses. She is the sole stockholder, with the token exception of the New York Post Foundation, which contributes in its small way to charitable causes.

One of the privileges of such ownership is not having to open the corporate books, but Dorothy admits that the paper does better than its detractors think, if not as well as the unions like to imagine. Two price increases in two years have helped keep the paper substantially in the black, offsetting a circulation loss. It still sells more than half a million copies daily.

The value of the Post has been put as high as $70,000,000, and as its production becomes increasingly automated, such a figure is going to remain large, even in a declining economy.

Dorothy's commitment to the paper is one which her grandfather, Jacob, would have understood. That titan of finance, who shared a height of five feet two inches with France's Napoleon Bonaparte and New York's Abe Beame, was dedicated in the same way to the direction of Kuhn, Loeb & Co. His firm is considered the Rolls-Royce of investment bankinghouses and it has now been served by four generations of the family. This con-

Jacob Schiff.

tinuing family loyalty to the firm might even have compensated Jacob for the move Dorothy's father and mother made to get away from Jacob's social orbit.

"They decided," Dorothy explains, "to escape from all that . . . background."

By "background" Dorothy means German Jewish, and by "escape" that her parents, Mortimer L. and Adele Neustadt Schiff, made Long Island their summer residence, instead of continuing in the shadow of Jacob H. Schiff's Rumson Road enclave at Sea Bright, New Jersey. They first rented a house, in which John was born and which Dorothy was too young to remember, at Roslyn, an area she describes as "very chi chi then, very different from what it is today." Before long, her father had assembled about 1,000 acres at Oyster Bay and built a mansion known as Northwood, thus becoming master of one of the area's largest estates, and obtained a founding membership in the Piping Rock Club, after the New York *Social Register* had let down its bars in 1904 and listed Morti and Adele.

Dorothy says her mother was the only member of the family not overawed by Jacob, "which is one reason we—the Oyster Bay Branch—weren't that impressed by him. I was amazed to learn how important he was, not that anyone ever asked my opinion of him or anything else. I was to be 'seen but not heard, like soup,' as my father said constantly. My mother called Grandpa 'the little giant,' and it's odd to think that the first time I was in Temple Emanu-El was for his funeral in September, 1920. He established it—at least, got people together for a Reform temple. It was on Forty-third Street then, opposite the Public Library, and I was called back from my first year at Bryn Mawr. Since my mother didn't approve of young girls wearing black, the thing that impressed me was that I was to have my first black dress. She bought it at a cheap store, Oppenheim Collins, saying I would only wear it once. It was satin, instead of crepe, which was all wrong, and naturally, I took it back to Bryn Mawr and wore it constantly."

The next most impressive thing about the funeral for Dorothy was that traffic was banned from a Fifth Avenue filled with Jews who had walked up from the Lower East Side. "Hundreds of immigrants in those hats, trying to get in and not being able to, standing out there, silent."

The death was front-page news, and the funeral received ample coverage. A family member remembers an old woman delaying the cortege by praying at a wheel of the hearse and says that not only did hundreds of that great multitude follow the cortege on foot to the Queensboro Bridge, but many walked on to the cemetery, Brooklyn's Salem Fields. Most pleasing to the widow, in view of Jacob's insistence on punctuality, was that the service began precisely as the hands of a large clock across the avenue pointed to ten.

In spite of the deceased's instructions calling for a simple service, Governor Al Smith and state military staff attended, as did Mayor John Hylan and a nearly complete roster of the city's financial, judicial and philanthropic names. Shops and business houses all over the city were closed, as were many courts. Numerous organizations were represented at the funeral and hundreds of people wept openly.

Many of the mourners had marched from the Schiff house, 965

Fifth Avenue, at Seventy-eighth Street across from the James B. Duke house (now the New York University fine arts department).

Dorothy is candid about how much she resented Jacob's hold over them all, and certainly his impact must have been as strong as the shadow he cast was long-lasting. Her aristocratic, even royal air is a reminder of his authoritative mien and is just one of the traits they have in common. Both were believers in the importance of routine, punctuality, anonymity in philanthropy, integrity in both personal and business affairs, and thrift. Just as Jacob collected string and saved used envelopes for scrap paper, Dorothy likes to remove stamps from rejected charitable appeal returns and turn off unneeded lights. In addition, these two Schiffs were good at taking well-researched risks and even better at coming up with the unexpected.

Fifth Avenue shop clerks are said to have set their clocks by Jacob's walk to work, so punctual was he, and his carriage was so imposing and his dignity so assured he hardly encouraged familiarity.

Dorothy remembers a visit she paid to Jacob at his 965 Fifth Avenue house when she was first permitted face powder. "He asked for the box when I told him what was on my face," she remembers. "Then he threw it out the window. I was furious and asked for the fifty cents it had cost. This was quite a sum for one with no allowance, but he never did reimburse me."

Not many people can have shown their fury at Jacob so readily, but then Dorothy's outrage was supported not only by violation of her dignity, but by what she saw as the injustice of having no allowance. In lieu of one, her mother insisted all she had to do was explain how much was needed and particularly for what. Dorothy wasn't given to arguing when the odds were against her, but she seems to have taken her mother's measure early. Her description is objective and is spoken in a brisk manner.

"My mother was very sure of herself and men thought she was divine. I was allowed to watch her dress for the evening, which her maid would help her with. She had rather a Charles Dana Gibson figure; she had a small

Adele Neustadt Schiff.

waist and was very good in the front department. Wearing a white chemise with lace at the top and no bra, she was always smartly dressed in the latest Pacquin outfits, but never overdressed. My father had given her a lot of jewelry, but she seldom wore it except for big dinners.

She belonged to a club of girlfriends before she got wholly into the non-Jewish set. There were four or five of them whom she saw at lunches, but never in the evening after she moved in the other set. They called themselves the Weepers and were always complaining about how ghastly marriage was and how dreadful their husbands

were. Instead of going to a psychiatrist, they told each
other their troubles and it seemed to help."*

Her cousin Carola Warburg (Mrs. Walter N. Rothschild) remembers Dorothy's mother as possessing great charm and having a wonderful sense of humor but adds that she could be
somewhat frightening in her sarcasm. "Aunt Adele wasn't warm
or cozy and wouldn't curl up and talk about things. She was less
a beauty than a *belle laide,* but very chic, liked parties and had a
very mixed circle of friends—some being absolute horrors—who
seemed to hang on forever."

The "horrors," according to Dorothy, were dropped eventually. By then Adele had penetrated the periphery of New York society, helped by her cooperative husband, Morti, a handsome
man with good features and very blue eyes, who was a little on
the plump side. He looked shorter than Adele, and she wished
he were taller. According to Morti's sister Frieda (Mrs. Felix M.
Warburg), the young Morti was always being punished, often to
be comforted afterward by Joseph, the butler. She blames Morti's difficulties on his rather violent will and felt that had the
cause of the frequent outbursts of temper been investigated, as
they would today, her brother's life would have been far happier. However, the perfection demanded by Jacob would most
likely have remained unattainable. Morti's remark on being giv-
en 932 Fifth Avenue as a wedding present reveals much. He
said, "It's wonderful to be the master of a house in which I have
been spanked so often."

Frieda credits her brother with "all the desired attributes—
good looks, good health, varied talents, exquisite taste and a flair
for art, in spite of being color-blind (as was his grandfather, Solomon Loeb)." Whenever Morti as a boy was not with his father,
he had to write him a daily letter in German. Eventually, Jacob
wrote him, "I notice you always write every morning. I would
prefer that you write late in the afternoon, because then you
could assure me that you've been a good boy and no trouble to
your mother."

*All comments directly quoted and set apart as here are from tape-recorded
interviews between the author and Dorothy Schiff. Other sources, such as Dorothy Schiff's memos, diaries and the author's interviews with others than she,
are so identified.

Morti attended Dr. Sachs' school in New York, which later became the Franklin School. He was often walked to it, a distance of thirty blocks, by Jacob, who recognized that he was a brilliant student but was concerned that the school judged him poor in deportment.

Morti wanted to go to Harvard, but Jacob decided he should start at Amherst, fearing Harvard would encourage his tendency toward extravagance, and he boarded there at $3.50 a week. When he bought a new, rather than a secondhand, bicycle, Jacob sentenced him to a second year at Amherst for his extravagance. That year, though, was largely lost because of scarlet fever, and then Jacob announced Morti was ready to go to work. Obligingly, James J. Hill found him a place on a road gang of the Great Northern to learn railroading from the bottom. What effect the art of tie setting and rail laying had on his future is unknown, but something else in the West came as an ugly surprise. For the first time he was exposed to anti-Semitism, and while it largely involved admission to a country club, the impact of the experience stayed with him.

After he had put in a year with the Great Northern, Jacob decided it was time for Morti to have a try at a few great banking houses. First he was sent to the Montagu house in London, then to M. M. Warburg & Co. in Hamburg. In London he lived well, being taken under the wing of Sir Ernest Cassel, who later told Frieda, "I don't think your father was too well pleased with what I did for your brother; I rather encouraged his spending money, because I believe a gentleman must learn how to spend gracefully."

Family members agree that Morti learned the lesson well. On his return to New York he stayed with his parents, and Frieda reports: "Designing mothers did their best, and in the winter of 1899 he announced his engagement to Adele Neustadt, an intelligent, witty girl, whose parents, the Siegmund Neustadts [Mr. Neustadt was a partner in Hallgarten & Co.], were old friends of my parents. Adele was very elusive and Morti, poor darling, never knew from one day to the next where he stood. He lost thirty pounds during the engagement."

Morti hadn't been Adele's first choice as a husband; she had wanted a brother of the Harry K. Thaw who shot Stanford White, but both sets of parents forbade the marriage. Morti was

Mortimer L. Schiff.

still a catch, though, and her father said, "To think of my daughter marrying the son of Jacob Schiff!"

According to Carola, Morti's Schiff temper "blew strong when it came but passed quickly, and then everything was lovely and you were supposed to forget it." He had an easy laugh, was very friendly and wished to be more of a country gentleman than duty, in the form of Jacob, permitted. Dorothy agrees with this, pointing out that the reason her grandfather never found out about Morti's American racing stable was that he didn't read the sports pages (nor does she).

"Grandpa was very hard on him and terribly critical of his accomplishments," Carola says. "Morti always wanted to have a little fun and fancied himself a sport. Although no athlete by nature, he made himself do things such as golf and polo, even if not top polo. He did all the things clubmen on Long Island did.

"The move to Long Island was a major one; Adele wanted to avoid being swallowed up by Jacob's New Jersey scene, and for Morti a new world of country gentlemen there was coming up. The elder Schiffs and the Warburgs did not look on it too kindly.

The Rumson Road place had belonged to my great-grandparents, and Friday evenings were always a full-dress occasion. Attendance was a must, and it was almost like the Court of St. James's."

Dorothy's feeling is that the move had much to do with her mother's lack of rapport with Jacob, her "little giant," and it does seem that all they had in common was a belief in the benefits of fresh air. In addition, she sees it as an attempt to get away from the restriction of "background."

A longtime observer of the Schiff-Warburg relationship says, "It wasn't so much that they were on the social make—really desperate to get into that Christian world—as that they simply went for the jet set of that age."

Dorothy was born into that new world in the 932 Fifth Avenue house Jacob had given Morti. It was 5 A.M. on March 11, 1903. Dorothy's recollections start at an early age.

"My first memory is at about two or so. I had been put in my crib in the night nursery for a nap after lunch, and my mother came in with two or three of her girlfriends. I was beyond diapers, I think, and didn't have to wear constraints to prevent thumb sucking—those aluminum mitts.

I stood up in my crib, and my mother said, 'Look, what she's done.' There were three drops of wet which I have never forgotten. I'm not even sure what they were—they looked like three drops of water. I wasn't a bed wetter—maybe I had cried or something.

Anyway, she just laughed and laughed, and so did her friends. I couldn't understand the laughter, and I was humiliated. This was a crime, you know, but she laughed. They weren't there long; she was always racing out. I just hated . . . was in a rage.

I wasn't sure what the punishment would be when my nurse came in, an English Canadian named Florence who replaced another nurse let go because it was thought she favored me. At least it wasn't nighttime, so I wasn't spanked. Florence usually spanked me when she came in to see if we were asleep, the 'we' being John and I. We shared a room until I was about eight, and while John always was asleep, I was usually faking with my eyes tight shut. Since my breathing wouldn't be deep, she always knew. On her night off an Irish chambermaid would take care of us. Her name was Dorothy, but my mother changed it to Katy for obvious reasons.

I was always trying to be good, and although I tried to do everything the way I was supposed to, I always slipped up. In Central Park, which was my life when I was small, I would feel very altruistic. There was a day when I had been given a box of chalk, the kind you write on blackboards with. I took out a long white piece, and when I tried to write on the pavement, it broke into small pieces.

There were quite a few children in those sitting-up prams, so I gave a piece to each while their nurses were gossiping. Each child, thrilled, immediately put the piece in its mouth, where it stayed until the nurses finally noticed. They were furious, and I was given an awful scolding for having given the children this terrible poison called chalk. I had only been trying to share, but I was utterly misunderstood. I felt very badly about that.

On another day I decided I was so crazy about dogs I would pat every one in the park. There were a lot of them on leashes near the Seventy-second Street entrance, which was the one we used. To my left, as I went my rounds, nurses were on benches gabbing to each other. Finally, I got to a dog which bit me on the wrist when I started to pat him. Much horror—nurses screamed, I was rushed home, the doctor was sent for, and the wound was cauterized. Whenever I have to specify identifying marks, I wonder if I should mention the scar, tiny though it is.

John was delicate and suffered from frequent attacks of croup, and many nights a croup kettle containing benzine—benzoin—would be steaming in the room. He sounded terrible, from way deep down, and there would be much hullabaloo of people coming in. I'd think, oh, God, another night of this! I was worried; he was my little playmate, and I thought he was going to die.

I would be half asleep, watching those shadowy figures running around, people giving each other orders, and I would say to myself I mustn't—you know—panic; he's had it before. Often, he was wrapped in a blanket and taken into the bathroom, where it was warmer. My mother was a fresh-air fiend, and there was a big window in the night nursery which had to be open. It faced on a courtyard, and I could hear cats all night.

The day nursery, or playroom, was on the Fifth Avenue side, and I had to sleep there when I had some disease, such as German measles. There were funny lights from the avenue and scary sounds—boys shouting 'Extra,' then the headline—but I could never make out what they were saying. It was always some disaster.

Between that room and the night nursery was a long hall with mirrors where William, the butler we had forever, came to get the linen. I would be put on the potty out there, and John would have the bathroom because he was sickly. Also, he got special privileges because he was a boy. As the son he had to survive."

Dorothy's brother, John Mortimer Schiff, has had *Social Register* listings showing membership in more than ten clubs. His wife, Edith, the daughter of the late (and second husband) George F. Baker, banker, socialite and clubman, was known as TeeTee and died in 1975. At seventy-one, John is a little stooped, but his six feet three inches make him a tall man, and his build shows the effects of tennis, golf, squash and riding. Although balding, he is strikingly handsome, wears a tan the year round, and his eyes are a grayish blue. They speak of shyness, doubt and kindness. He is as known for that quality as he is for integrity, a sense of noblesse oblige and dedication to duty.

John's childhood memories are scant and not very visual. He is certain that there was no parental favoritism and is equally certain that although brought up by nurses and governesses, Dorothy and he were close to their parents. He points out that as a girl she grew up more quickly than he and that she tended to dominate.

According to Dorothy, the reason their early education was at home by tutors—"French, German and carpentry, endlessly"— was her mother's fear of other children's infections. The fresh air of Central Park afforded protection against disease, Dorothy's mother decided. But it didn't diminish Dorothy's anxieties. They included leprosy and trick-or-treaters, known then as ragamuffins.

A Miss Clemens gave the two children religious instruction at home in the form of the Old Testament complete with a wrathful

God ("always frowning at me, probably not without reason").
Dorothy explains that her grandfather, Jacob, visited their house
each Friday night to bless them, murmuring the hope that the
Lord's countenance would shine on them. She never dared ask
what countenance meant. But then, she never dared tell him that
she was given to reading the New Testament, knowledge of
which would have bothered him less, probably, than her attendance with a school friend at St. Bartholomew's, a Park Avenue
Episcopal church just a little less social than Fifth Avenue's St.
Thomas'. Her visit to a Roman Catholic church wouldn't have
pleased Jacob either. This was done in the company of Mademoiselle, a convent-educated French governess, engaged when
Dorothy was eleven ("Parisian, of course; my mother said they
had the only good French accent").

Mademoiselle brought companionship, guidance and the
world of books to Dorothy. They read in French together often,
leading Dorothy to explore the extensive libraries in the family's
town and country houses. In time Dorothy became so close to

*Dorothy Schiff, her brother, John, and a nurse at Northwood, her father's estate
at Oyster Bay.*

Mademoiselle she couldn't go to sleep until the latter was back in the house after her night out. By the time Mademoiselle came into her life Dorothy had been attending the Brearley School for a year, and the winter routine was well established, she recalls.

"The mornings would be cold and darkish and some-body, nurse or governess, would tap us on the shoulder to wake us up. There would be a gas fire in the grate with a rounded screen to keep children out, and there were mar-velous fake logs with little holes in them for the flames. You turned a little spigot on the side of the hearth and lit a match. . . . I wasn't allowed to, of course.

Curiously enough, I can't remember bathing, but I think the first thing we did was take a bath. Then came dressing and all the underthings, which were home-made—at least those not bought in Paris. These were made to order with real lace edging and frills, and the flannel petticoat had scallops embroidered around the bottom. The homemade things were run up by two of the maids or by a dressmaker who would come in spring and fall.

After a ribbed cotton undershirt—like a man's, no sleeves—came this corsetlike waist thing with large yel-lowish buttons sewed on with big tapes, and everything hung from that. There was a large bone button in the front, on the sides and in the back for the panties, which stopped above the knee with a frill, lace and stuff. The flannel petticoat came next, then the regular, nonflannel one, and over them some kind of dress but not long; my mother believed in the French style of dressing, short.

Once I was dressed, it was down the front stairs quietly to the breakfast room. After that came good-mornings to our father and mother, who had separate rooms. He would be up and shaving in an undershirt, sharpening a big razor on a thing called a strop, and she would be in bed in a darkened room with a headache, or something—looking sick and unhappy. Then came the potty business, which seemed to take hours, followed by that awful line 'Let me see what you've done—there's nothing in it.' Ev-erything retreated, and that meant punishment—laxa-tives, purges—and so the day began.

Lunch was served in the breakfast room by William, helped by a footman or waitress and goodness knows

how many in the kitchen. Sometimes I would be asked
out to lunch by girls near Fifth Avenue, but there were
some who lived farther east. Their brownstones were
smaller with only an Irish maid to serve lunch, but the
food was much better—hot chocolate with whipped
cream instead of our ice water. Occasionally, mothers
would appear at these lunches, less fashionably dressed
than mine, but kind and nice.

After lunch, it was the park again; I spent so much time
there I wanted to be important like the people whose stat-
ues are all over. We went even on the coldest days and my
frozen cheeks would have to be rubbed with ice in a face
towel to thaw them when we got home. The various lessons which came after the park were not done with much
interest; I was forced to do them. Piano was twice a week
with daily half hour practice consisting mostly of five-
finger exercises—scales. While I wanted to play jazz,
which I heard at friends', it had to be Chopin, and this
went on until I went to college. A whole group of us had
the same teacher, who conducted what she called recitals
for her students once a year. I was never able to play at
one, being paralyzed with self-consciousness or something.

No parents were visible at supper, which John, I and
our governess had in the breakfast room. We had to finish
everything on our plate, in spite of my father's always
saying if my tummy got any bigger, he would call the
doctor to cut it off. After it we would join them for a short
time in the library, where conversation would be limited
to 'How was school today?' Sometimes we played Par-
cheesi, which my mother always won. I got absolutely
fed up with it, but I just couldn't beat her. I don't think
my father ever played, and anyway, he wasn't around that
much. John was not good at parlor games, but he was always good in other ways and never got in trouble; I was
the bad one.

The only time we had meals with our parents was Sunday lunch. Sometimes there were quite a few people, and
once I knocked over a glass of water and was sent from
the table. A couple of Sundays later my father knocked
one over, and I screamed with laughter, but I was told
this was not the same thing before being exiled. I learned
later that even when he was a grown man and married,

his father had sent him from the table for some such crime.

Our day ended eventually with an escape back to the nursery and bed, followed by that spanking. This, I suppose, was child abuse or whatever it's called. In a funny way I loved Florence, and perhaps, she me. On her day off a housemaid took over, who wore a black uniform with a strong body odor. We would roughhouse with her, rolling around on the floor, with much laughter. And when it got to be too much, I would be pushed away. . . .

One nice thing in our house was that a man from Tiffany came to wind the clocks; there were clocks in every room, great big gilt clocks with black Roman numerals. I liked watching him with his clocks, using a big key, and I used to tag along as far as I was allowed to go in the house. Certain areas were *verboten*—the drawing room, for instance, where grown-ups would be. I don't think I was ever in there, even with a nurse or governess.

There was one dreadful French walking governess, who always took us to the park and into that tunnel with the echo near Seventy-ninth Street. She would invariably squat in there for a 'Pee-pee,' which we thought was absolutely fascinating. But, of course, we knew she was French and that they did things like that."

That Dorothy and John were allowed to play with only Fifth Avenue children, as she overheard Florence once saying, is nonsense, according to Dorothy. She says their friends were Upper East Side dwellers, if not quite as far east as Lexington Avenue, but although she knew there was a West Side, somehow they never met anyone from there. Occasionally, Dorothy's friends were asked for weekends at the Oyster Bay estate, Northwood, which she calls the graveyard of her childhood.

"It was thought good for me, so various little impecunious girls were dragged out there. Not having country places, they might spend a weekend with Joan Whitney and so on, doing the rounds. The girls who had country places didn't visit me, or I them, just as English dukes don't visit each other. It's rather the way Nelson Rockefeller and Jock Whitney have of sort of eyeing each

other with suspicion, both being American dukes with
big country places.

The little friends who came on weekends were sort of
like satellites—very nice and very accommodating. A lot
of time was spent on those weekends with my telling the
friends how miserable I was and that my mother
wouldn't let me do anything I wanted and so forth. They
would listen politely, and if they did say anything, I
don't know what it was. I wasn't interested in what they
wanted and besides, their lives were open books; they
went to school and came on weekends."

There were endless lessons in sports at Northwood, Dorothy
remembers. She found riding lessons a bore, and these she was
also subjected to in Paris by an English riding mistress. They
gave her a stitch in her side, which she blamed on so much jog-
gling, and she had no use for putting on riding habits either, to
say nothing of the horse smell. Dorothy remembers it this
way.

"At Oyster Bay I was forced to ride every day for an
hour and a half. We'd go first this way, the next day that
way, always with our coachman along, who was in
charge of the stable and grooms. It was all so boring, and
I wasn't crazy about giving the horse I had to ride sugar. I
did it the way you're supposed to, but I still wasn't sure
my hand wouldn't be eaten off.

There was swimming, among other sports. I never
dared dive, having been taught the breaststroke with my
head always out of water. With pools, unlike the limitless
ocean, you know where you are and that you can get
back. There isn't that undertow which could carry me
out; I had read lugubrious tales about that and quag-
mires, too. I didn't mind bicycling, as long as there was
an occasion, and I rather liked roller skating. Ice skating
was beyond me; my ankles were weak and turned over.

I much preferred curling up in a leather chair in the library, working through the sets of leather-bound classics,
but there was always my mother's insistence on fresh air,
so I did much of my reading under the big maples. This
omnivorous reading may have something to do with an
early ambition to write. When I told my English teacher
at the Brearley that I wanted to write about a girl at
boarding school, she said, 'Write about something you

The formal gardens at Northwood.

Dorothy Schiff, age nine, driving a hackney at a Piping Rock Club horse show.

know.' So I didn't write it, and she committed suicide eventually, not that there was any connection.

On some mornings at Oyster Bay, Florence would let me in her bed, which was a comfort, but there was a sensuous element, too. She was a stocky, peasantlike brunette, but things never went very far. It was always time to get up and get going. She kept looking for a man—even thought the Oyster Bay druggist was in love with her—but without success. Since John was delicate, in quotes, and I wasn't, she took things out on me. Eventually, a woman in the next cabin on a liner heard her beating me and told my mother. I had never told her because Florence said she'd kill me if I did."

The Brearley School was at Park Avenue and Sixty-first Street then, which meant a walk in that mandatory fresh air thirteen blocks down and two east each day, but Dorothy didn't really mind and was never late for the nine o'clock beginning. Her father's sister, Frieda Warburg, was the first of their "background" to go to the Brearley, and Frieda's daughter, Carola, and Dorothy were the only ones of their generation there then. It was more of an academic than social school, Dorothy says.

"The Whitney girls did pass in and out rather rapidly though, Abbey Rockefeller, too, and then there was Alice Astor, whose father went down on the *Titanic*. She wore black that year; until then I had only seen old ladies in mourning.

The classes were of about twenty girls, divided into A and B divisions supposedly on an alphabetical division. I was always in A, although I never did any work. It never occurred to me that they thought I was intelligent, and I couldn't believe it when I won a debate between the *Iliad* and the *Odyssey*. I ran into Carl Van Doren, the Brearley headmaster, years later, and he remembered me as having dark hair and red cheeks and just sitting there looking sullen, as though I were daring him to teach me anything. I didn't really think the *Iliad* was a better book when I chose it; it was just that everyone wanted the *Odyssey* and the unpopular side let me be different.

There was a sense of isolation at the Brearley—the family money and 'background.' The few girls there who lived as I did had only the first, and for them there wasn't the problem of Christmas. Grandpa Schiff didn't permit it. It was pathetic—no tree—and we had to wait for New Year's presents, which is what our Christmas presents were called. Friends were given 'birthday' presents, and they, of course, didn't have a Grandpa Schiff lurking in the background, coming each night at Hanukkah to light a candle.

My mother would have had Christmas, but my father was too frightened of *his* father. The maids were given presents, though—several yards of black alpaca to make themselves new uniforms and, I suppose, something besides.

Otherwise, the 'background' wasn't directly a problem at the Brearley, although there was one girl . , . she went bohemian later, as my mother called it. I remember she was giving a party and said I couldn't come because of it. Later on I was walking with Mademoiselle on the west side of Fifth Avenue, feeling miserable and thinking the most terrible things. Just as we came opposite our house, I was struck by something; it wasn't as bad as being black."

Dorothy explains that she doesn't know how, or when, John found out about the "background," as they never discussed it, but that she was twelve before she made the discovery. The recitation is clearly an effort for her and is done in a low voice.

"One summer we were taken to the Adirondacks because of a polio epidemic, and there were two Canadian girls there whom I liked. I saw them a lot until the day they came and said that they wouldn't be allowed to play with me anymore, and why.

Mademoiselle was very helpful; she called it something else—*Israelite*. That does sound prettier, doesn't it? Then she put her arms around me and held me, kissing me. I cried a lot when I was a child, and I guess I did then."

Everything about herself seemed wrong, Dorothy says.

"My clothes were different; my shoes were buttoned with white tops and black bottoms, while other girls wore brown oxfords. Instead of white stockings attached to

that hideous straitjacket thing, they had black ribbed
stockings. But then, my mother thought that everything
from Paris was better and that nothing good came out of
America.

I suppose she was the most different thing about me;
her clothes were Parisian, and she was much better
dressed than other mothers, really very smart-looking.
When she came to school, she smelled of perfume; they,
with their tweed suits and mannish blouses, didn't. They
were down to earth, while she was very glamorous. She
would appear in a Renault town car with a basket weave
body, stay only briefly, then be driven off. There might
even have been a footman out in front with the chauffeur,
as in the carriage days when they drove with the coachman on the 'box.'

It was all most embarrassing, and I kept wishing she
wouldn't come. I never told her, though; I didn't dare,
any more than about getting away from things—the
money and . . . being Jewish. And having said that
word, it sounds all right. Or, at least, as all right as such
things ever could in those days."

Among the contemporaries Dorothy was close to during her
school years was Ellin Mackay, the daughter of Clarence Mackay, whose subsequent marriage to Irving Berlin was a social
sensation. As Ellin Berlin she has drawn on her social background for several novels, the most recent being *The Best People.*

"I don't think the *Social Register* ever had any importance for
us; it was just that once you were fourteen, people could find
you," Ellin said in a recent conversation with Dorothy.

Dorothy agreed, saying she hadn't known there was a phone
book in her schooldays. "I looked up my friends in the *Social
Register* when I wanted to call them. But I haven't owned one
for about thirty years, although the *Post* library may have one."

A discussion about the inclusion of Jewish names in its early
years resulted in Mrs. Berlin's claim that it had always listed
them.

"Very, very few," Dorothy objected.

"Well, because there were very, very few Jews. I found this
out when I was doing research for a book on my grandmother

Mackay. I was obliged to tell my daughters that there was absolutely no anti-Catholicism in this country until my grandfather got here, and there was no anti-Semitism until their father, Irving Berlin, came."

"I don't know why the Warburgs weren't in the *Social Register*, although the Kahns and the Schiffs were," Dorothy said.

"I imagine with your family it was automatic; there was Piping Rock and all that sort of thing. They went to everybody's parties, and originally this is what it was all about."

Scandal that got into the papers made the kind of society represented by the *Social Register* uncomfortable. One *cause célèbre* involving her mother and father has not been entirely forgotten to this day. Dorothy first knew something was wrong when she noticed the servants whispering in the hallways, but it was some years before she discovered what it was all about. The ominous whispering, no matter how much it worried her—and it did, considerably—wasn't to be mentioned, let alone inquired into. Even now, as she speaks of it, she looks a little apprehensive. "It had to do with a footman who, in his madness, delivered a billet-doux to my mother. Before it was over, it created an enormous hullabaloo."

The Brandt case was a big one, and the paper which made the most of it, and out of it, was W. R. Hearst's New York *American*. It is an irony that the New York *Post* is now housed in the building the *American* last used, after being merged by Hearst with the *Journal*.

The billet-doux addressed to Adele was written in uncertain English by the footman, who claimed royal Swedish blood and called himself Lawrence De Foulke. His real name, it developed during court proceedings against him, was Foulke E. Brandt. His note included a postscript: "This is a free country and I have a right to love you."

When Morti returned from the office and learned of the letter, he discharged Brandt with wages but without a reference. A few days later, on the night of Friday, March 12, 1907, after the Schiffs returned from the theater, Morti was reading in the study before retiring to his darkened bedroom and heard a noise in the adjoining dressing room. As he turned, he was struck a blow on the forehead with what turned out to be a tenpin. He switched on the lights to find his former footman threatening him with a hatchet-shaped ice pick and a carving knife. Later Brandt admitted that he had entered through the cellar, where he picked up the tenpin in Jacob Schiff's old bowling alley.

Morti gave Brandt $50 and talked him into coming the following Monday to Kuhn, Loeb for further consultation. Brandt collected his shoes from the cellar, and Morti let him out the front door. When he came to the office, Brandt was arrested by detectives, and two doctors examined him for sanity.

New York American *headline on Brandt case (March 12, 1907).*

The case filled the newspapers for days. In an effort to still rumors, Morti's lawyers persuaded Adele to make a frank statement. "A man who is insane enough to write me a love letter . . . would be crazy enough to do anything, the wretch! Who knows what would have happened if he had assassinated Mr. Schiff?"

The judge gave Brandt thirty years, a harsh sentence though the youthful offender had been in trouble several times before. Five years later Brandt appealed to the governor for executive clemency, but the appeal was rejected after due consideration. The Hearst press did not let the matter drop. Ultimately, so many public figures become involved and so many rumors were spread about the possibility that the family had conspired to obstruct justice that a grand jury was impaneled.

Morti's lawyers, among them Paul D. Cravath (credited with Piping Rock's founding), made application "for full disclosure of all matters pertaining to the case to the end that the scandalous rumors and misconceptions with which the press has teemed for weeks should be dispelled." Except for the Schiffs, for whom sympathy was building, no one came out of the case looking good, least of all Brandt. Investigation revealed that he had been guilty of theft in Sweden and perjury in New York and had been discharged for dishonesty by several employers.

The *American* stuck to its aggressive editorial line to the end and, although the grand jury found that there was no evidence of conspiracy and recommended that the charge of burglary be reduced to that of grand larceny on a technicality, still editorialized that the finding was "a warning that selfish men with money will not soon forget."

New York Governor William Sulzer at last freed Brandt in 1913, and he is said to have joined the Russian army in World War I and to have been killed in action. If, indeed, this was the end of Brandt, it still wasn't the last of the case the Schiff family would hear, for it came up in a mayoralty campaign in the 1970s. Dorothy rebutted the story in a radio broadcast, but it revived her anxiety about those ominous whisperings from her childhood.

The most distasteful element of the case was the Hearst allegation that family influence had conspired to railroad Brandt with an unjustly long sentence. No such evidence was produced, nor was any that would indicate he had encouragement which would have prompted his billet-doux.

"The insinuation was ridiculous," Dorothy says. "Anyone who knew my mother was aware that her set offered more interesting possibilities. Brandt may have been handsome, but everyone engaged footmen in those days with an eye for how their calves would look in knee breeches." Aside from anything else, Adele was clearly too socially ambitious to have taken a chance with the servants' hall.

The family went abroad regularly, spending much time with what was known as the international set, and in later years a house in Paris was redone, where Adele spent a few summers, though Morti preferred his quarters at the Ritz.

Dorothy recalls one spring voyage to Europe when there was weeping by cabin attendants on the old *Olympic*, on news of the *Titanic*'s loss. Equally vivid is her memory of a voyage home without Morti, who had refused to travel with them because he didn't like his wife deceiving the customs agents. To avoid paying duty, Adele insisted on getting off the boat wearing several layers of Paris gowns, which enraged him. Outwitting the customs agents was a popular game then, but Adele dropped it after one of her friends was arrested. Morti went to Europe frequently on his own; the trips were largely on behalf of Kuhn, Loeb, but he was fond of taking cures, too, and after Jacob's death he had his French racing stables to busy himself with.

Dorothy had a way with her father, according to Dorothy's cousin, Carola.

"You had a lot of fun together," Carola added. "Isn't that true, Dolly?"

Dorothy straightened and answered after a pause: "I wasn't aware of it."

John, not unsurprisingly, sees their parents as having no favorites, but in her early years Dorothy's relationship with Morti seems to have been special.

"When I was still preschool, I used to roughhouse with him in the library; I'd be in his lap in a big armchair, and I would tickle him under the chin or something. We'd laugh together with my mother sitting there sternly, and when we'd get quite violent, she'd put a stop to it, saying, 'That's enough, Dolly—you're playing too rough.' And she would speak very sternly to him; I think our obvious animal enjoyment worried her. It was all so frustrating; I mean, nothing ever came to a conclusion. There was always that, 'That's enough—stop it!' and then her cold disapproval....

Eventually, this stopped happening; I was not allowed to sit in his lap anymore. Later it became all scenes between them until I think my mother didn't want him around, so he found other interests. A mutual friend, Sidney Smith, of whom my father was fond—always taking him out on his yacht when he wasn't abroad—began to visit more and more. He had a great sense of humor and wasn't a bit stuffy. I loved Mr. Smith.

I think I must have been a hyperactive child. I was always rushing up to everyone, flinging my arms around them, usually to be pushed away. My mother used a German phrase about me, *ausgelassen*. A hoyden, she called me—not a tomboy exactly, but wild and madly impetuous. I wasn't daring on trapezes or with horses and things, but kept taking dogs in my lap and hugging them. I sensed my mother's disapproval, and my father, too, became more the same way, remote. . . .

I don't know how my mother felt about me then, but I didn't think I could be their natural child. I knew about stepmothers who are mean to stepchildren because so many stories dealt with wicked stepmothers. I thought I must be a stepchild because I was so badly treated, but I never mentioned that to her, either. She was so . . . sure of herself.

It may have had to do with my feeling that I was a girl and not a boy, although the first Schiff grandchild, and my birth was overshadowed for my grandfather by the Kishinev pogrom in Russia. Less than a hundred Jews were massacred, but it was a major disaster until Hitler's time.

What I wanted passionately was to grow up; I was desperate to be free. Marriage was the only escape in those days, since you couldn't take an apartment on your own at eighteen. That was all I cared about, getting away from things. . . ."

II

"I used to read a lot, which the Philadelphia girls joked about, saying that I was this peculiar combination of a party girl and an intellectual."

A film of the family was made at Northwood about 1916 as a birthday surprise for Jacob, and in it her father plays unexpectedly roughly with Dorothy while her mother is aloof in a long skirt and picture hat, avoiding both her white-stockinged daughter with the long ringlets and the robust knickerbockered father. John, seemingly a movie extra, takes direction dutifully.

This same, almost desperate attempt at activity is repeated in the indoor, heavily palm-equipped swimming pool. Here Morti seems bent on hitting Dorothy with a large rubber ball, ducking her and holding her under just a little too long. John keeps out of harm's way, and Adele does a serene breaststroke. She seems almost tea-gowned as she comes up the swimming ladder, oblivious, while Dorothy handles the ladder clumsily, being a bit on the plump side. Morti clambers up with a gusto reminiscent of Theodore Roosevelt.

There is a riding sequence, too—Adele is an elegant figure riding sidesaddle—and another sequence illustrates the perfect functioning of family carriages and cars. In a final scene the grandparents, Mr. and Mrs. Jacob Schiff, are caught in an unguarded moment being served demitasses by a tailcoated William on a stone veranda of the great house. Jacob is the picture of dignity, his back ramrod straight even when sitting alongside his surprisingly stout lady. Dorothy thinks everyone else in the film was trying too hard.

The Schiff family: Mortimer, Dorothy, John and Adele on a four-horse brake at a horse show, about 1912.

"I thought it was rather tasteless—the English house bigger than anyone could have needed, the English grooms and butler. My mother had made a scene about being photographed, I think—she couldn't be touched by me, always saying she bruised and it might cause cancer in the breast department—and John seemed more delicate than I remembered.

I was depressed by it because it is a dead time, and I can't understand how children raised like that can survive—just riding and learning how to play games. It seems so sad how hard my father tried to show *his* father what a happy family we were, just to please him. We weren't, and the whole thing was untrue."

The outbreak of World War I caught Morti and his family at Aix-les-Bains, in France. The fashionable spa offered both a cure and gambling, relaxations of which he was fond, though neither held any charms for eleven-year-old Dorothy, as she recalls the historic moment.

"All the chambermaids were crying, which I was told was due to their husbands and brothers having been mobilized. I was eleven and John ten that August, and with the war suddenly on, the problem was how to get out of France. My father had done well at the gaming tables, luckily, and had enough cash to get hold of a private train in which we could reach the Channel, where we could cross to England. It didn't take a whole train for us, of course, although there were four in the family, and then there was a valet, maid, nurse who was leaving, new French governess, Chow dog and Pekinese. This meant considerable space for the transatlantic voyage, what with all our luggage, and eventually we secured passage on an old liner, the *Lapland*. Aboard her I met Walter Wanger, who was then about twenty-one, and I fell in love with his marvelous stories. A few years later I saw him and was again madly in love. But this time it was with him, and I cried when my mother told me he had married a famous showgirl.

At home we did what we could for the troops by having a Red Cross thing set up in the old squash court at Oyster Bay, where we made dressings. There was also a canning kitchen, knitting and canteen work for the soldiers. I was with older girls mostly and became very close to the very social widow who ran the kitchen end. A great beauty who was the model for the World War One Red Cross poster, she had great gashes on her face from an automobile accident in which the two men with her were killed. Since she had no money, my father lent her a cottage on the place, in which, being a Christian Scientist, she surrounded herself with books by Mary Baker Eddy. She meant a lot to me, gave me tips on makeup and dress, and later chaperoned me to a dance at St. Paul's School. Eventually she committed suicide. Another older woman who was very kind to me in those years was Irene Gibson (Mrs. Charles Dana Gibson), one of the beautiful Langhorne sisters from Virginia (another sister was Lady Astor, leader of the Cliveden set and a Member of Parliament).

A German teacher who taught us on walks in the park stopped coming after 1914, when the war started. The Warburgs kept theirs, their father having been born in

Germany, but in our world there was much talk of *les Boches*, the Huns and such. Our French governess helped us with the war work, with which I became more and more involved. Maybe it was all that canning, dressing making and knitting that got me interested in doing things for other people. That may sound Lady Bountifulish, but anyway, it was good for me and kept me from sitting around all day doing nothing like my mother."

When Dorothy tries to summarize her childhood, she recalls that as a little girl she used to wonder what was across Central Park besides the West Side of which she had heard. Finally, she decided that on the other side of the park was another little girl who saw herself as a stepchild and also wondered what was on the other side of the park.

It seemed to Dorothy she was always being asked to go through the motions. An example is the Bar Mitzvahish ceremony for her and John conducted by a rabbi in the Northwood library for the purpose of what she calls her confirmation. The appropriate words were said and responded to, however unOrthodox the setting, and before she knew it, she was part of something to which others had decided it should appear she belonged, no matter how alien it seemed to her then.

"Years later, in a conversation with me about having children, my mother said that although of course they loved me, they had been afraid to show how much; I needed to be slapped down so I wouldn't be spoiled. It was all to do with my being so wild and extreme—so passionate and so excitable—but, actually, I think she thought I was hopeless.

My father may have rather liked me, but I don't know. If he said anything complimentary, she always ordered him not to spoil me. Naturally, he obeyed; he was afraid of her.

If I had to put my childhood in a word, I guess it would be misery . . . misunderstanding. Everything I tried to do ended up in disappointment, and as Ted [Thackrey, her third husband] used to say, 'He blew it in so sweet, and it came out so sour'—a horrible phrase. Anyway, nothing turned out the way it started."

Drawing by Charles Dana Gibson done at Dark Harbor, Maine, of Dorothy at fifteen.

An important influence on Dorothy was her mother's friend Sidney Smith. Once she reached her teens, they began having long talks in the library at 932 or on the Northwood verandas while her mother dressed for dinner. Much of their conversation concerned religion, and Dorothy says that this "great agnostic," as she thinks of him, could interweave that topic with her views and experience of young men then both minimal. This association on an adult level meant much to her, so much, in fact, that she began thinking of Mr. Smith more as her father than as her mother's friend. Because of the many weekends he spent at Northwood, Dorothy was shocked one day when her governess raised the possibility that Mr. Smith might be having an affair with her mother. She laughs as she recalls the moment, but the laugh is not one of the ones that light up her face.

"I insisted that it just couldn't be, because of our night watchman. He was on regular patrol with one of those key things in a leather case to be sure he didn't miss a round, so how could Mr. Smith have managed it?

I was certain that every morning he was in his own little guest room at the far end of the house, where he belonged. As to his relations with me, any passes he made were purely verbal; he loved that kind of chatter."

Strong words, Dorothy was told, should be kept for suitable occasions. She was reminded of this when she said she "hated gym" at the Brearley, being unable "to climb up things." "Hate" was such a word, and so was "love"; she still doesn't use the word "feel" as an alternate to "think."

The Brearley School class of 1920. Dorothy Schiff is sitting at the left end of the second row.

At thirteen, Dorothy once escaped the Brearley gym in the afternoon to sneak off with a classmate to the Plaza Theater movie, where she wanted to try smoking. She found out that there was a choice of brands and that she liked the illegality of the act more than the smoking. And at the Brearley she did the expected by graduating, just as she would also do the expected at Bryn Mawr by not staying after her freshman year.

"My mother, afraid of my becoming a bluestocking and that no one would marry me, didn't want me to go to college, but I wanted to get away from home. Some teachers at the Brearley who were Bryn Mawr graduates took us there, and while I wasn't overcome by the campus, I thought I might find out some answers. I suppose if my mother had let me, I would have gone with a missionary, Dr. Wilfred Grenfell, to Alaska . . . Labrador—I always get them mixed up—the summer after my freshman year.

My first class was at ten A.M.; I never had breakfast, just leaped into something with a raccoon coat over it and got through the morning that way. My set, which lived in the chichi hall—Pembroke East or West—went for meals to something called the College Inn, where we ate mostly ice-cream sodas and apple pie, which strained my monthly allowance of twenty-five dollars.

I learned about lemon meringue pie from Southern girls there and a great deal else from girls from other states. We'd sit up all night talking; I had never met anyone outside New York except in Europe. Until then I hadn't even been in a public conveyance, except for ocean liners. I had never heard of lesbianism, although some girls were expelled for it while I was there, and I didn't understand why two girls couldn't, but three could, go to the movies. As for sex education, they had lectures in something called hygiene—a couple of girls fainted; I didn't faint.

I took Greek instead of Latin, knowing Latin was impossible, but the Greek was even harder, and so all I learned were a few phrases and the alphabet. I didn't get what I wanted at Bryn Mawr, courses in psychology and sociology.

The dean, a formidable lesbian type and huge, so petrified me, I answered yes, when she asked if the Jacob Schiff who had just died was my father. That must have meant money to her, so they assigned me to history of art, which meant slides and stuff to look at. I flunked every single course, which is pretty hard to do, and the dean sent for me to tell me that I had dragged down the freshman average by getting zero. I'd had an earlier interview with her over my bobbing the girls' hair; she said they wouldn't be able to get teachers' jobs with short hair.

The reason I left after my freshman year was due to having to 'come out' at eighteen—with the debut they had planned for me, there wasn't room for more than that

Dorothy, Adele and Mortimer Schiff at a race meeting. Dorothy is about sixteen.

in one winter—and then there was my academic progress, nil. Obviously, I didn't do much for Bryn Mawr, not even my homework, which was enormous—six hours a day. I just sat up all night and talked. But it did a lot for me, and I loved it, even though I couldn't go back."

By the time Dorothy left Bryn Mawr she had lost her plumpness and no longer engaged in shoving contests. Vogue offered her $100 to model her legs, which her father forbade. Boys liked talking to her, partly because she was able to ask "a feeble question at the right time" which showed she understood what they were talking about. This, for many of them, included boasts about the chorus girls they took about.

"I considered these confidences flattering, but maybe it was just a line. My mother used to say that I was very gullible and that I must learn to be suspicious. I never really did, though; I fell into every trap set for me, thank God!

She thought I was hopeless and I knew that as the ugly

duckling—awkward, inadequate—I was a dreadful problem for her. The only thing I was trained to do was to attract men, and even that she didn't think I was very good
at. But I guess there, at least, I turned out better than she
expected. . . .

You know, it's very nervous-making, being made to
look back at one's life in a whole piece. It's hard to believe that any of it happened, really . . . particularly to
the one least likely to succeed.

And I don't like seeing that there was no joy in my
growing up. But there was no joy, none . . . absolutely
none."

Dorothy wasn't keen about having to go through the motions
of being presented to society, but it was expected that she would
come out, and by this time she'd had ample training in honoring
expectations. Debuts now are not what they were, but for some
parents getting a leg up socially by a daughter's presentation
still has meaning.

The coming-out routine began with a series of predeb dinners
and dances, some proffered by the Junior Assembly, a group of
socially impeccable parents. Dorothy was looked over by a sister
of J. P. Morgan for inclusion in the list, and a businesslike compromise was arrived at. She was invited to attend one dance out
of a scheduled three. Her acceptance meant that exile had been
avoided, though hope of full acceptance was abandoned. Generally, a Junior Assembly membership leads to the Junior League,
but here Dorothy was passed over altogether. A friend puts it
down to the Brandt affair, and Dorothy felt bad about it; she had
hoped to work in such a social service organization.

"Once you were on the list, you were invited to endless
parties, a lot of them at the old Ritz Carlton. A boy would
have to ask to take you in for supper, which used to make
me a little anxious—about not being asked—but I always
was. These parties, which my mother thought so important for me, drew the fortune hunters and no-goodnicks.
The first-class boys were too smart to come to them; they
were out with the Broadway girls, getting into trouble
and having fun, but later on they'd be after us. Anyway,
those parties weren't much—just a coatroom, ballroom
and maids waiting to chaperone the girls home."

According to Dorothy's brother, John, their parents didn't insist on her being chaperoned if he was at the parties and saw her home.

"It got me to deb parties when I was about sixteen," he says. "But when I'd say it's time to go home, Dolly would say, 'Oh, don't bother—I've got someone to take me.' "

John assumed their parents knew but preferred to overlook it. Dorothy, on the other hand, is sure that they didn't know, but in any case, her father's chauffeur, Gillespie, and the Rolls-Royce with the Brewster town car body always had to wait for her. Owing to the number of parties she attended, Gillespie must have put in a tough winter, even though her mother's chauffeur assumed morning duty. It was bound to have been cold, too; a town car's chauffeur sat out in the open, except in bad weather, when a fabric top and side curtains were permitted. The car's heater supplied only the tonneau.

It seems likely that Dorothy's parents were less concerned that she end up with the right suitor than that she should be safe from the wrong one. Almost as if she felt obliged to disappoint them, the one who took her fancy was popular but without means. Richard B. W. Hall's charm and good looks almost guaranteed both that he would become her husband and wouldn't remain so, as Dorothy recalls it.

"I met Dick when I was seventeen at a predeb Christmas *thé dansant* in the Plaza's small ballroom. He had sleepy, slightly Asian brown eyes and dark hair, slicked down. He was tall, had a way of looking down his nose contemptuously and was both more sophisticated and mysterious than other boys. This was due partly to his being older—six years older than I—and he had served as a lieutenant in the World War I navy on Vincent Astor's yacht, which had been converted into an auxiliary for North Sea service and was based at Brest, France. He enjoyed it all so much, he never did get over it, especially the young French countess.

He was quite sarcastic, saying biting, yet funny things, and had a terrific chip on his shoulder because he hadn't been born rich. Everyone he went out with had a lot of money, and it galled him terribly. Although he was really quite bright, he never had a chance. The only job avail-

Dorothy Schiff at the time of her debut.

able was as a bond salesman on Wall Street, which he hated. Before that he sold vacuum cleaners or something in rural areas, and he said the housewives all wanted to go to bed with him.

His father, a Son of the American Revolution who died young, had held a small Republican job and always hoped to sell some property in the Adirondacks for a lot of money but never did. Dick's family lived with his maternal grandparents on the upper West Side, but they were in the *Social Register*.

Although Dick did do a year at Williams, he really hadn't been to the right schools or college. Still, he was the best-looking man at parties and since I wanted to be independent—have my own little nest and a lot of children—I went after him."

When Dorothy went to the movies with Dick, she would be chaperoned by Mademoiselle, who sat behind them. Once Dorothy took Dick's hand in hers, which he thought sweet; she thought it risqué. The number of parties Dorothy attended that winter were so numerous that by the time her own was given at 932, with literally hundreds of guests, it didn't bother her a bit, she says.

"What did bother me was a ghastly girl who walked in uninvited, Dorothy Gardiner, the stepdaughter of Pierre Cartier. His was the number one jewelry shop until Van Cleef and Arpels became it. Dick Hall had done some flirting with her, and I was amazed to see her, having crossed her name off the list. She had blond hair and was quite fat in a pink and white something; she looked like a pig, a pink pig, and I hated her out of jealousy, I suppose.

When this ghastly girl came waltzing down the receiving line, I told her she couldn't come in. She said she was only going to stay a few minutes, but of course she stayed for hours. My mother, horrified, said what a terrible, rude thing I had done. I was outraged; all I cared about was Dick and how soon I could get married and out of that house."

The gathering was a *Social Register* one, with the exception of a young man recently taken on by Kuhn, Loeb, whom Morti had once brought home. This man was Lewis Strauss, who later became a rear admiral and eventually chairman of the Atomic Energy Commission.

"He was more interesting than other boys, having been Herbert Hoover's assistant, and he wasn't bad-looking either. My father thought he was terrific, but he wasn't what my mother wanted for me; she saw him as a shoe salesman from Richmond, Virginia. Later he was stolen from Kuhn, Loeb by the Rockefellers, who always got the best.

He married the daughter of a K.L. partner finally, but I should have told my mother how much I liked him, instead of letting her throw him out. Once he discovered there were no Jews at my party—virtually none—he was appalled and didn't stay long, he told me the last time I saw him, when we were reminiscing many years later.

Neither the young man's disappearance nor its cause kept the party from being a success, and while Dorothy recognizes the effort it involved on the part of her parents, there is a feeling that they, too, were going through motions in giving it. It did nothing to help her overcome her feeling, nor did it bring reassurance about belonging. Even now, she can speak as an orphan, and its effectiveness in getting the compassion of others is considerable.

"Dick and I saw each other only at parties until my eighteenth birthday in 1921, when I asked him for dinner. I was given a string of Oriental pearls by my father, who had been giving me a pearl each year. He added to it to make it long enough, and it had a diamond clasp.

There were only ten for dinner, and after it we went dancing, my mother's escort being Sidney Smith. When we came home, I said to her, 'Isn't that the most divine boy you ever saw?' She didn't think so at all and said the attraction was physical. Dick was very quiet, hardly ever saying anything, and had to be drawn out. I didn't understand then that the problem was in *him*. Although my father was around very little, he was opposed, too—afraid of what his family would think because of the religious difference, I thought."

Sidney Smith did a little research and came up with the fact that not only did Dick Hall have no money, but he owed some. Brooks Brothers had yet to be paid for his navy uniforms, and it seemed the reason that he had been turned down for Racquet Club membership was bills owed the Williams Club. Aside from his financial problem, Dorothy's feeling now is that had Dick been a Harriman or Whitney, he would have passed muster with her parents.

His older sister, Marian, was to become almost a staff interior decorator for Adele and later for Dorothy. She had been a classmate of Carola's at the Brearley. "As with all the Halls, Dick had charm," Carola says. "They had hearty laughs, were sophisticated, and they knew where the bread was buttered and how to play it. He had a terrific sense of humor, and you couldn't dislike him. But I don't think he had any depth or solidity."

Dick Hall had been taken by Dorothy a couple of times to Carola's, a place where in Prohibition drinks were served readily, and knowing this, Adele called Carola. "I wanted to play it safe," Carola explains. "I said I had seen him but didn't know him well. She wanted to know if I thought him attractive, and he was, until he grew older. He did put out a lot of sass, though, being fresh off Vincent Astor's boat, always 'our ship.' Anyway, it was clear Aunt Adele thought Dolly wasn't going to have a terrific time if she married him and that he wasn't a very solid person. She was right."

Dorothy was not forbidden to see Dick, but it was discouraged. They continued going to parties together and, in addition to speakeasies, went to nightclubs such as Harry Richman's and the Cotton Club in Harlem. For the boys the standard drink was the orange blossom and for both the dance was usually the fox trot.

Dorothy was in Oyster Bay in spring and fall and Europe for the summer, on which journeys, she says, Dick was not invited.

> "I remember being taken to England in June because that's when the season is, my mother and father making a big effort to introduce me into society and young men. I was not presented at court, but I went to parties in London quite a bit—terrible parties. I was very surly, and they got very angry with me. My father was interested in racing, so we went to Ascot. And I met a lot of people who were completely nameless and faceless to me, and it didn't work."

Ellin Berlin told Dorothy that she was put through the same thing because of the Mackay family objections to her future husband, Irving Berlin. They met six months after her chaperone had been let go, its being considered she was old enough to be safe on her own. The lady was promptly rehired and dispatched with Ellin to Europe.

"That was always the thing," said Dorothy. "A trip to Europe to break it up, and it never worked."

"Nothing really works, said Ellin Berlin. "All you can do is delay things, and delay may not be so bad, I think now. One can be so dazzled by somebody, one might marry them because of, or in spite of, who they are."

"How long was your marriage to Irving delayed?"

"A year and eight months."

"That's not very long."

"It seemed long to me. I often think of Consuelo [Vanderbilt]

Ellin and Irving Berlin, just after their elopement.

and what a brilliant thing she did to get married. She had her appendix out, and as she was coming out of the ether, she asked her mother to let her marry Earl Smith."

Remembering Earl Smith's father, her mother's beau, Sidney, Dorothy laughed. "I can't believe Mrs. Vanderbilt said yes. She was not easily moved."

"But she was very practical; when Consuelo and I were carrying on about what school to send our girls to, she said, 'Why don't you just stick them in Spence and forget about them?' Always a very sensible woman, Mrs. Vanderbilt."

In New York Dorothy's days were spent in learning shorthand and typing at the YWCA and taking correspondence courses in "everything from accounting to psychology." Among other things, she had hoped such training might help her to get a job at Kuhn, Loeb. When she felt up to it, she spoke to the senior partner, Morti, but he turned her down. Her evenings, whenever possible, were spent with Dick, and their outings, on the proceeds of opera matinee subscriptions given Dorothy by Morti, then sold by Dick, included burlesque and movies.

"One day, in the spring of 1922, after the family had moved to Oyster Bay, I came in to New York to dine with my father at the Colony Restaurant and go with him to the theater. I planned to stay at our house at 932 Fifth Avenue. The following evening I had been invited to a dinner party at the large house of a well-known banker. The Gould daughters were friends of Dick Hall, and I was much looking forward to the party.

While having dinner with my father (both of us dressed in evening clothes), he happened to ask where I was going the following evening. When I told him, he became furious, saying he would not permit me to enter the house of this man, but he didn't tell me why. I said I was going anyway.

My father then said, 'In that case, we will leave the restaurant immediately. You will go home and change your clothes and Gillespie [the chauffeur] will drive you straight back to the country.'

We went back to 932. I changed my clothes in a fury and went down to get in the car, but the car wasn't there. Delighted, I walked quickly around the corner to Madison Avenue and, in a pay station in a drugstore, telephoned Dick, whose phone did not answer. I got into a streetcar and went to the YWCA at Lexington Avenue and Fifty-second or Fifty-third Street, where I had been taking my secretarial course, and continued to call Dick, who lived nearby, but his phone still did not answer.

Around ten thirty, I got scared and called a school friend who lived with her mother in an apartment on the East Side. She was at home. I told her that I had been out for the evening and forgotten my key and couldn't get into my own house and asked if I could spend the night with her. She said certainly. I had very little money in my purse and had to borrow money from her to buy a pair of stockings because mine had run.

I had dinner as planned at the banker's house and spent another night with my friend.

The next morning, early, there was a telephone call for me. It was the woman who had worked in the Red Cross and had been so kind to me in the war years. She asked me if I would join her for breakfast at Longchamps, which I did. She said my parents were terribly worried about me, and if I would go home to Oyster Bay that day, the matter would never be mentioned. I agreed to do this.

My mother, as so often, was in bed, looking upset, but didn't bawl me out. I could imagine the dreadful scenes she and my father must have had about the whole thing. How they tracked me down, I don't know to this day."

Among the ploys to distract her from her involvement was the importation of a possible suitor, and Dorothy enjoys telling the story.

"They dug up a Rothschild, a French one. He arrived at Oyster Bay and was pretty unattractive, I thought. We had a French cook at the time, and he went into the kitchen and talked French to her endlessly. That was all right, but he was in trouble.

He had brought his mistress with him but couldn't get her into the country—moral turpitude, or whatever they worried about in those days. So he sent her to Canada, but there was a big scandal, and they shipped him back to France.

A couple of years ago, I read in the paper that this same man, having been widowed, married a coat-check girl, aged eighteen. So it was just as well that plot didn't work."

Two years went by before Dorothy's parents accepted defeat. Returning from Europe in August, 1923, after a second try at the field of overseas eligibles, Adele told her she could be engaged. The announcement made all the New York papers, was picked up in other cities, and says Dorothy, "to my horror, some people thought I was marrying a Hallgarten—not Hall." (The Wall Street firm belonging to Dorothy's maternal grandfather was Hallgarten & Co.)

"The minute they gave up I was much less interested— the challenge of forbidden fruit, I suppose. I had doubts about Dick; I got scared about his anti-Semitism, his interest in money and material things and his lack of warmth. But I was still attracted to him.

He was very critical of me and wouldn't hesitate to tell me he didn't like my hat and so forth. I wasn't what he had planned for himself; he did want to marry an heiress, but I was far from his first choice. He would have pre-

Dorothy Schiff at the time her engagement to Richard Hall was announced in August, 1923.

ferred Barbara Whitney, Sonny's sister, who was my age, but he couldn't get anywhere with her. Maybe he tried too hard. When I finally told my mother I didn't want to marry Dick, she told me a lot of girls get these feelings before a wedding. 'It's too late,' she said. 'You have three hundred wedding presents, guests will be arriving for the wedding tomorrow, and you've got to go through with it.'

I didn't talk to my father about it—I never talked to him—but a few years later when I told him I wanted to get a divorce, he said that wonderful thing, 'When you've made your bed, you've got to lie in it.'"

Among those surprised by the announcement of the engagement was Dorothy's brother, John. It wasn't that he didn't like his future brother-in-law, though.

"At her age of nineteen, I could see her marrying someone twenty-five," John says, "but to me, at seventeen, a man of twenty-six looked awful old. It was beyond my comprehension. And he wasn't a terribly good athlete, but he worked like hell on his golf."

The wedding, at Northwood on October 17, 1923, was as big as they come, consistent with good taste. The groom was as described by Dorothy—handsome with hair slicked back and looking down his nose—while for her part, she has been described as appearing something of a houri, which she defines as a belly dancer. In the wedding photographs she is certainly regally dressed, and they and the news stories tell more of *who* she was—granddaughter of the late great man of Kuhn, Loeb and daughter of its senior partner—than what she was.

The officiating cleric was the Right Reverend Herbert Shipman, Episcopal Suffragan Bishop of New York, who, when still rector of the Church of the Heavenly Rest, the Halls' church, had confirmed Dorothy in his denomination after due instruction. Thus, she was blessed twice over—spiritually and socially—but there were Jewish relatives who were shocked by the Christian service, although there was no kneeling. The matter of bridesmaids was something else; she had wanted her best friends, Consuelo Vanderbilt and Ellin Mackay, to serve, but they refused. Dorothy doesn't know why, but her guess is that, as with the Assembly and Junior League, the Brandt case was behind it. Other people, she says, felt that the problem lay with "Dick Hall and his pals; he wasn't considered first class."

In addition to the fact that Adele disapproved of the marriage, since Dick was not up to her standards, Dorothy had a problem on her wedding day of an unexpected nature.

"I had developed poison ivy. I got it necking in the bushes, and it broke out all over my arms, so I wore long white gloves to hide it. I slit the ring finger of one to be sure the ring went on.

On the way to the St. Regis Hotel for the bridal night, Dick had to leave off his laundry. The night was not very satisfactory; I was a virgin. I would have, but he wouldn't, and my experience was so limited that once, in an active moment, I mistook a petal of a white carnation on the sofa for something else. Finally, I said, 'Well, go on . . . ?' And he said, 'That's all there is.'

The morning after that I had put on a silk peach wrapper with maribou collar and sleeves to greet him at the table in our St. Regis suite. He said, 'I never could stand women in the morning,' and that was our last breakfast together. Of course, that whole experience was a horror. In Montreal he gave me too much white wine, and when I awoke during the night, throwing up, he sent for the maid and moved to another hotel. Not surprisingly, we came home earlier than had been scheduled, and my mother was furious, as we had to stay with her.

I had my Willys-Sainte Claire roadster, which my father had given me on my nineteenth birthday (and which I never drove once, as Dick was mad about driving), and our honeymoon was spent driving to Montreal and back because that's all we could afford.

Morti Hall was born on July 21, 1924, nine months later."

Adele, who furnished their New York apartment, on Seventy-third street between Lexington and Third avenues, tried to talk Dorothy out of a double bed. This, Dorothy supposes, was due to the fact that as long as she could remember, her parents didn't share a room. Those three hundred wedding presents went a long way toward furnishing the place, and well they might, being the joint efforts not only of family and friends, but also of business associates of Kuhn, Loeb. Dorothy did make some exchanges, but for the most part the wedding presents from that marriage were far more durable than the union; in fact, they not only saw her through the next three marriages, but serve her today.

With the apartment settled, Dorothy then had the family finances to consider.

"My father gave us a fourteen-thousand-dollar allowance in the form of a joint account at the bank, but he wouldn't take Dick into Kuhn, Loeb. He got him a job as a sort of intern with a brokerage house, which paid only a hundred dollars monthly, and I signed most of the checks. With my father, it wasn't so much that he disapproved of the marriage or Dick's lack of money as it was his view of his personality. But since we were married, he wanted to do all he could to help make it work.

Prices were high in the twenties, and there was never enough money, not nearly enough. Dick lost a lot of money at backgammon, so I took some jewelry my father had given me and hocked it at a place on Seventy-second

Street, called the Provident Loan Association. I never re-
deemed it, and it was years before I learned the place had
been founded by my grandfather and that my father was
president."

Although Dick had his losses in backgammon, Eddie Warburg
points out that "he made expenses at evening bridge sessions;
my mother liked to think she was a bridge player." Eddie's sister, Carola, agrees. "Dick looked forward to the evenings with
great enthusiasm. Mother played for practically nothing a point,
but Dick would raise the ante."

During the first years of the marriage Dick and Dorothy saw
much of the latter's friend Consuelo Vanderbilt, at that time
married to Earl Smith. While Consuelo can't remember the reason for not being part of the wedding, she has a very vivid recollection of Dick, who she says was great fun to go dining and
dancing with, even if "he wasn't perhaps the most brilliant man
that ever lived." Aside from the fact that intellectually he didn't
have much in common with Dorothy, she thought them well
suited. Dorothy, she feels, was prettier than her mother, but her
most important quality was that "she was never mean; she was
always the most ungossipy person." Between his bachelor
friends and golf, Dick was out a lot, and Dorothy found herself
reading more and more.

"I found out about a magazine called *The Bookman*
that was current at that time, and it gave reviews of the
books on the best-seller lists. Much later a book was written about the Great Books, and although I had never at
that time heard of Dr. Eliot's Five-Foot Shelf, which was
made fun of, Great Books was sort of that. I decided I was
going to read everything. Of course, I got nowhere, but I
read more than most of the people I knew. Always search-
ing for answers to, I guess, how to be happy, how to function and how not to have a nervous breakdown, which I'd
never heard of before.

But then we'd go to parties or nightclubs, and I learned
about alcohol. I drank too much, then decided that was
no good and went back to the books. The books would all
say, get into life, and I'd go back into life and get disgust-
ed and go back into the books. I still do that."

Dorothy's mother had told her that childbirth was the most terrible experience she had ever had, and as Dorothy's time approached, she began to wonder if she would be able to go through with it. She told herself that she had to ("there's no getting out of this"), and the situation wasn't helped by Dick's remarking after a dance at Sherry's that no one had asked her to dance. As she remembers it, her face hardens. "I told him once I had this baby, they would. And they did."

All went well with the birth of Mortimer Wadhams Hall. The W below the M within the H made a perfect monogram. The event didn't change Dick's life particularly, but it did Dorothy's. The apartment became small and diaper-filled, and Adele was hardly an indulgent granny; the one time she came to dinner, she didn't take to the menu, and the evening was a disaster. As for her father, Dorothy feels he was rather ambivalent; the baby he saw as a Hall, not a Schiff. In addition, he still considered himself a man-about-town and felt that if he had to be a grandfather, he would rather that John produce an heir named Schiff.

Dorothy says at that time she was very immature for twenty and knew very little. While it was true that she had always wanted to have a home and children, she found herself wishing that she were less tied down and could have more of a life on her own (even though there was a nurse at $70 a month and a cook at $60).

Thirteen months after nine-and-a-half-pound Morti, came the 5 A.M. birth of Adele Therese Hall, weighing 10 pounds ("we ate for two then"). The senior Adele commented that Dorothy was "having litters like a bitch." This made Dorothy wish she could "invent a device so it wouldn't happen again, a piece of rubber, sort of, for me. Dick wouldn't use one of those things we were always finding on beaches."

"In the twenties, with the exception of the rhythm method, all birth control was illegal. The diaphragm could be bought in certain drugstores, and the way I found out about it was on a boat coming back from Europe, when a boy called Ryan asked me to smuggle in a book called *Married Love* by Marie Stopes. The only other book I ever smuggled in was a book for Gilbert Seldes, *Ulysses,* by James Joyce. I was fascinated by the Stopes book because it had illustrations, and it showed a picture of a diaphragm. I found out it could be bought in a drugstore on Madison Avenue.

On that particular day the clerk behind the counter was a man. But I went right up to the counter, and I told him what I wanted, and he said, what size? I didn't know they came in different sizes and just stood there. So he looked me up and down and said he thought a medium one would do. So I said, okay, and I asked how much and he said five dollars, which threw me because I thought it would be about twenty cents. But it turned out to be a good investment. It lasted for years."

Now that she was twice a mother, Dorothy began to look about her. A summer was spent in Southampton, where the club issue arose. They were elected to the Beach Club there but not to the Meadow (tennis) or Shinnecock (golf) clubs. Dick Hall blamed Dorothy for his blackballing, and it is clear that she is still bitter about it.

Another summer was spent without Dick at Biarritz, which Dorothy refers to as "utterly frivolous," and springs and falls were passed at Oyster Bay. Winters were based in New York, but there were southern visits to White Sulphur Springs and Palm Beach. At White Sulphur, Consuelo and Dorothy agreed that exercise was a waste of time, and while their husbands played golf, they limited themselves to cards and talk of their children. Palm Beach life was not as simple, Dorothy recalls.

"My parents had shared a house with Otto Kahn, a Kuhn, Loeb partner and Metropolitan Opera sponsor—he occupied it in February, and they in March, as they didn't believe in being away simultaneously.

In addition to the house, we shared use of a private car, and its blacks, as we call them now, doubled as servants. The house, which was pink stucco, was near Bradley's gambling house, and there I developed a system for winning at roulette; at least, I thought I had. I lost one thousand dollars one afternoon and was desperate. Having no money, I saw Colonel Bradley and agreed to pay him back over a couple of years. When I told this to Herbert Swope, he said, 'My God, your father lost twenty-five thousand dollars the night before in the big room upstairs!' This was before I was married.

I thought Palm Beach was divine—flowers, bougainvillaea and stuff—and later sold my mother on building a house. I took the children there, and Dick would come

Adele Schiff's Casa Eleda in Palm Beach.

down for a short vacation. I heard recently that his mother said it was no wonder he strayed, because I was in Palm Beach all winter. But he strayed long before that, having come home with lipstick on his cheek one night. I was so innocent I believed him when he told me that if I were unfaithful, he could tell by feeling my arm.

There were a lot of women there and some extra men with whom we'd go to nightclubs and things. They told me that one night they would take out the ladies and the next what they called the bims—the bimbos. These were older rich men, not from New York as much as from Pittsburgh and around the country. One of them was quite a friend of mine—very good-looking, like a lion, but terribly stupid.

Dorothy Schiff in Palm Beach in the 1920s.

Girls from Philadelphia, Main Liners (now it means something else), visited me a lot. At the Beach and Tennis Club, where we had a cabana, there was a lot of . . . pouncing, we used to call it. You couldn't change your bathing suit without somebody trying to break in; older men, many of them married, made passes at us. I fended them off by making a joke of it, then running away.

Athletics were limited to walking around the golf course occasionally with beaux, and they always tried to get me to take a mashie shot or something. We played a lot of backgammon in the late afternoon, and since I couldn't afford the bridge stakes, when a fourth was needed, my mother would back me, but I didn't like bridge; I couldn't concentrate. My mind was on other things, and I used to read a lot, which the Philadelphia girls joked about, saying that I was this peculiar combination of a party girl and an intellectual.

So when they were all horsing around, I would be reading in my room. But when evening came and it was time for making what we called whoopee, I would be ready for the evening's activities—out-of-doors dance floors and drinking. Even then I was smart enough to take my own car, so I could get away and not be dependent on one of those drunks to drive me home.

My mother, who loved to entertain, had a bar in the house. Even though it was Prohibition, there was always plenty of liquor, and people would drop by in the late afternoon. Among them was Joseph P. Kennedy, brought by Averell Harriman, and none of us knew anything about this redheaded Irishman, who didn't drink. He was just one of the older men who took us out and paid the bill. For me, he wasn't a pouncer, but I heard he was with others. We were very good friends for years, until he had a stroke."

Palm Beach meant both a more sophisticated social life and more elegant staffs. One nanny was so haughty she had been known by a former employer as the Duchess, a warning Dorothy failed to heed. An English nursery governess taught the children to read, but in time, she, too, presented a problem; how could they learn to speak French when it could be learned only from one who spoke no English? The answer was a mademoiselle.

"There were stages in those days; it was time for the children to have a governess. The girl this mademoiselle had brought up said, '*Mademoiselle est très autoritaire,*' which she was. She was sort of a bore, but wonderful because she was very definite. She was marvelous for Morti as he grew older—she would try to think of things for him to do—but she was mean to Adele. It was sort of what happened to me in a boy-girl sibling situation; the boy would be allowed to play in the garage with the chauffeur but not the girl—stuff like that.

The nursery governess, when I let her go, made a speech. She was quite severe with me, saying I ought to see more of my children. She used to read to them at night, and they'd huddle up next to her. It made an impression on me, although I thought I had done rather well with them; other people left their children at home with servants when they went on trips, but I always took mine along; I don't think it hurt them, and it was good for me. My son, Morti, used to say to me, 'A woman's place is in the home,' and when my hair turned gray in my thirties, he was delighted. He said, 'Now you look like a mother.' "

Dick Hall with his two children, Adele and Morti.

There were times when Dorothy's life seemed a series of private cars, which were used for runs as short as to Philadelphia. On one such trip, Dorothy remembers that although the girls were in their twenties, the men were middle-aged, including a lawyer with three daughters, named Faith, Hope and Charity.

"I had met him in Southampton, where he pounced on the beach after a party. I had on a diamond bracelet my father had given me, which I lost in the sand. It wasn't

Marian Hall, decorator and sister of Dick Hall, with her niece and nephew.

the first piece of jewelry I had lost that way; one went in Palm Beach and another at White Sulphur. Men were very rough in those days and would tear at you.

The jewelry I was always losing on roads and in the sand was real, but although they were insured, I never reported the losses. The thing was, all the girls wanted to be taken out, but all that lost jewelry meant the price was high. Sometimes, though, it would be returned by the police.

On the private car there were a lot of drinks and dinner with these older men, all of whom were unloved and certain that women were interested in them only because of their money—true and very sad. I suppose they might have been interesting if asked the right questions, but I was too green to know that. They weren't self-made, just poor, little old rich boys looking for some kind of solace. They got nothing from their wives, nor did their wives from them. It's all rather somber, this, but maybe through the experience I gained some understanding."

Dorothy with Adele and Morti.

The late twenties were a period of restlessness for Dorothy. For Dick, they were a time for even more bridge, backgammon, golf and pals—male and female. Along with these interests went alcohol. Orange blossoms had long since been abandoned for dry martinis, and often enough of them were taken to put him asleep in his living-room chair after dinner, "so I started stepping out." He and Dorothy still went together to parties, at one of which she met a czarist prince. It was a 1930 Fourth of July fancy dress affair at the Piping Rock Club, and she was asked to dance by a tall, elegant man with aquiline features, wearing, appropriately, a Cossack costume. Serge Obolensky says of Dorothy, "She was very attractive, amusing to be with, very intelligent, with a number of beaux, and she had—how should I say—an aura about her."

Dorothy recalls:

"It was a storybook romance, even if it did last only ten months. Serge was very good-looking, danced divinely, and the girls all flipped that night. I did, too, and when he phoned the next morning, I thought, why me?

He invited me to lunch at a place I'd never heard of, the Grand Central Oyster Bar. Later he took me to a marvelous Russian restaurant where all the émigrés went and there was a pool of live carp or something. He talked about the University of St. Petersburg, the Russian Revolution and galloping down treelined grass avenues of his family estates. We were in evening clothes, and after dinner we danced at the Casino-on-the-Park. This became a ritual, and no matter how late, he would see me home, and Dick never woke up. Serge had a marvelous apartment on East End Avenue with a big portrait of himself in uniform in the living room, by Sorin. Lunches, of course, were less of a problem.

Serge Obolensky.

Serge was separated then from that school friend in mourning Alice Astor. After several more husbands, she died mysteriously in her town house, which smelled of incense as used at rites. I didn't know that Serge wasn't

about my age, twenty-seven, and was amazed to learn
that he was forty. I suppose the affair was more infatua-
tion than love—he was a fascinating man, charming and
different—and he knew how to court a woman. And yet
he was shy.

He asked me for a weekend at his Rhinebeck house,
where he had a marvelous chef and a butler, later at the
British embassy in Washington. There was a stranger at
the house party, and I was surprised to find myself put in
a downstairs guest room next to an attractive, very good-
looking Englishman. I didn't know if Serge was testing
me or what, but the Englishman came into my room, I
thought just to talk. But I was in love with Serge. The Englishman married an heiress later.

All weekend Serge was acting as if he barely knew me,
and when I asked why he had put me next to this man, he
said he hadn't dared put me upstairs with himself because it might compromise me. I didn't understand any
of it and finally decided he just didn't like me enough."

Averell Harriman appeared in Dorothy's life again, this time
in France. His father, E. H. Harriman, had been supported by
Jacob Schiff and Kuhn, Loeb, his bankers, in an epic battle on
behalf of the Union Pacific against J. J. Hill, allied with J. P.
Morgan, who controlled the Great Northern. It was one of Jacob's greatest victories, accomplished with a minimum of the
fast dealing for which rail magnates became noted, and it
brought a new measure of professional acceptance from Morgan.

Dorothy had always been attracted to Harriman, who had just
gotten a divorce from his first wife and was a star polo player. He
was older than Dorothy by twelve years and one Saturday in Paris asked her to spend the day and dine with him.

"This charming man with the beautiful voice and perfect manners was the kind who demanded complete attention. I rather like that kind of demanding man.

A friend of his, who was in France with him on a German reparations mission, thought the tennis at St.-Cloud
boring and suggested we go to Longchamps to watch one
of my father's horses run. I told Averell we'd be back in
an hour, but what happened was that we had a lot of little

brandies at the track and we came rolling in, laughing, and arm in arm. Averell was not amused.

If I had known that my watching the tennis meant anything to him, I would have stayed. He had hired a car, and about five of us drove back to Paris. As we reached the Arc de Triomphe, he took my hand and turned it over. Then, in front of the others, he said, 'Your hand looks like a hotel register.'

A dead orchid was left at my hotel later, with a note saying he had to leave for London immediately. I cried then, being very disappointed; we had had a previous dinner together, and I was looking forward to our date that Saturday night. Also, I had heard he wanted to marry my childhood friend Marie Norton. She had been married to Sonny Whitney, which meant that with Averell she'd grabbed the two catches somehow or other; God knows I didn't!

In a while, Jim Forrestal [the future Secretary of Defense] called me; he had been with us and watching. He asked if I were free for dinner, which I certainly was then, and came right over. He talked about his friends and professors at Harvard and philosophy and stuff. But I was thinking about how I'd messed up my life and wondering if the dead orchid could have been the florist's mistake. And if that line about my hand really meant what it said."

How Morti's horse did at Longchamps is not an item of interest for Dorothy, nor was how her father was doing. Their rare meetings were limited to family occasions, and while there was no estrangement, there was a wide difference in life-styles and friends. His stable in France, appropriately enough for the sport of kings (and bankers), was run by a titled sportsman, the Vicomte Sebastien Foy. He admired Morti greatly, and his fondness for him may have prompted her to do some thinking about the remote father-daughter relationship when she came back to the United States, and made her more receptive to a dinner with Morti alone at Northwood, where she had been spending June as his hostess ("not that many people came around").

It was after his golf game and nineteenth hole moment at Piping Rock. Adele was in her house in Paris, and John was out for the evening. Nothing had been planned for Morti's fifty-fourth birthday the next day; in fact, both Dorothy and John had engagements. In the smoking room after the dinner served by William and a footman, Dorothy asked for a brandy, in spite of Morti's opposition to women using hard liquor. ("I reasoned that I was a married woman, even if Dick and I were rarely together.") Morti settled down with kümmel and a cigar and began a conversation such as they had never had and never would again.

He spoke first of his experiences in England as a young man learning banking. On a weekend in the country he had spent the night with a titled English lady, also a guest. A week later he was shocked and hurt to receive bills from her Paris dressmakers, and now, so many years later, "It was still uppermost in his mind that he was expected to pay for things she had bought before she met him; he had thought she liked him."

Dorothy sees Morti as having always been victimized by women and quotes some of them as considering him the kindest and most generous of men. ("He gave them terrific presents, got them jobs, set them up in shops.") Women and his inability to match that strong, dominating father were agonizing problems all his life, in Dorothy's view, and it occurred to her for the first time that night that he was a man to be pitied. She recognized his positive qualities—his concern about others, generosity to poor relations, philanthropies, strong sense of duty—and is certain that he never enjoyed himself without feeling guilty, saying that "he was terrified his father would hear about his racehorses, gambling and women. His wife, of course, couldn't have cared less." Of all the women he talked of that night, Adele was not mentioned.

Dorothy feels that her father, half playboy and half do-gooder, was never able to resolve the conflict. He was essentially an Edwardian while Jacob was a Victorian.

Morti mentioned Dick Hall, too, saying that one of his regrets was that he had been unable to communicate with him. Dorothy says that in spite of her father's warmth and jollity, Dick didn't like him. Morti's generosity, however necessary, was probably a contributing factor; acceptance of in-law financial support can make for harder work than earned income. Dick did allow himself to like Adele eventually, which Dorothy feels was due to the Jewish female being more socially acceptable than the male. She points out that the reason Lord Rosebery achieved the last of his three wishes in life—to be Prime Minister, win the Derby and marry an heiress—was that his lady was a Rothschild. "They permitted their females to intermarry but never the males (not true anymore)."

Morti, Dorothy says, "worshiped" his mother. In spite of those short legs so obvious in the film, Therese also would sit with one tucked under her à la Dorothy, however hard it is to imagine. The blue of her eyes, combined with that of Jacob's, has contributed to that striking blue of Dorothy's.

As her father talked on in the Northwood smoking room, he revealed that he thought himself a failure. He explained that instead of enlarging the fortune left to him by Jacob, he had lost half of it in the '29 crash; instead of expanding the operations of Kuhn, Loeb, he had merely confirmed its good name; instead of having real contact with his "fellow religionists," he had only succored them through funding; instead of finding one to whom he could give his love, he had given presents; and instead of being loved in return, he had been thanked. There were times when there was no more joy in this man than in his daughter.

Still, Morti's loss of half his fortune left him with holdings which can hardly be called penury, and few would see his life as a failure. He never lost his belief in ideas, saying of Lewis Strauss that if only one from his endless store worked in a year, he earned his partner's share of Kuhn, Loeb's profits (said to bring him $1,000,000). Dorothy further remembers:

> "I think he must have been without a mistress at that moment. I have been told that he was very much in love with my mother, who rejected him. Although this was sad for him, I never saw him depressed until that night. He had always been gay, and would feel so badly when he lost his temper, then try to make up for it.
>
> He was a man of extremes, either being a teetotaler or drinking and having to take cures and sit in a hot box contraption at Oyster Bay with his head sticking out to lose weight. And of course, he was a gambler on everything, yet always so conscientious. . . .
>
> After hours of talk that night, we went upstairs. It was cooler in my mother's empty room, and I had moved in there at his suggestion, as it had three exposures. It adjoined his room, and he told one of his rather off-color

stories as he saw me to my door. As usual, he laughed heartily at it, which my mother always pointed out to him. After kissing me good-night, he said, 'Well, we're like an old married couple.'

I didn't know anything until seven A.M., when I heard William knocking and knocking on his door. Then he knocked on my door, calling my name. I went out into the hall and asked, 'What is it?'

He said, 'I don't seem to be able to rouse your father.'

We went into his room, and there he was in an armchair, wearing a silk brocade dressing gown with brownish lapels, a Jaeger lap robe folded neatly over his knees. I had never seen a dead person before, but it wasn't scary at all. He just looked peacefully asleep, his hands on his knees. . . . John's room was up on the third floor, and William, who used to call him Mr. John, knocked on his door, saying, 'Good morning, sir. Your father is dead.' John suggested that we telephone Paris, which was seldom done in those days, to get a cousin to tell our mother. He said it would be a shock for her, and I didn't dare tell her. This being before transtlantic air travel, the funeral was delayed a week. She arrived on the *Bremen* and was taken off at quarantine by the Kahn yacht. When she came into the smoking room, she went over to the big round table by the bay windows; on it were a lot of magazines—the *Tatler, Spectator* and so forth—and also the Boy Scout magazine. Since my father had been their president, his picture was on the cover with a broad black band around it. She picked it up, turned it over, and slapped it down, saying, 'How tactless of you to have that here when I come home.' Later she said, 'He was the kindest man I ever knew,' and 'The only thing I ever did for him was to give him you two children.' "

The service was held in the drawing room of the great house; outsiders consisted of a few friends, business associates and employees. Rabbi Nathan Kraus, of Temple Emanu-El, officiated, and for many of those present it was their first exposure to a Jewish ritual, even a Reformed one. Interment was in the Cold Spring Harbor Memorial Cemetery, which was chosen by Adele for the same reason as had been Oyster Bay. Dorothy says, "She had no idea how soon it would be needed by both of them. She just wanted a simple place and found this beautifully landscaped, very expensive-looking place." For the mourners, almost as unusual as the service was having taps played by three Boy Scouts. The notes were clear and without quaver.

Morti's chief bequest to Dorothy was not in his last testament but in his last testimony that night in the smoking room. With that exposure began her growth, and so his end was to become her beginning.

"After he died, I lost twenty pounds," she says, with real wonder. "And I cried a lot. I can't imagine why."

III

"Max told me he would make me the toast of London; I guess I was already the talk of it."

Although Morti's estate was only half what he had once expected to leave, it was, at $30,000,0000, comfortably large without being vulgarly so. Jacob would have been pleased that of the million left to charity, more than half went to Jewish causes, and he would also have approved the bequests to the Henry Street Settlement and black institutions. The Boy Scouts of America received $100,000 from its late president and holder of the Silver Buffalo decoration, and neither Kuhn, Loeb employees nor household staffs were forgotten.

Adele received three-fifths of the residuary estate, Northwood in trust, and, outright, 932 Fifth Avenue, plus two private garages (212 East Seventy-fourth and 174 East Seventy-fifth), and their collections and furnishings.

John received $1,000,000 outright, one-fifth of the residuary estate in trust and the privilege of substantial borrowing from the estate in order to maintain a major Schiff interest in Kuhn, Loeb. However, he was obliged to assume direction of the firm and thus accepted a life of service to institutions in the tradition begun by Jacob, rejecting the more congenial role of gentleman-sportsman. In committing his energy, talent and ambition to the worlds of investment banking and society, he had as ally his wife, TeeTee Baker, whose father's yacht was even grander than Morti's.

At first Dorothy thought she was on an equal basis with John, being also favored with a one-fifth interest in the residuary estate, plus $750,000 outright and a share in the three-fifths of the

*John Schiff with his wife,
the former Edith Baker,
in 1934.*

residuary upon termination of Adele's trust. However, the quarter million left to Dick came out of what might have been Dorothy's cash bequest, the residuary share was for the children "in proportion of two parts to the son and one part to the daughter," and of course, Dorothy had neither the privilege of borrowing from the estate, as did John, nor the very considerable emoluments coming with a Kuhn, Loeb partnership.

Dorothy has never commented on this unequal inheritance owing to respect for Morti's wishes and her acceptance of being "merely a daughter." In fact, she had thought until recently that John received two-thirds of everything not left to their mother and that their mother's will had made a similar division. This she mentioned in association with her early fantasy of being adopted.

"I can't understand why he left me anything," she says. "He was a believer in primogeniture and hadn't liked my marrying Dick."

In spite of being born to wealth, Dorothy has never been able to relax about money. Over the years she has had fantasies in which she has seen herself destitute, made so, if not by husbands, by the New York *Post.* Yet even before she arrived at wealth, it had a way of cutting her off from others. An example is her embarrassment in being unable to treat school and college friends owing to the absence of an allowance. She doesn't like speaking about how it feels to be well off.

"I remember being furious whenever it was mentioned. People even said, not entirely joking, 'Come on, give me a million. You won't even miss it.' But still, I didn't think of myself as having money, and I never spent money even for things I really wanted. There was a pair of little Rousseau primitives at the Marie Harriman Gallery, which Averell set up for her. They could have been bought for five thousand dollars, but I had never heard of such a price—the last pictures I bought were three Grandma Moses for three hundred dollars each. I wish to God I had bought the Rousseaus, though, and not just for what they are worth now.

There has always been this thing about spending money on myself, so I'm used to being asked why I don't buy a new coat or dress. I don't know if it's fear of being self-indulgent or a puritanical guilt, but spending just isn't easy for me."

Dorothy's horizons broadened suddenly and dramatically when a new man came into her life or, more accurately, when she was ordered into his. He was the renowned British press lord Beaverbrook, born William Maxwell Aitken and knighted prior to his peerage.

"It was August, 1931, and my mother had planned to take me and the children back to Europe after the funeral. Reservations had been made on the *Bremen,* a fast ship, but after Hitler, I didn't use German ships. My mother had one of her attacks, so the children, their governess and I were put aboard, with arrangements made for them to eat at the first seating in the saloon and for me to share a table with family friends, the Gordon Douglases, in the Ritz Restaurant, which was à la carte.

You know, those liners were terrific—the romance of the whole thing and the whoopee. It's funny, the men I met that way. I remember meeting Jim Forrestal on a ship, and before we docked, he asked about our sharing a roomette on the boat train together to Paris. I said, 'Sure, but I have a couple of children and a governess in tow.' 'Oh,' he said. 'Well, let's meet in Paris then.' We did, but we certainly didn't sit together on that boat train.

We always dressed for dinner in first class, and the first night out on the *Bremen* I wore a black lace dress with satin slip. As arranged, I was at the Douglases' table and across the dining room we noticed two unusual-looking men—one, a big fat man with a red complexion, and the other was a little man with a huge head. The big one came over to our table and introduced himself as Valentine Castlerosse, who I knew was a peer even though he wrote a gossip column for Beaverbrook's *Daily Express*.

'The big boss over there wants to meet you,' he said to me. I knew who the 'big boss' was, of course; a stag dinner had been given for Beaverbrook on Long Island, and I had been irritated because all the men I knew had gone. May Douglas whispered to me that she knew all about the press lord and I was to sit right where I was. She told Viscount Castlerosse, 'Bring him over here, if he wants to meet her.'

Castlerosse said, 'Well, he won't do that. Just join him for coffee and a liqueur; then I'll come and bring you back. He's very easily bored.' So I said, 'He sounds interesting from what I've heard, and I think I will.'

I joined the press lord, and before long he asked if I knew how to set up a backgammon board; he had one in his cabin and had forgotten how. I said that I did know how to, but that was about all I knew—stuff like that. Castlerosse came over at that point and was told, 'Valentine, you may go back and join those people. Mrs. Hall is going to show me how to set up the backgammon board.' We went down to his cabin, which turned out to be a suite, and made a few moves—backgammon ones.

One of the first things he asked was if I were the granddaughter of Jacob Schiff; my father's death had been in the papers at home and abroad, of course. I said, 'Yes, I am. But it's something I have tried to conceal for years.' After a while we went up for a walk on deck, and he told me that when he had come to New York as a young man to raise financing, he had gone to Morgan's. They had

Max Beaverbrook.

turned him down because he had no collateral, and then he went to my grandfather, who gave him the loan on his personality—or so he said. Anyway, he repaid it and became very rich. The memory meant a lot to him.

Presently, he surprised me by saying that he had always wished he had been born a Jew. I asked, 'My God, why?' He said he was fascinated by them; they were brilliant, knew more than other people, and so on. Then he suggested we return to his suite for a drink. The next morning three dozen roses arrived at my cabin with a note, saying I was to sit at his table for the rest of the voyage and Castlerosse would sit at the Douglases'. As to the roses, I could say that I'm not sure anymore if I had earned them. I could also say, 'Sort of.' "

The press lord and the future publisher were together almost constantly for the rest of the voyage, and no matter where they were, cables for him kept appearing. Dorothy says that she was fascinated by the way important news of the world seemed almost to seek him out, although at first she thought he might be having them sent to impress her. They were delivered by either his secretary or valet, "both male, small, inconspicuous and looking exactly alike."

Beaverbrook, then the same age as her father would have been, has been described (in A. H. P. Taylor's biography *Beaverbrook*) as having "an enormous mouth which often offered an urchin's grin, yet had the appearance of a Presbyterian minister." While tough and highly energetic, Beaverbrook was high-strung and suffered frequently from such emotion-connected illnesses as asthma and gout, particularly after periods of intensive work. A hypochondriac, he had many theories on diet, kept a medical log on himself and was careful to take exercise (often tennis). He was not an elegant dresser or even a tidy one and was given to blue serge suits, black overcoats, Trilby hats and white shirts with frayed collars and cuffs with buttons, not links. The latter, he felt, were not consistent with his proclaimed working-class background.

In spite of his view of his origins, he was the son of a Presbyterian minister in New Brunswick, Canada. Like Jacob Schiff, he showed youthful business promise, going to work at fourteen and by the time he was twenty-one having his own finance company. He was soon on his way to creating a cement trust so invulnerable it encouraged him to make British acquisitions, which included stock in a newspaper. Before long he took an active role in management to protect his investment, and this led to the gradual creation of the *Express* newspapers, a chain second only to Lord Northcliffe's. His energy, ideas, intuition and hard work made him even richer and more influential than Jacob. He was also less scrupulous and dogmatic.

As the *Bremen's* voyage neared its end, Dorothy was under increasing pressure to accompany Beaverbrook to London and stay with him at his elegant Stornaway House on St. James's Park (later destroyed by bombs in World War II). She declined the invitation since her children had to be properly settled in Paris in time for Adele's arrival. Instead, a couple of days later, Beaverbrook moved into the Ritz in Paris, and Dorothy found herself being Rolls-Royced between it and Adele's house at 73 Rue de la Tour. The couple also found time to visit an Indochinese exposition, complete with a reproduction of the Angkor Wat, about whose history Beaverbrook asked her to write an article, which he then corrected and returned.

There wasn't time for much backgammon in Beaverbrook's Ritz suite, the hours being taken up by other games.

"Suppers," Dorothy remembers, "were invariably lobster and champagne. It makes the suite period seem like a bad B picture, I guess."

After Adele, who said she had heard Beaverbrook was "a cad with women," was settled in, he was brought to tea. She then pronounced him "the most dynamic man I've ever met." His view of her was concerned with her guilt about Morti, which Dorothy feels was probably tied up with Beaverbrook's own guilt about his late wife. Beaverbrook, the same age as Adele, was horrified when her recurrent illness was diagnosed as cancer. "To think," he said, "that a woman of such vitality could have something like that!"

That he had impressed Adele so favorably didn't displease Dorothy, and she points out the other men with titles she knew hadn't earned them.

"In Biarritz I had a Spanish grandee beau, Pepito, who was the cousin of a king and became a duke. When crossing the border from France to Spain to go to bullfights with me, he would offer his card instead of a passport, and the guards would say, '*Passar el conde.*' He was not all that attractive—he had a Mexican friend who was—and I never brought him into the house. My mother thought I'd never do anything interesting, so I had to collect all those scalps to show her she was wrong. Most of the relationships were short on sex, though; there was talk, of course, but they were scared that what they called the 'ladies' would get in trouble. It was easy enough for them since they had girls they went to bed with.

When Pepito came to Paris to see me, he arrived as I was having a manicure. In he came and kissed my bare arm up and down, saying, 'Ma chère Dorothée' over and over, then kiss, kiss, all the way up."

Paris appears to have ranked with ocean liners for whoopee, and during that period Beaverbrook wasn't the only title Dorothy found time for. Still another was the Vicomte Sebastien Foy, a gentleman stable manager, who took care of Morti's French racing affairs, as well as ran his own stud farm in Normandy.

"Bastien was devoted to my father, even if he didn't understand his taste in ties. My father was color-blind, as was his grandfather, and so is my son. Bastien didn't understand his use of bay rum, either; in France they use cologne. He told me that his father, a count, was a well-known homosexual; Bastien, of course, was not. What he was was an aristocrat with a beautiful voice who was charming and divine—a good ten years older than I—and really lovely. Also, he was very fat; in fact, quite ludicrous-looking. He had pink cheeks, terribly white skin, poppy pale blue eyes, and with all that weight, he looked silly on the golf course.

Still, he had a good sense of humor, was very well read, and nice—just terribly sweet. He worshiped my father, which is probably why he spoke to me about my reaction to a present my father gave me. My car, a Citroën, had been smashed up by a driver who was taking it to Biarritz, and my father thought it was a big joke. He went to Cartier's and had them make a replica in sapphires and diamonds. It was a pin, and I thought it was in terrible taste; I mean, who wants something like that? I said so, and later Bastien told me I was terribly hard-boiled. He said, 'You're the toughest girl I've ever met.'

Of course, a lot of us in those days put on an act of being hard-boiled; it was the 'in' thing to be, and then, he didn't know many American girls. Still, he was very attentive, and I needed him. He knew all the best restaurants and would spend hours discussing the menu and wines with the maitre d' and sommelier, all of which I found very boring."

Because Dorothy refers to so many of her admirers as "good-looking" or "divine dancers," it is surprising to find her involved with a Bastien so overweight he looked ridiculous and with a Beaverbrook described even in his obituary as "gnome-like" and a "golliwog." She speaks of Beaverbrook as having lost a lot of hair on top of that huge head but having gained a potbelly and with it a wart on his face.

"He really did resemble a bull frog," she says. "And in spite of the little valet, he was rather unkempt—almost seedy. He would wear brown shoes with a blue suit. He was not what we used to call an Arrow collar type."

Bastien supplied understanding and reassurance to Dorothy at a time when she had lost a father, planned to dispose of a husband, found her mother a burden and was attracted to a press lord she knew was dangerous. It may be that the very absurdity of the figure Bastien cut reassured her. Besides, he amused her, and if his consultations with restaurant staffs bored her, at least he was not given to the kind of practical jokes Beaverbrook took pleasure in. Such as the latter's insistence, on one notable evening at Robert's, where he was not known, that Dorothy do the ordering, for Beaverbrook spoke no French. It didn't bother her at first, and in fact seemed rather fun, until at the end of the meal he had her call M. Robert to their table and claim that they had no money. After Beaverbrook had enough of Robert's discomfiture—"he was terribly upset"—Dorothy was ordered to tell him who Beaverbrook was. Their shocked host gave a slight bow and murmured, "It is not nice to fool old Robert."

Dorothy says that she early developed a maternal feeling for Beaverbrook, although at fifty-three he seemed an old man to her twenty-eight. She felt his need for her and was flattered at being pursued by so illustrious a figure. His Svengali quality was strong, and her natural curiosity propelled her toward him. As a young woman looking for answers she had found the right man. Beaverbrook was a mine of information, his experience was broad and his self-confidence strong enough for him to ask her why she bothered to read books when she had him to tell her things.

Bastien took a very dim view of Beaverbrook, calling him "a terrible man—dangerous and evil." On reflection, Dorothy agrees that this was probably true and suspects that it was one reason she was so drawn to him. In fact it took very little persuasion on Beaverbrook's part for her to follow him to London after his Paris visit. Adele was horrified when told by Dorothy that she would be staying with him at his house and would put the children and governess up next door, at the Hyde Park Hotel, which he owned. However much Adele had been charmed by him, she warned Dorothy that he had a bad reputation with women and was "a thoroughly wicked man." Says Dorothy, "I told her I didn't care; good-bye, I'm off to London."

A. H. P. Taylor speaks of Beaverbrook as knowing that he could not make a good husband and supposes that this was due less to his quick temper and inflexibility than to his capacity for intense but short-lived concentration. Taylor writes:

> He thought himself free to turn the tap on and off at will. With his women friends he formed the habit of giving each of them 100 pounds for Christmas and another 100 pounds on his birthday. In the 1930's, the list was not more than half a dozen ladies . . . by the 1950's it was costing him 2,500 pounds to celebrate Christmas and another 2,500 pounds to celebrate his birthday. Though he was in fact the most captivating of men, inspiring love in the most differing characters, he could not believe that people liked him for himself. The presents of money and other things were a way of making sure. Also, they were a compensation for the way he switched his friendships on and off . . . the regular cheques were a reminder that he loved them all the same.

True to form, Beaverbrook tried to press money on Dorothy; she thinks he knew that Morti's estate hadn't been settled. When she refused his offer, he told her to buy anything she wanted.

She pointed out to him that she didn't need any money, as all she planned to do was visit museums and libraries, though all she had was a $500 letter of credit. He couldn't believe her refusal, saying, "You're the only woman I've ever met who won't accept money from me."

Dorothy was installed in a fourth-floor bedroom, the windows of which opened on treetops. It was the room used normally by his daughter, Janet, whose first husband was Ian Campbell, later the Duke of Argyll. Their daughter, Lady Jean, was briefly the wife of Norman Mailer.

"Jeannie did arrive at one point while I was at Stornaway House, but being only two years old, she didn't register on me. The thought of her nanny reminds me of what a happy time my maid had there in that great house; she was thrilled because her meals were served by a tweeny in the company of the butler, housekeeper and valet. Bastien came to see me one afternoon when Max was out and didn't like the atmosphere of Stornaway House or anything about it. He didn't stay in London long, probably being on his way to Saigon to buy horses. I had needed him in Paris, but I didn't need him when I was in London.

I was hardly thrilled at finding myself Max's hostess in London, and being naïve, I didn't understand about the lack of competition; the women were in the south of France for the summer, and the men were in town because of a general election coming up with which Max was involved. He held a sort of men's salon every night— just these very bright young men and me with a few older established names thrown in. Mostly, there were writers and politicians—people such as Michael Arlen, H. G. Wells, Sir John Simon, Liberal Party leader, and the royal physician, later Lord Horder, William Gerhardi and a tall, good-looking, successful young writer with one of those English names the pronunciation of which has nothing to do with the spelling—Edward Marjoribanks but you say Marchbanks. He saw me off on the boat; I don't know why. . . . Later he committed suicide in the poolroom of one of those great country houses, and although Max said it was on account of me, I know I had nothing to do with it.

Leslie Hore-Belisha.

Then there was a Member of Parliament who was ten years older than I, Leslie Hore-Belisha. He insisted on its being pronounced Bel*ee*sha, not *i*sha, which apparently sounds Cockney. The name became hyphenated when his mother, Lady Hore, remarried. Leslie was brilliant, had been head of the Oxford Union (the famous debating society) and was very proud of being a Sephardic Jew. He said he would never think of coming to the United States because he understood Jews couldn't join the good clubs and he refused to visit them as a guest. I didn't at first realize it, but he fell for me madly and in spite of my living at Stornaway House. He simply had no idea of anything going on with Max, and after I left for home, he told Max that he wanted to marry me because I seemed so chaste and pure. Max told me he was terribly embarrassed and didn't know what to say. Naturally, whatever he did say wasn't the truth.

As hostess at Stornaway House I did manage one big dinner, for which I dug up some Americans and a very aristocratic British Rothschild who had known my father.

It went off all right, too—you know, sherry first, even though I was used to cocktails, then wine and champagne—but it wasn't easy for me. It never has been easy, entertaining, and never will be; all my life I have been running houses, and I still don't like telling people what to do. I'd rather do it myself.

But I have discovered most employees vastly prefer precise instructions to vague pleadings."

Running houses, servants or anything else he found necessary to provide the life he desired seems to have come easily to Beaverbrook, but then, as Taylor points out, he lived as a very rich man, maintaining three houses always kept ready, and his country place, Cherkley, which Dorothy calls "huge and ugly," employed twenty-one servants. He supported both yachts and private aircraft, and before he became bored with racing, his stable is said to have cost him well over a million dollars. Other than his involvement with possessions, Beaverbrook's life was simple as the customs of the rich go. His dinners at Stornaway House only occasionally meant more than six at table, his Cherkley weekend parties were small, and he spent as little on clothes, relatively, as does Dorothy. In addition to checking his bills carefully for overcharges, he would deduct 10 percent for early payment. While he was given to Rolls-Royces (partly out of loyalty to the firm he had once controlled) and enjoyed his private screening room (mostly Westerns and the Marx Brothers), the stock of fine cigars and wines was for his guests. For years he did indulge in a daily glass or two of champagne, as a youth having once resolved to do so once he was rich, but he didn't smoke and had little use for it in others, particularly by women. The numerous cigarette boxes in his houses always were kept empty.

Beaverbrook was fascinated by money, and his brashness let him ask Dorothy, on her first dinner at Stornaway House in front of a dozen black-tie guests, if she was as rich as Doris Duke. He called for a clipping of Morti's will, so shocking the royal physician he apologized to Dorothy for their host. She, though, says she was merely amused. "Besides, I wanted to know what was in it, too." According to Taylor, Beaverbrook liked checking on the value of his own possessions, once asking in front of guests the price of a Gainsborough in his gallery, saying, "I detest a man who conceals the extent of his wealth—it is as bad as leaving out the date of one's birth in *Who's Who.*"

He told Dorothy he once had his own orchestra and race-horses, but they bored him and he got rid of them.

Dorothy feels that Beaverbrook's major contribution to her future was what she learned about politics rather than newspapers. Much of his time was spent with political thinkers, candidates and officeholders, and many observers felt that if he hadn't accepted his peerage, he might have become a Conservative Prime Minister, even though he was both maverick and Canadian. As friend and adviser he was close to Winston Churchill, and the support of the *Express* had meant a great deal to Churchill's career. But at first Churchill didn't impress Dorothy much. "He came to tea, this heavyset man with a big head thrust forward, and all he did was grunt a few times. But then he was out of office."

It was watching the way Max used his power that fascinated Dorothy during those exciting weeks she was at the center of his world.

"Max told me he would make me the toast of London; I guess I was already the talk of it. But it wasn't a cheap affair; I thought it was terrific and I was very proud of him and just couldn't believe it was all happening to me. He talked about me a lot, as usual always asking questions. About my marriage he said, 'That must be broken; that's not for you.'

We used to walk endlessly in St. James's Park, and he'd tell me all kinds of fascinating things about people, such as Jack Churchill, self-made and first Duke of Marlborough, and Sarah Jennings. He loved gossip and knew exactly how many mistresses and lovers people had. He could be funny, but he wasn't really witty—just terribly cruel—and he knew everything about everything and was extremely sophisticated. He was a full-time job.

He liked to find talent and develop it, and I think he introduced me to so many young writers on purpose—perhaps even pushing Leslie at me—to see what would happen. They didn't interest me one tiny bit, the young writers; only Max did. Once he told Leslie to escort me to a political meeting at which he, Max, had to speak, and we sat in the front row together. Max said he was so upset it ruined his speech, and later he told me never to do that again.

Max used to discuss marriage a lot, arguing with himself about whether it could work. He said I was too young at twenty-eight and that after a couple of years I would be taking on a young lover. He was terribly jealous, and for no reason that I could see. Of course, the whole thing lasted less than a month, as I had to take the children back for school before the end of September. I had no choice, and besides, I thought things would keep on ice until he came to New York in November.

When the morning for the boat train came—they left at some unearthly hour—he had gone down to his room and was in bed when I came to say good-bye. He couldn't believe I was really leaving and was terribly upset, saying, 'Never say no to your lover.' As I tried to explain once more that I had to, he said, 'But you can't do this.' Then he turned to the wall, his back to me, and I heard my maid in the hall. She was waiting with the luggage. . . . And Marjoribanks, to my surprise, was downstairs to take us to the train."

IV

"Here was this interesting, stimulating, almost primitive man and so wicked, and I had literally thrown it all away."

Dorothy was a conscientious mother, and while she saw Morti and Adele as a responsibility—"They were always with me, so I didn't have a guilt feeling about leaving them three thousand miles away"—she didn't regard them as a burden; they were part of what she had got into through her marriage. During her stay in London their mademoiselle brought them each day from the hotel to see her at Stornaway House, and thus Dorothy could reassure herself that they were all right and that Mademoiselle was carrying out her duties satisfactorily. Dorothy remembers her as "a marvelous person with a wonderful, lovely face, who I thought never approved of me." After she was let go, Mademoiselle always sent flowers on Dorothy's birthday with a note, courtly and old-fashioned, signed *"Respectueusement toujours. . . ."*

In an album belonging to Mortimer W. Hall, Dorothy's son, there is a faded picture of Mademoiselle and Dorothy going up the gangplank, followed by Morti and Adele, who was eight. Today Adele is Mrs. Robert Sweet, a tall, very slender and dignified matron with upswept hair and something of Dorothy's profile. Her memories of her mother do not go back before the age of five.

"She was someone I wanted very much to please, and the level of expectation was very high," Adele Sweet says. "Standards, which were higher for herself than others, had been set. Achievement was a constant theme, and disapproval was painful; she could be very abrupt. It was disappointment rather than anger—she was totally nonviolent—but I think disappointment can be harder to deal with than a swat. In fact, there wasn't much physical demonstrativeness.

"I may have had the feeling that she was so positive it wasn't particularly useful to have a contrary opinion. I remember being taken like a tray of hors d'oeuvres to be looked at by her mother, dressed to the teeth in a little Paris dress. Her mother made it hard for her to relate to people; the blanket she put over such things may be why there were no demonstrative scenes with me as a child. That watching owl would have laughed at her if Mother hugged me and mussed her dress in the process."

Adele Sweet's view of Beaverbrook is largely concerned with Dorothy's and his relationship. "I was aware that he was part of her life, but not in a romantic way. I had no idea adults *had* romances. I recall him as a charming and fascinating man who hung around a lot and had torn hankies—they had holes in them—which fascinated me. I expected titles to have monograms.

"I had a hang-up about being attractive, because of my father's having said once that my brother, Morti, was such a beautiful child, while I was intelligent. So I suppose my awareness of Beaverbrook was more concerned with my effect on him than his on me. But he was a presence—unforgettable."

Morti Hall does not resemble Dorothy; in fact, he could be called portly, an effect enhanced by his use of Churchillian cigars, and he lives on holdings which he likes to refer to as his "little pile" in upstate New York, where he rides to hounds with Franklin D. Roosevelt, Jr., the hunt master. Morti's new wife, formerly Penelope Wilson, brings the number of his spouses up to Dorothy's (but he has divorced only once).

His early memories of Dorothy stress traveling, and it seems that much of his exposure to her was at tea time when he was presented by nurses. He remembers Beaverbrook as a short, plump, very bald man with a great deal of authority. Morti was taken aback one morning to find Dorothy in an enormous bed in what he calls the "master bedroom of his nibs' London house."

Neither child saw Beaverbrook as a threat; he was an exotic part of their mother's world. Predictably, John Schiff was less concerned with Beaverbrook's qualities and their effect on Dorothy than he was with the appearance of their relationship. As a student at Oxford he had known Beaverbrook, and Dorothy thinks Beaverbrook's daughter, Janet Campbell, was in love with him.

"I used to go down to Cherkley for weekends before Dolly knew Beaverbrook," John says. "By the time Dolly came along, he was having an open affair with what's-her-name . . . the Honorable Richard Norton's wife."

On the voyage home Dorothy did considerable reading on British politics and history, together with a lot of thinking about Max and those she had met with him. The discovery that politicians do not just happen but are really creatures of the imaginative thinking of others intrigued her, as did the idea that a woman as young as she could exert an influence on politics.

All of Dorothy's books carry penciled comments in the margin and an index of item and page number on the reverse flyleaf. She began a diary on her return to New York; much of it is concerned with Beaverbrook and the views others took of him:

> Those endowed more generously with brains say Max is a genius, but mad. The mediocre people say he is a bad speaker, which is ridiculous. I am bored with stupid people and thank God for backgammon, which spares me ghastly conversational nonsense after dreary meals. My chief worry is that I never have time to read books I am longing to get at.
>
> Otto Kahn [a Kuhn, Loeb partner and husband of a founder's daughter, Addie Wolff] says of Max that all who know him think him a good man and not wicked at all. Sometimes I wonder if such thinking isn't the result of Max's hypnotic effect; I came under it, too, and although I love him, am aware of something esoteric. Mr. Kahn, a man of enormous self-confidence, is rather rotund, wears a white mustache, is pompous and very smart. He is socially ambitious, and there are many jokes about him. My father loathed him, possibly out of jealousy.

Years after Dorothy's return to New York, Beaverbrook spoke to Max Lerner, columnist and lecturer, of his still-vivid sense of loss on Dorothy's departure and referred to her as "a willful woman." This she undoubtedly was, but not so much so that she wasn't deeply influenced by her press lord and his power. As Dorothy told Geoffrey Hellman for his *New Yorker* profile, in her teens she used to be dragged to Jacob's Friday evening dinners, after which the men retired to the smoking room. She was convinced they spoke there, out of earshot of their banished ladies, of great events and ideas. She was determined to find a way into that room someday, and the press lord, if he did nothing else, let her have a good look at a world that could be her very own and that others "would be dying to get into."

Of more immediate effect was his advice about getting rid of Dick Hall; it had taken root. Once she had the children settled in New York, she made plans to go to Reno, *the* place in those days, but a cable arrived from Adele in Paris saying that she was sailing home because of further illness and with instructions for a doctor to meet the boat. This sounded as if it must be more than one of her mother's usual malaises; she had told Dorothy that as a girl she had such painful stomachaches she would hang herself over a chair for relief.

Following consultation, a hysterectomy was performed and a malignant uterine tumor was removed "large as a melon." Dorothy's dedication to Adele during these somber weeks of slow convalescence was partly inspired by her awareness of Adele's rejection of her father, and Adele, too, was affected by a sense of remorse.

Dorothy's concern about Adele and the past she represented did not take up all her time in those weeks, however; what she hoped would be her future occupied her, too. The press lord arrived as planned in November, and Dorothy was happy in the thought that she would be in closer touch than through the reports she had been sending him. He had suggested she write him about the Prohibition situation as a way both of keeping him informed and of training her reportorial eye. In their exchange of cables there had been nothing to indicate she hadn't been forgiven that early morning farewell, and in Dorothy's experience, while people might turn to the wall, it was done as a gesture and not as an expression of inviolate rejection. Her involvement with Beaverbrook was deep enough to make her certain that distance between them, whether geographical or emotional, would not be long-lasting.

She had been invited to lunch at his Waldorf Towers suite, which was commodious enough to offer, among other amenities, a dining room. Dorothy found the company suitably dazzling, but at that moment her interest was in Beaverbrook and in him alone.

"I simply didn't like the people at lunch and I thought
they might be why things didn't seem the same. Max and
I had barely a word together, and when he suggested a
walk in Central Park after lunch—as usual, he was mad
about walking in parks—I thought it would be all right
when we were alone. But there we were alone, and . . . I
knew it was over.

I told him about my mother and things, but it was all so
different. I thought he wanted it that way, and I heard afterward that he had been seeing a woman he had returned
to. [This was the Honorable Richard Norton's wife, Jean,
whom Taylor says Beaverbrook 'transformed from a
tousleheaded Scotch lassie into a woman of the world'
and one so sophisticated she accepted 6,000 pounds a
year.]

At first, it was hard to believe—that I had lost him. I
was hurt, too; I mean, here was this interesting, stimulating, almost primitive man, and so wicked, and I had literally thrown it all away. I knew that he was already the
major influence in my life and that I would miss him for a
long, long time.

Of course, I don't *know* that if I had not deserted him
in London, he would have married me; he wasn't easily
talked into things, and then I wasn't divorced. All I am
certain of is that our walk in the park made it clear he was
through with me. The trouble was, I wasn't through with
him. As I can see now, it may not have been love exactly—fascination, perhaps—but it was unlike anything I
had known. In fact, ever would know and now it was
gone."

Beaverbrook had told Dorothy that his heart was in her keeping, and it is her guess that this changed once her aura was removed by her return home. He had, she says, "come to his
senses" and realized that she was more than he wished to take
on. Certainly, her aura was strong enough to affect others' judgment—indeed, is still—and her guess about Beaverbrook seems
accurate. Had he been more secure in his relations with women
than his biographer tells us he was, he might have remained
committed. Still, he wasn't about to give up all thought of Dorothy; if he couldn't have her for himself, he could still have control. Thus, he tried to sell her on Hore-Belisha, who, being
"mad" for her, needed no selling. However, the lordly match-

maker had overlooked Dorothy's resentment at what seemed to her abandonment. And she was hardly flattered at being considered a suitable match for a man who was almost a staff member of her adored, to say nothing of the arrangement being created to suit the latter's convenience.

Beaverbrook does seem to have made the journey from jealous lover to promoter of a Hore-Belisha union even faster than he did most things, but then he saw this future baron and Minister of War less as a competitor than as an intimate and possession in the sense the gossip columnist Castlerosse was. H.-B.'s seat in the House of Commons brought him about $2,000 a year and he picked up extra income through writing his column in one of Beaverbrook's papers. In spite of H.-B.'s being a Liberal and constantly at odds with Beaverbrook's Conservative stance, they were very close friends. Also, they were surprisingly similar in ambition (each could see himself becoming His Majesty's First Minister), energy, tempo and taste in women (H.-B.'s name at one time being linked to Barbara Hutton's). Both were brilliant speakers (H.-B. munching grapes before public appearances in lieu of William Pitt's glass of wine before his), very hardworking and full of ideas.

Although H.-B. was plump, his sartorial taste put Beaverbrook's to shame; in fact, H.-B. was known as being even more elegantly dressed than his good friend Anthony Eden. In London H.-B. had squired Dorothy about at the request of Max, who was often busy, with such conscientiousness that when he took her to Sir John Simon's for tea in very distinguished company, Sir John referred to H.-B.'s candidacy, asking Dorothy, "How do you think our boy is doing?" She says she was horrified, as "Leslie was not *my* boy!" One reason for her shock might have been that he was as little the physical type she went for as was Beaverbrook, and she says of H.-B. that he was "very strange-looking, rather like the fish footman in *Alice in Wonderland*." In his favor, she was impressed by his Continental manners and beautiful French, in addition to his intelligence and intensity of political involvement. His age, too (thirty-eight) she felt was about right, and she found him almost as interesting as Beaverbrook. But it takes more than a checklist of pluses to attract her; "he just had no sex appeal."

At a ball Beaverbrook gave in London, Dorothy found herself gravitating toward H.-B. for protection and reassurance owing to his almost fatherly manner, which made him seem older than Beaverbrook. The latter was convinced that Dorothy and H.-B. had a strong bond because both were Jewish. It may have been one he envied, and she was touched by H.-B.'s pride in being Sephardic. Although she understood his need to try to inculate in her something of this same pride, it didn't take ("it was still a bloody bore").

Hore-Belisha, who was noted for his single-mindedness and persistency, didn't drop his suit easily. He wrote that his mother, the Lady Hore, would act as chaperone if Dorothy would spend the summer with them in an English lighthouse he had rented. Dorothy declined politely but soon received a letter from H.-B. proposing marriage. This offer, too, was rejected but, as she fears now, perhaps not gently enough. She adds, "It seemed so odd that a sophisticated man would propose without first having been with a woman. But now I realize how naïve I was."

In general, Dorothy's admirers have not been as determined as she in ending their relationships, and they have a way of turning up again. This is due less to the fact that the world in which they all moved was small than the fact that her charms were not easily dismissed. Beaverbrook continued to call her on his visits to New York, and she always found flowers from the press lord when she came to London. This constancy is one reason that mention of him still brings a warmth of voice and an engagement of manner no other man's name can for Dorothy.

Beaverbrook's departure left Dorothy to organize one of her own—that of Adele, children, staffs and herself for Palm Beach. The house was big enough to accommodate them all comfortably, just as it was grand enough to project the image of substance Adele was used to, even if now she could hardly enjoy it.

In addition to the changes illness had brought to her life in Palm Beach, there was a change in how much she saw of Dorothy. As a suddenly dedicated daughter the latter spent as much time with her as she could take and it appeared Adele could handle.

While Adele's true remorse over Morti may have not been great—it sounds more like guilt—her regret at the loss of the faithful Mr. Smith was real. For, although fond of fantasizing about the life bohemian and her dislike of wealth, Adele had always had to face the fact that Mr. Smith had no money. She had a comfortable inheritance from her father, but becoming the wife of Mr. Smith would have meant giving up much of the life she had become used to since marrying what her sister called the "crown prince of her set." Thus, in refusing to give up her regal way of life, Adele gave up the very thing that had made it bearable. Mr. Smith had been the real estate salesman whom Morti asked to assemble the Oyster Bay acreage which became Northwood. And so that which brought them together—property—was their undoing. For now he had married and left her.

"My mother couldn't believe it when she heard his news. She was shocked, appalled—absolutely furious. And those houses she had decorated in such a hurry in order to move on to something else, that she ran with such an iron hand and with such good food, were now meaningless to her. She wanted glamor and dancing—twirling around and laughing—and seeing the right people instead of 'Our Crowd,' whom she thought impossible. She never made it socially really, although John married into it. And had she been alive, that might not have been possible either.

I tried to teach her how to knit—I could always do things like that and found it helpful—but she just couldn't learn. She and Mr. Smith had been utterly frivolous, so now there was just the money and the houses and her boredom. Of course, she had always been athletic—golf, tennis and swimming. Although she had found Piping Rock terribly boring, at least she was doing something, but in Palm Beach now all there was for her to do was sit and twiddle her thumbs. Occasionally she read popular novelists of the time, and when she would be feeling really unwell, she'd have a tiny glass of rye whiskey. Then she would get hysterical and silly—sort of off her rocker—and embarrass me at the table.

Perhaps it was because she liked much younger people I keep hearing that she was sweet, but she was not sweet; she was very caustic and rarely had a good word for anyone. Being extreme in her reactions, she either admired people tremendously or loathed them. Her rapport with her children, I think, was zero. Of John, I remember her saying that if you try to kiss him, he always butts—puts his head down. I think we bored her, too.

In marrying my father, being unable to get the man she wanted, she was pleasing *her* father, whom she absolutely adored. She was crazy about him—it was almost incestuous. He, Sigmund Neustadt, who came from Darmstadt, was a heavy, tall man with a red beard. He was very gay, wonderful with children, and was always giving people nice times, such as hiring a brass band to play under their windows in Europe, or on the trip to Japan with the staid Schiff grandparents meeting the geisha girls. Toward the end of his life he kept shelling out gold coins to servants. When we'd be taken to his Sixty-ninth Street house, he would receive us on the john, which used to surprise me.

His wife was a Richard, a family who had been in this country a long time. My mother thought them nitwits— they seemed to live forever—but his wife wasn't that type at all; she was dignified, very beautiful and cold. On her wedding night in a French hotel she had run screaming down the hall with horror, not glee. Twelve years after the two girls—my mother and her sister—she had a boy, Maurice, who changed his last name to Newton in World War I. He was very good-looking, very tall, had three wives, and I loved him as a child. A close friend of Uncle Maurice was Bobby Lehman, whose art collection was recently installed in a special wing at the Metropolitan Museum. Another friend was the top-paid producer in Hollywood, Walter Wanger, whose body was covered with fur. His second wife was Joan Bennett, and he shot one of Joan's beaux in the groin, for which he went to jail. Mother's sister had a terrific sense of humor and married a Frenchman, Casimir Stralem, a partner in their father's firm. He used to come home after work and have sandwiches of white bread and milk chocolate, which fascinated me."

Adele became well enough to entertain quietly, and among those who came were the Herbert Bayard Swopes. They brought along a houseguest, George Backer. Then thirty, only a couple of years older than Dorothy, he was more mature and sophisticated than the only man near her age she had been close to, Dick. As a fringe intimate of the Algonquin group he offered charm, wit and occasional seriousness with which he made country week-ends shorter and heavy black-tie dinners lighter.

The fact that Dorothy was drawn to him surprised both of them; he wasn't her type of beau, although he became that almost at once, nor was she the type of woman who had attracted him in the past. His first impression was of her detachment, as if she were without focus and dissatisfied.

"She was not," he said thoughtfully, "a beauty. The mouth and nose were very Schiffian, a little too full for beauty but nice for handsomeness. She wore her brown hair with a little salt in it short, and she had certain aspects of beauty—the eyes were wide apart and a very good blue, and she had very nice skin.

"The most attractive thing about her was an immature belief that knowledge was contained in men. Not knowing the difference between wisdom and wise men, she thought that all problems were answerable in terms of a single human being. It was easy for one to think himself brilliant by explaining little primary things to her, such as that the *Nation* was a magazine. She was a good listener, absorbed things very quickly and had great but unfocused curiosity. The reason she was dependent on men then was that she was in search of someone who would be herself—in whom she could find herself—rather than being in search of herself.

"It was this, more than a sensual quality, which at best was secondary, that composed her charm. She did not have a sense of humor, which is a Schiff failing, because a kind of directness precluded humor. There's a difference between wit and humor, but she didn't have wit then either. In the end I think what attracted her most was power. I don't know if she ever found out the difference between what men know and what knowledge is."

Dorothy's view of herself then is that she knew she was in deep trouble. Adele was dying; there was the Beaverbrook disaster and before that her father's death. Her divorce was still ahead of her, and she had a feeling of general unease regarding the children. As she looked about her, nothing seemed to have been too well done, and she doubted herself as woman, mother and

George Backer.

daughter. In spite of all her reading, there weren't any easy answers, and worse, there was no one to whom she could talk.

"I told George my mother was dying—I hadn't told
anyone else except Max—and he was sweet and sympathetic. He was very good-looking—Semitic and Byzantine—and attractive physically. He wasn't very tall—

about my height—and not a bit aggressive. He was just a love. I introduced him to my mother, and afterward she said, 'My God, what is this? It looks just like what I've avoided for years.' I knew what she meant—the Jewish thing—but as soon as I told her he was a friend of the Swopes, he was more acceptable.

His father, who had been a contractor, had become involved in a building trades scandal and died shortly after. A Tammany figure, he was a Polish immigrant, and his wife, George's mother, was a Russian one. When George was a boy, his father used to take him on the Atlantic City boardwalk, telling him he wouldn't amount to anything because he wanted to be a writer instead of a businessman.

George used to tell me about his fascinating friends— Alexander Woollcott, Harpo Marx, George Gershwin, the George Kaufmans, Harold Ross and the Algonquin crowd—and he was pretty thrilled with them; they thought he was a darling person. He was delighted in Palm Beach by the gossip he caused; he said people couldn't make out whether he was Mrs. Swope's lover, her daughter's fiancé or Mr. Swope's boyfriend.

George thought he was much brighter than I, much. He kept talking about books, such as *War and Peace,* Russian novelists, Pitt the Older and Pitt the Younger, and Charles James Fox. I stayed home a few nights to read *War and Peace.* When I made a comment about something in it, he couldn't believe I had read it. That bothered him a bit.

I think my mother's reaction to him made me wonder if I didn't have the same reaction myself. I thought maybe I should hide him because so many people I knew might not understand his good qualities. But it wasn't necessary, as it turned out; everyone liked him immensely. In those days I thought it was important to be married, and since the substantial, older ones had enough sense not to marry me, there wasn't much choice. There wasn't anything else around in the United States."

One who was around—at least, came around—was Bastien. Dorothy says that he was still an awfully nice person, understanding and loyal, but something was lacking. For one thing there was his appearance, and for another, she realized with some shock, there was George. "And so I had to get rid of Basti-en. There wasn't a scene or anything; he thought he'd see me again, he was such a faithful type. Of course, it didn't occur to me then that one Christmas Eve years later, when I was desperate over some unhappy love affair, I would call him in Paris. He said he'd come right to New York, but I just wanted to talk to him."

While George was sympathetic regarding Dorothy's concern about her mother, he had no sympathy for her sense of loss in the Beaverbrook affair. George saw Beaverbrook as an evil man, and he thought it accounted in part for his attraction for women.

"He corrupted the young," George later claimed, outrage in his voice. "Respectable writers and journalists, all of them, yet he would get them under his influence and teach them how to drink more good brandy and spend more money than they should. He would get them girls, too, this terrible man.

"Still, he was a charmer and a wit. I used to stay with him, though I hated him. I was attracted to him and couldn't help it, he was so disarming. I was having lunch with him at the Wal-dorf once and getting rather hungry, but the preluncheon chatter went on forever about Lord this and Lady that. There was an Irishman there, St. John Gogarty, and Beaverbrook turned to him and said, 'Gogarty, are you a Papist?' He said he wasn't. 'Good,' Beaverbrook said. 'Come in to lunch; I don't treat Papists.'"

Palm Beach afforded Dorothy an opportunity to do some growing in those months, and her view of the place, in the past a little jaundiced because of the emphasis on the life social, changed. Her diary notes: "The time has been spent partly in adult observation through the influence of Bastien and George Backer. The place is not impossible, if only one can import people and ignore the regular inhabitants." In addition to her view of Palm Beach being altered, the views she held about the men in her life at that moment changed. The comparison Dorothy drew between George and Bastien impelled her toward the for-- mer, and he, George, through his criticism of Beaverbrook, whom he had yet to meet, did much to get her over her nostalgic longing.

So effective was George's criticism, on Beaverbrook's next trip to New York the diary notes:

Max arrived with his entourage in high spirits and filled with his political importance. He acts all the time, and now that I know him better, he has ceased to impress me. He seems to be making a great noise about nothing, has fascinated himself and appears to get much pleasure from his synthetic life. Yet he has courage and is a good sport, not being downhearted when people and events turn against him. I suppose the reason is he likes to fight.

In her comment on this entry, Dorothy credits the influence of Bastien and George with her release from what had become a self-destructive nostalgia and she adds, "Poor Max never made a success in his own eyes, just the world's." She must be one of the few people to whom it would occur to feel sorry for a self-made man of such power and renown, but then, she is capable of noting an omission in her diary which says much, both by way of fact and in its recognition. "It's curious that in this diary there isn't a word about my mother's dying of cancer."

The omission suggests that in her months of attention to Adele, Dorothy became so involved with the effort of caring *for* her she lost sight of what little caring *about* her there may have been. Adele hardly helped matters by her withdrawn attitude, in combination with a projection of boredom and depression. The latter condition was largely due to the absence of Mr. Smith and her inability to circulate socially. While she may have suspected her illness was terminal, she said nothing to indicate that suspicion, even upon undergoing a second operation after her return to New York. It was performed by an eminent Mount Sinai surgeon at home, in spite of being major surgery, in Adele's sheet-draped bedroom at 932. Being operated on at home was consistent with Jacob's way of doing things; lawyers, doctors and rabbis called on him.

All it accomplished was confirmation of the diagnosis and the suspicion that the disease had spread. Particular care would have been taken by a Mount Sinai staff member treating a Schiff in view of the family's munificence. He would have known the story of a meeting when Jacob Schiff, then on the board of Mount Sinai, found a Wall Street member who that day had declared bankruptcy. At once Jacob announced he would not permit himself to be in the same room with a man who would not honor his debts and, with a stiff bow to the others, withdrew. After an awkward silence the man left for home and later that night committed suicide. Jacob resigned from the board and founded what is now known as Montefiore Hospital. He also sought out the man's son and brought him to Kuhn, Loeb, where he became a partner. Dorothy was put on the Mount Sinai board eventually, feeling as useless as she did on others, and it was then that she learned of Jacob's stern judgment. It is one she doesn't envy him.

Adele's convalescence progressed even more slowly this time, and Dorothy moved into 932 to be with her. She did have some distractions, though, among them H. G. Wells, who had come to New York. At a Colony Restaurant luncheon, he told her he had "a loincloth soul," as if by ringing in Gandhi he could give the lie to his reputation as a womanizer. Feeling safe with his desire to appear ascetic, Dorothy accepted his invitation for a drive around the park.

"It didn't occur to me," she says, sounding a little surprised still, "that a great writer, who was so much older and not very attractive, would proposition me. I was flattered but frightened and escaped only by saying I would be late for my hairdresser."

In the future she made Wells concentrate on his views rather than his desires, and her diary comes up with some of the former.

He said that virtue is its own regret, and that Chesterton and Kipling should have died of alcoholism, rather than Kipling being made to work so hard by his wife and Chesterton being seduced by Roman Catholicism. Bertie Russell and wife, he said, are running a country school for children and are extremely broad-minded—she goes to London twice a week to be unfaithful. He feels that those who destroy gods must replace them, that all children should be illegitimate and that in bad times people paint their cars in drab colors so as not to excite the poor. He begged me not to send him a cold remedy, saying his bathroom is loaded with bottles and jars from Margaret Sanger.

George's effect on Dorothy was enough to make her think of him frequently, and she finally called him. He asked her to join him and Alexander Woollcott for dinner, and, she adds, "At least, that's what I thought he said. As we were sitting in the bar of the restaurant, Alec came in with a large party. He waved and that was having dinner with Alexander Woollcott."

She did see Woollcott again, however, and from then on received more than a mere wave. Before long, George and Dorothy went on a weekend to the Adirondacks with the Irving Berlins. Ellin told Dorothy how fond they all were of George but that she didn't think he was anyone to become involved with. "You're going to get yourself into a peculiar emotional thing," she warned.

Dorothy didn't understand at first, then decided it must mean that some of his friends were homosexual. She says it didn't worry her, adding, "Of course, men loved him; everyone did. And besides, he functioned perfectly as a man with a woman."

Among the friends Dorothy knew before George was Dorothy Parker, about whom the diary notes: "She has the nearest thing to a salon of anyone here, though it is a speakeasy variety one. Her black maid has a son called Harold Lloyd, and a boyfriend educated above her whom she addressed as Mr." For Dorothy, time spent with the George Kaufmans, Alexander Woollcott and the playwright S. N. Behrman was a look at a new world and one she liked. George's friends, but not Woollcott, conducted a soft-sell operation on his behalf, and it was one that Dorothy responded to with caution at first. Woollcott, she felt, had contempt for her as "a rich kid," and she recalls a line of his at the card table to George Kaufman, when he swore. "Oh, George! What will Mrs. Hall think? *If* she thinks at all."

Herbert Bayard Swope held that a man likes following a series of lovers because he thinks he can show the woman how much better he is. George, she learned, was impressed only by women who'd had distinguished lovers, but Dorothy wondered if another man wouldn't be scared off by having to meet such a standard.

"A line from a play of the time said love affairs should be consecutive and contemporaneous," Dorothy observes. "Obviously, men like it, but I think more than one affair at a time is promiscuity. Besides, because of the emotion that goes into it, how can a woman handle more than one man at a time?"

Dorothy's awareness of Adele in those somber weeks prompted some thinking about the relations between parents and offspring, too. John once told her he felt children owed their parents everything and should always make sacrifices for them, but she disagreed vehemently, calling it absurd.

"Children," she argued, "are often brought into the world for the personal satisfaction of their parents."

The move to Northwood was made in early June, and it meant a major effort for her; she had to see even to such details as the Northwood caretaker's being transferred to town for the summer. While she did have qualms about the children living in the same house with a terminal illness, she doesn't think they were aware of the situation. Doubtless, the size of both the place and the insulation of nursing and household staffs prevented that, but the atmosphere led to some diary entries:

> Even to an unsentimental person, death brings sadness. Life after death seems a coward's fear of the unknown, and therefore it serves as a religion for the weak made by the strong. I have never believed that the meek should inherit the earth, unless the word is taken to mean the nonconceited.
>
> We must be able to protect ourselves from the devil, and as with courts of law, religion should be accepted by believers and agnostics alike. F. P. Adams wrote that "In the past the lower types had to be coerced by spiritual or material fears to meet the standards of the higher." This agrees with my view of the Catholic Church, in that I accept the comfort it gives to those who need it, but it is comfort of being forgiven by a frightening and stern parent after having been naughty.

While the essence of these views of the diary has not changed over the years, Dorothy now feels that her opinion of the Catholic Church should apply to all religions and "the objective should be to make life tolerable. I have never believed in life after death, and when I was asked by Edward R. Murrow to be a guest on his program *This I Believe,* I refused. Such topics were taboo, being thought controversial."

The reason she lost weight and wept for days after Morti's death, Dorothy decided, wasn't that she was mourning him. It was due to her discovery that the shackles upon her freedom had been removed at last. His assent to her divorce from Dick was no longer necessary, nor was his financial assistance. She could do what she wanted with her life at last, she thought, but Adele's illness soon made demands on her which were both new and uncomfortable. With them, as the illness dragged on, came guilt.

"I had been unsympathetic in pooh-poohing her illness in order to hide the diagnosis from her. She would send for me at cocktail time—she wasn't the kind of person you just went in and saw—and tell me I didn't realize how sick she was. She talked about her pain, complaining that the doctors didn't know what they were doing, and I would tell her that there was nothing seriously wrong with her. Each time they tapped her abdomen to remove fluid, she would send for me later to reassure me that she felt better. She was pitiful, but I didn't feel pity for her then, although I do now. I was pretty hard-boiled, and so was she.

After the second operation, drugs and pain-killers didn't seem to work, and I begged the doctor to put her out of her misery, but he wouldn't, saying they might find a cure tomorrow. And so her agony went on. I did think about doing it myself, but I would have had to get the pill from him, and besides, I was afraid of being arrested. Years later a doctor friend told me how he handles the thing—he leaves some pills with instructions to take one if the pain is bad; if severe, two; and if it's unbearable, to take them all. And that is what I would like. . . .

The servants hated my mother and, perhaps, their saying so made me their ally. My father wanted to please her, instead of trying to understand me, and so I was the victim of both and felt rejected by both. I suppose if they had ever suddenly embraced me, I would have cried—disintegrated. Of course, it was too late for that.

My mother couldn't marry the first man she wanted because she was Jewish and the second years later because he didn't have enough money. To please her father, she married the catch of her set. He came to call with a carriage and matched pair, and his affinity to England meant their honeymoon was spent there. She cried all the time; it was freezing cold in those great country houses, and she was miserable.

She said my father was so awkward and had such clumsy hands, he left black-and-blue marks when he touched her. When she produced me in much travail and agony, which she thought was a terrible thing, I wasn't a son. The husband-wife relationship, to put it in the old-fashioned way, ended with the birth of that son seventeen months later, and she said, 'No more.'

She objected to my father's family; she thought they were gauche and without taste. She said each time she bought a dress one of them would buy the same thing, and it would be *just* wrong. And when my father would give her a diamond bracelet and wait, all smiley, for her to open the box, she would say, 'Not another Cartier bracelet.' Later one of 'them' would show up with a bad copy and from the wrong jeweler.

There was an awful lot of 'not in front of the children' when I was young. I remember almost nightly scenes between them during the two years when 932 was being rebuilt and we had rented a house just off Fifth Avenue that belonged to the Woolworths. I would appear after my supper, right in the middle of a scene, and try to make peace. They would turn on me, saying, 'Don't butt in.' I would run from the room, crying, and they would go out to one of their dinner parties. . . .

One night near my mother's end, she sent for me to tell me she thought she must have cancer. I told her she couldn't have or I would have been told. (Her mother and sister, who knew and saw her in New York only once, did not come to Oyster Bay; they said it was too much for them.) She was silent, this woman brought up in the German tradition of wasting nothing, then said, 'Wear everything, Dolly.' She meant, don't let it be too late.

That was the last time we talked, for she went into a coma for three days, bereft of lover and with guilt about a dead husband. It was odd; she hadn't had a manicure for weeks, yet her nails were a bright red, as if just done. But then she didn't do what I do under stress—pick at her cuticles.

Just in time I was sent for and sat with her. It was the eve of her fifty-second birthday, July 7. I don't know what the significance is of my father's having died on his birthday eve, too, and that both times it was a Thursday. She went into a death rattle, Cheyne-Stokes breathing I think it's called, and then it was over. There was some foam on her lips, and the nurse said I could kiss her, but not on the lips. I was surprised; I hadn't thought of kissing her."

V

"I didn't need a psychiatrist now; I had a President."

Her mother's death caused Dorothy neither to cry nor to lose weight. Leaving John to take care of the arrangements, she locked herself in her room for a couple of days, lay on her back and thought about future plans. These included Dick, and she remembered that when they were still new to each other, she had asked him what he most wanted from life. He had answered without hesitation, "For someone to die and leave me a million bucks."

When he arrived after being informed of the death, they strolled on the lawn, and Dorothy recalls, "I said, 'My God, Dick, I'm rich now at last.'" The next line was delivered in her bedroom where he had followed her. "I said, 'And now I'm going to leave you.' He was enraged and asked me to repeat it. Then he came up to me in front of the mirror and raised his fist. I said, 'You'll never get into the Racquet Club if you do that.' His ambition in life, of course, was to be a member. And that sounds pretty sad."

Adele's funeral service, which was conducted in the Northwood drawing room by Rabbi Jonah Wise of Central Synagogue, was even simpler than Morti's. Before the interment, alongside Morti at Cold Spring Memorial, Dorothy's grandmother (Jacob's widow, Therese) asked to see Dorothy alone. Dorothy refused, giving no reason but knowing that Adele had disliked her mother-in-law, as she had the rest of the family. This decision Dorothy now regrets. "She was probably a nice person, and I should have gotten to know her."

There may have been an additional reason, a healthy one Do-

112

rothy was not aware of; she had to get out of that house of death. Not unnaturally, she had arranged to see George in New York, but then, she says, "I behaved badly that night—selfishly. I guess I implied I didn't like him any more than I thought he really liked me. I know I told him how crude I thought him for suggesting we stay together with my mother's funeral barely over."

Nevertheless, the effect of the encounter encouraged Dorothy to consider a life with George. In speaking of this period, George admitted he had his doubts. "To lose two parents in such rapid succession tends to make one uncertain about life. Of course, the courage with which she faced her own may have impelled her into wishing to marry sooner than she might have, but I give her the benefit that she did so because she wanted to, not because of circumstances forcing her into it.

"Her father's history—his anxiety about having racehorses, his effort to impress by building that tremendous place, Northwood—had something to do with it all. I don't mean Morti was a second-rate man, but he lived a second-rate life. He tried to be a rich man, but old Jacob didn't think about that. He was just an old Jew who had a lot of money with a nice, comfortable house and a lot of carpets; what a Jewish banker would have but not to impress. Alec Woollcott spent a night in Adele's old room once at Northwood, then wrote Beatrice Kaufman, 'I was ensconced in Mrs. Schiff's room, which had all the intimacy of Grand Central Station.' It was sort of a silly era without background or taste—pretty second-rate stuff, really."

On her return to Northwood, Dorothy had to face the disposition of Adele's things. She discovered what she calls "an atticful of fur and lace trimmings cut off things which had been given away. They had been too good to let go, but now they were all either moth-eaten or yellowed with age."

Adele's will, which disposed of an inventory requiring 530 pages, did not make very interesting reading for Dorothy, since most of the bequests benefited John. In addition to the jewelry, she inherited what she calls the "nits and lice"—the Palm Beach pleasure dome and the "old" garage (on Seventy-fifth Street and later given to her daughter Adele as a residence) and a third of the Northwood acreage without buildings. Until recently, Dorothy thought she had also inherited the Paris house at 73 Rue de la Tour and later sold it, which shows how confusing wealth can become. With her share of the residuary estate, left to her in trust, she then had the income from roughly $8,000,000.

To John went the Fifth Avenue house with the adjoining property around the corner on Seventy-fifth Street, valued at $900,000. The latter had been bought by Morti, not so he could choose his neighbor, as alleged, but to preserve light and air. With the house went the library at $800,000, the art collection at $1,000,000 and the so-called new garage (on Seventy-fourth Street and bigger than the old garage), furnishings, Northwood and the Paris house.

Except for the fact that Dorothy does not wish possessions taken from her, she is not interested in them. It is one reason she doesn't object to John's outweighing her in their parents' estates, although she did hope for at least one of the Fragonards. Nor is she bothered that she did not inherit the library of 3,000 items of fine bindings, rare titles and manuscripts.

"The value of a book for me was always the content—what I could learn from it. My father was very interested in his library and every Saturday would work on cataloguing it. It was a hobby, like my needlepoint; something which didn't require intelligence and was a way to pass the time in winter. He didn't show me things much, but what he did show me was enough to get me interested in learning bookbinding. When I took it up, my teacher didn't think much of my working on Boccaccio.

The library room wasn't terribly large. It was on the second floor of 932 and was done in a blue Renaissance decor. In the shelf-lined walls was a secret door to a vault containing things of special value, and it all brought him a lot of pleasure. He said once that inheriting collections was no fun; the joy was in the collecting. He thought all collections should go to public bidding to make them available to other collectors. In spite of his Long Island life and that constant travel, he was a great reader. The night of his death he was plowing through Trevelyan's *History of England.*"

Dorothy boarded the *20th Century Limited* on a hot July afternoon, headed for Reno, the first step toward freedom. Little of the mystique of the West rubbed off on Dorothy during her stay at Lake Tahoe. A news shot of her leaving the courthouse in company with her Reno lawyer shows a well-dressed, attractive woman with fine legs in mid-stride. It shows, too, an air of certainty, as if she knew what she was about and why, but it says nothing of fun and games; her Reno lawyer warned her against some local charmers who were bootleggers. These appointed themselves her protectors and warned her, in their turn, against some local gangsters. Nor does the picture hint at the possibility that she found a new interest in her last two weeks there. She did, though, and they rode east on the same train.

This man, a fox-hunting Connecticut type, was far closer in style to Dick than the man she expected to marry, George. Her Reno interest was tall, good-looking, aristocratic, reasonably successful and the age she had a thing for, fifty-four. He was a very real temptation and possibly could have been hers. Dorothy lets the answer to the question hang in time, rather as she does the memory of the affair, which worried her. For if she could so easily be distracted by another man, how real was her feeling for George?

Dorothy's children do not have unpleasant recollections of this period of the divorce. Adele Sweet remembers little of the tensions between her parents and says about her later relations with her father: "My father and I would have lunch, painful lunch, at the Plaza from time to time. My main concern was which fork to use. The seeing of him was sort of when the spirit moved him; I don't remember spending the night with him or being taken as a little daughter to Bermuda, for instance.

"He seemed terrifically glamorous to me and witty. His Ritz Towers apartment was absolutely papered with pictures of gorgeous ladies that had, I thought, very risqué inscriptions on them. Clearly, the women in his life were knockouts—you know, great beauties—and I didn't feel that was going to be my role in life. He really wasn't an influence, and the deepest relationship I had with him was years later in California, when he became financially dependent on me. He was in bad shape, and the experience was painful—excruciating."

Morti Hall, too, was aware of his father's lady friends (in later years one was the mistress of a friend of Morti's) and of the total of his marriages—five. What seems to have most impressed Morti was Dick's fund of stories, mostly dirty ones; He saw Dick more as a treat than parent until he became aware of Dick's anti-Semitism, as when Dick complained that Dorothy's being Jewish had kept him out of the best clubs or that Morti's walking with his toes turned out was evidence of this lineage.

George Backer did not relish the prospect of succeeding Dick as Dorothy's mate; he had known Dick slightly, and as he explained, "I certainly wasn't someone in that classification. It didn't seem to me I was ideal for her purpose in any way; I knew how impressed she was with Beaverbrook, and I wasn't for that, either. I think what attracted me to her was the feeling I could supply some element . . . perhaps fill an area of nonknowledge.

"Her brother, John, is not an ungenerous fellow, but unfortunately he received from his father some inhibitions. He's an incredibly reactionary man politically—his social sense about life. He thinks it's all compartmentalized and shouldn't be changed. He and his father couldn't be Jews—in their own souls—but she got away with it. While I don't know if I helped her with it. . . ."

George, in his candor, went on to say that he was flattered that Dorothy had picked him out of the crowd of men available to her and that she thought him clever. He wasn't sure that she loved him, in spite of their spending much time together in New York after her return from Reno, and he began to wonder if she wasn't drawn to him as a kind of escape.

"Ellin Mackay had as much drive," George continued ruminatively, "but being cleverer, when she decided to marry Irving Berlin, he didn't know what hit him. He didn't have a chance, and it turned out to be wonderful for both of them. But Ellin wasn't doing it out of dissatisfaction with life." Dorothy doesn't see it this way but doesn't care to expand on it.

The exact moment when Dorothy decided to marry isn't clear in her mind, and as she has with so many things, she let it happen, rather than made it happen. In preparation for the event and even before she told George he was to be "it," she decided to abandon her conversion to Christianity. Years earlier Bishop Shipman, who had confirmed her and performed her marriage ceremony, happened to be aboard the night boat from Newport to New York.

"I told him I couldn't be sure about God," Dorothy remembers. "The bishop said, 'You must have faith, my child.' This was small comfort, as I had expected him to say a kind of two plus two equals four."

Perhaps it was the influence of Beaverbrook and Hore-Belisha that determined her to return to the faith into which she had been born. Always a believer in dealing with the top, she sent for Rabbi Jonah Wise. Like Jacob, she expected him to come to her at home. His answer gave her something of the letdown she felt with the bishop. She was not to worry about it; she was still a Jew, he said.

In something of this spirit of taking full part in the action now that she knew where it was, Dorothy made an investment in a play George had written ("it was god-awful, but I didn't dare tell him") and kept it going for six weeks since he hoped for a movie sale. There were no returns on the investment; but *Dead End* did well for her and, as with other plays she backed, gave her a feeling of being "in" by attending first nights when they were still glamorous.

George's Eastern European Jewish and mid-level Tammany background presented a problem for the Warburg-Schiff clan, so conscious of its German Jewish Republican aura. First-generation contractors' sons just didn't marry heiresses of private bankers; at Kuhn, Loeb, not only was a man meticulously screened before he was invited to be a partner, but the source of clients' money was looked at, too.

"Actually, I was rather well received by all of Dorothy's relatives," George recalled, "and was taken to see her grandmother. If you wanted to be a Kuhn, Loeb partner, you had to be passed on by Jacob's widow; I didn't, but I had to be looked at anyway.

"Dorothy's brother, John, at first thought I was an adventurer. I tried not to intrude and I saw him a bit in England during the war. He said, 'You know it's not my fault; I'm very fond of you.' By then Dorothy's aunt, Frieda Warburg, was fond of me, too."

John's early view of George, Dorothy says, was "no likee," It was Carola Rothschild who prepared Jacob's widow for the marriage. "Grandma had very high standards," Carola says. "I explained to her that Dolly didn't want to tell her because she was afraid she'd be upset, and she asked, 'Why? Isn't he a nice man?' I told her that apparently he was very nice, and she said, 'I hope she'll be happy. It will probably last seven years.'"

George was unable to remember when he married Dorothy

("some things I just don't remember; this sounds very ungallant, but I don't even know how it came about"), but Dorothy not only remembers when they were married, but knows why.

"He didn't want to marry me; *I* married *him.* Of course, I had doubts, but I felt he was a kind man and one I could cope with. Even though he seemed terribly thrilled and pleased, he was sort of scared of me and of a lot of things about me. But he loved his friends, and they were so impressed. . . . Naturally, my mother wouldn't have permitted it—George was beyond the pale—but I suppose my father would have accepted anything.

We were having lunch somewhere, and I said, 'Well, when are we going to get married?' He laughed merrily, saying, 'But we can't this afternoon. You have to show your divorce papers.' I took them out of my purse, and we went down to City Hall. He looked terribly frightened, poor George. Afterward we went back to my apartment, but we didn't tell the children or anyone—certainly not John.

Three days later the story was leaked from City Hall, and his brother insisted I meet their family. George had told me that as Eastern Europeans, they were Yiddish-speaking; he was always deprecating them jokingly, as I found out later. That was his idea of humor. But they were absolutely charming, divine people; they couldn't have been more attractive and better-looking. I had expected to see Orthodox-type immigrants with *sheitels*— those wigs—the way he described them, but his mother was terribly pretty, although she did speak with an accent. His brothers and sisters were sophisticated New Yorkers.

Eventually, we moved into 932 with John, and that was dreadful. Obviously, George adored John, who ignored him. The whole thing was embarrassing, and when George and I went to London, I introduced him to some of the people I had met, but not to Max, of course. It was a terrible letdown for me after the glamor of his entourage, but to George it was a big leg up—Lady Colefax and people like that.

In the spring we went to Paris, where I had a miscarriage. The doctor I was referred to was French, and the midwife who presided explained that they don't shave you, as is done at home. Then the doctor came in, kissed my hands and said, '*Les messieurs n'aiment pas ça.*' I thought it was absolutely fascinating—so French and so right."

Dorothy kept hoping to overcome a feeling of ennui of which she had been increasingly aware in her relations with George. There was something wrong, or at least missing, in the marriage. Although she liked their life, based as it was largely on the writers, actors and musicians he had known, it didn't match the excitement of the people she had known with Max. The politicians George knew didn't impress her; they just were not in the same class. As her lassitude increased, more and more she let things happen rather than made them happen.

One of the things Dorothy thought she was doing in marrying George was escaping from that Long Island where her father's ducal domain and club life were. She and George did visit his Sands Point friends, though, and gradually she found herself accepting the idea of building a simple house on her 300-acre share of Northwood at East Norwich on Route 25A. While a house does not mean a home, she knew, it could help a marriage, and it might even help a life in trouble, too.

The $85,000 it was to cost was a lot in the Depression. An ex-relative, Dick's sister, Marian Hall, experienced in interiors and Schiffs, took charge.

Marian decided the place would be called Old Fields. Dorothy, who thinks place-names pretentious, jokingly honored Jacob's birthplace, Frankfurt-am-Main, by referring to it as "Frankfurt on 25A." Dorothy selected an architectural firm noted for its Palm Beach mansions. The result was a showplace of old Virginia brick executed in a super-Williamsburg style—an attractive, yet wasteful, mansion designed more for elegant entertaining than comfortable living. Indeed, members of the Pine Hollow Country Club, the name by which Old Fields is now known, blame poor golf scores on the awesome atmosphere of the nineteenth hole. Dorothy remembers being consulted on the number of rooms she wanted.

"I said, 'Well, a room for me, a dressing room for George in which he could sleep if he wanted to, three

children's rooms'—I was determined to have another
child—'and a playroom.' There were to be a couple of
guest rooms, the usual public rooms and, as it turned out,
a downstairs guest room, using the space they didn't
know what to do with.

I didn't have any more idea of square footage, having
lived in that enormous house at Oyster Bay, than an ability to read plans and statements. I knew nothing about
money—Kuhn, Loeb handled all that—and George knew
nothing about money either; he probably never did. Marian, of course, must have thought my inheritance would
be a bottomless well."

By April 1 the eighteenth-century English furniture collected
in London was moved in along with the entire contents of her
New York duplex. The previous two months had been spent by
Dorothy in rigorously keeping *out* of things and *in* bed, the doctors being worried about her pregnancy. In April, her seventh
month, it was considered that both she and the house were far
enough along for her to have a look at what had been wrought.

"I was horrified; I couldn't believe it. Here was this
enormous house against all my principles, and I felt so
guilty; I had made such a botch of it. I remember telling
the architect that it was ridiculous to have such a house
for two little people with three little children. Unless it
were an embassy, it was absurd. He said he couldn't
imagine better people to be living in such a beautiful
house.

Marian Hall thought it was divine—her masterpiece.
She couldn't even handle two people for dinner at her
apartment, yet thought I could run the goddamn thing.
John didn't think it so enormous, and of course, it wasn't,
compared to his. He was so busy talking about how expensive the New Deal was tax-wise, he never asked about
the cost.

This monstrous house ran about a million, instead of
eighty-five thousand dollars. The bills were paid by
Kuhn, Loeb, and I don't remember anyone pointing out it
was all getting to be too much. The blame for what happened belongs partly to me for being such a sucker, and
maybe to George; his father's firm was handling it all.
But I think he was unequipped to say, 'Too much—stop!'

Old Fields.

He probably just shrugged his shoulders because he didn't want to get involved in crass material things. His friends thought it was lovely, and everyone said it was marvelous to have provided so many jobs in the Depression.

I was wearing a green maternity dress that day, and as I crossed the front hall and started into the drawing room, I slipped on the parquet floor and fell. Sarah-Ann was born about six weeks later with a birthmark on her forehead, and I used to wonder whether a blood vessel had burst, but I was told that wasn't possible because a baby floats in fluid.

My first night there everything felt so strange. My room was enormous and had a dressing room, bathroom, sitting room and sun porch, which I don't think I was ever out on. My dream had been to live in something like that development in Manhasset—Munsey Park—with one house on top of another and lots of neighbors and things. Instead, I had a house which was exactly what I didn't want.

What I did want was that baby I had been having a lot of trouble with even before the fall. But George didn't want a baby; he said he had no paternal instincts. So it was my baby, my house, my everything and no partner."

Dorothy with Sarah-Ann.

George was at as much a loss to explain the house as Dorothy—"I never quite understood how we got into it. . . . I didn't think it was my place to interfere." As time went on, he saw Dorothy's money as an increasing threat to their relationship, a view common to American men who marry into money larger than their own, one calling it "the hardest work I know." George was careful to point out that Dorothy was always generous and never talked about her money, saying it was there to be used and that she never used it as a weapon.

"Still," he added, "sometimes she could be rude in the Schiffian sense of forgetting that it does set one apart. No matter what the husband of a richer wife tries, it doesn't quite work. And in the long run, I think that's what busted. . . ."

George's dressing room, described by Dorothy as a monk's cell, soon became more than that. He withdrew to it—"very wisely keeping out of things"—and this withdrawal was paralleled by Dorothy's. At first it was an enforced one for a couple of weeks at the Doctor's Hospital after the birth of Sarah-Ann, June 23, 1934, followed by a period of convalescence at Old Fields. Her bedroom, by its enormousness, hemmed her in. And then, once more, she was *locking* herself in; even maids with trays were not always admitted.

To her surprise, she missed her mother and now recognized her for the excellent manager she was: "very firm and very positive; she knew exactly what she wanted, as far as running a house was concerned, and got it." Morning interviews in Dorothy's bedroom with the cook were a daily trial, and people kept coming for orders, orders that Dorothy didn't know how to give, nor even what they should be. A more serious problem— drinking by the staff—then appeared, and she switched to an all-woman staff. That didn't work either; the cook insisted on a kitchen maid. And there were outside staff problems, too. Instead of one chauffeur, there had to be two. The formal gardens and pool house, modeled on slave quarters meant not only a head gardener, but a staff of six "fixing the borders every five seconds."

Finally, Dorothy was advised the only solution was to engage a housekeeper to run everything. For a while, this kept problems from her, and it looked as if things were falling into place, although the Hunt Club continued to course along the fields in front of the house "and wake me up at the crack of dawn; then said they'd pay for the damage they did tearing up the lawn." The housekeeper approach didn't last long, though; once, when Dorothy and George went off for a visit to Alexander Woollcott's, they came back to find the house a shambles, a large party having been given in their absence.

In discharging servants, Dorothy used to wish she could put the burden on George, but he wasn't the type. At least, she knew enough when writing obligatory letters of recommendation to leave out such key words as "honest" or "sober," depending on the case. Later on she solved the problem simply by moving to a hotel, where she would stay until she ran up against *their* housekeeping problems.

By the end of summer she had a problem with a different kind of dependent. Her son, Morti Hall, ten, had been sent to camp, which he hated so much he lost twenty-five pounds, and claimed he had been tied to a tree and left out all night. This, not unnaturally, brought Dorothy to the rescue; she was already concerned by his reaction to the newborn Sarah-Ann.

Many of Dorothy's bedroom days were spent on household bills, and her discovery that the grocery bill alone was running $700 a month didn't help. Such was her dislike of the place that there were areas of the house she never did see, and her suspicion of the servants, with their constant discord and complaints, grew to the extent that she caught herself wondering about Sarah-Ann's nanny. Could that be a bottle for herself, rather than for the baby, she carried about in a shoe box? Or was she, Dorothy, verging on a nervous breakdown? If not, why was she, she asked herself, unable to sleep, prey to cold shivers, always crying or about to, and terribly frightened? And what was this fright about—inadequacy, failure, a sense that the nothing she felt herself really was?

At least, she thought over and over, she was up to seeing the children still. But she was not up to the web in which she was caught and absolutely not up to climbing out. She was locked in, just as she was locked in that bedroom which closed in on her, in that house she hated. And she was locked into remembering her mother in the morning in her room, too, with headaches keeping people away, the shades drawn, eyes closed, lips tight and hands clenched. And her mother hadn't had to face simultaneously a house she couldn't accept, a staff she couldn't handle, a newborn child with a birthmark, a son regressed to bed-wetting in protest and a nostalgia for a lover whom she had failed, not to mention guilt about withdrawal from a monklike husband who kept to his cell. And so, it wasn't just the house that was too much; life was.

A physician of note, who was a friend of George's, was consulted in mid-August, an alleged homosexual who had resigned from a prestigious medical board on pain of exposure and then been brought back. He suggested that a psychiatrist be consulted, a term of which Dorothy says that in spite of her thirty years, she had never heard. Nor had she heard of the referral, Dr. Harry Stack Sullivan, a highly original psychiatric pioneer and teacher whose reputation has continued to grow.

He based his approach to psychotherapy on interpersonal relations, since he held that mental illness involves how we deal with others and they with us. He focused on helping the patient regain his or her self-respect and sense of value. Anxiety, according to Dr. Sullivan's research, produces protective defenses which, in the long term, can lead to schizophrenia, an illness which he demonstrated could be treated successfully by psychoanalysis, in spite of Freud's dictum to the contrary. As a therapist he functioned as a participant observer, both monitoring his patients and interacting with them, and as a consultant he was in great demand owing to his diagnostic insights. He must have felt on familiar ground with Dorothy's case, having developed the theory that prolonged loneliness resulting from lack of early intimacy can lead to neurotic disturbances, and she undoubtedly served as confirmation of his feeling that few of us realize our potential.

Because he was a therapist who regarded money as an incidental—his New York practice was set up on borrowed funds, his own going to help friends and advance his research and training interests—one wonders what Dr. Sullivan's reaction was when he was picked up in New York and driven by Lincoln town car to that elegant house so much too much for Dorothy. She was in her drawing room, ready to receive him, and the fact that she had been able to leave her suite and meet him halfway, at least within the confines of the house, was a good beginning in her mind.

He entered, she says, with a walk which was that of an automaton. He was very pale, neither tall nor short, was dressed in a dark suit and was without warmth or personality. He chose his words carefully and spoke slowly, and while she was surprised to find him so wraithlike, she had wanted "a faceless healer."

She recalls that Dr. Sullivan began by asking what seemed to be the trouble, and so she ran down her checklist: despair, fear that she was going mad, a desire to be dead, but without dying, and a sense of nonbeing. She added that although she knew how to drink, she hadn't been doing much; there was no one to drink with.

"I told him all I wanted to do was hide in my room," Dorothy goes on, "and repeated that I felt I was going out of mind. He reassured me by saying this would not happen, although I might become increasingly afraid of it. He called my condition an anxiety neurosis and suggested I come to town the following Monday to begin treatment. I felt better already; that would get me away from the house and all that was in it."

Dr. Sullivan's East Forty-second Street suite consisted of two rooms and could have been a business office. In the austere consulting room there was a swivel chair and desk with side chair and, of course, the couch, so dreaded by new patients. He said that he hoped she would find it helpful in their five-day-a-week sessions and that the fee was $15 an hour. This Dorothy thought steep, but she didn't "dream" of saying so.

By the third day she was on the couch, and it didn't bother her a bit; as with the Oyster Bay commute, she even found it rather enjoyable. Classically, Dr. Sullivan sat behind her out of view, equipped with pad and pencil. When he asked for dreams, she would try to oblige; when she couldn't, he suggested a favorite tool, free association. "He told me to just say whatever came into my mind, but an awful lot of the time I was complaining about my cook and stuff."

The reassurance which appeared with these early sessions was reflected in her ability to begin functioning again; the bedroom was no longer a refuge, and she became involved in her surroundings. As far as she can remember, no one remarked on this change in her, least of all George. In spite of their being husband and wife, her therapy was never mentioned, but she learned later that Dr. Sullivan consulted Marian Hall, which Dorothy sees as a breach of trust, and she wondered about George. He never was contacted, but forty years later he said, "I think she suffered from a sense of personal failure—inadequacy—and I lay a lot of this to the loss of her parents. There weren't tensions in the marriage which could have caused it; maybe that was one of the difficulties. There was not very much in the way of communication."

The family moved to the city that fall of 1934 and, in order to solve Dorothy's perpetual servant problem, took up residence in the Carlyle Hotel. They occupied two apartments—one for her and George, who went to Poland shortly, and another for the children, governess and nurse. Dorothy was impressed by Dr. Sullivan's socialistic ideas, but not to the extent that she was pleased by his reaction to the effects luxurious hotel life might have on the children.

She says he called it pretty fancy living, but that he supposed her kind of children would have to live such a life. She hadn't thought the place all that great; it wasn't as if it were the Ritz in Paris.

"The fact is, Dr. Sullivan simply didn't approve of the lifestyle of the rich. Of course, I didn't know then that he was both an arrested alcoholic and homosexual."

Dorothy recalls that he was patient about her ideas, even if he didn't seem impressed by their originality. His response to appeals for guidance in decisions convinced her that "he didn't really think it mattered very much what a person like me did. His attitude was so very much 'no comment,' I often wondered if he were even listening."

This distance and coldness had a way of depressing her. He was her only confidant, and she was without "chums" or a husband she could lean on. She resented having to relate via a monologue instead of two-way conversation, and as their work became more difficult and threatening, she saw her life as being largely devoted to trying to deal with servants ("the staff was still out there, eating their heads off"). Again there were times when she envied her mother "hiding for days with blinds closed and curtains drawn," and there were times, too, when she would remember an escape she had made from the Old Fields dining room at a housewarming dinner; without bothering to excuse herself, she had strolled from the room and then sneaked up to her bedroom.

"Other people in analysis seemed to enjoy it so," Dorothy says, a little bitterly. "Beatrice Kaufman, the playwright's wife, was with Dr. Gregory Zilboorg and talked all the time about the emotional things she was going through with him. I met him at her house—odd-looking man—and I thought things would happen to me, too, but it didn't touch me at all.

"Dr. Sullivan was so cold and unemotional I had the feeling he was bored with me and had his mind on his training and research—that he was treating me because he needed patients who could pay. I never dared mention it because I was afraid he would throw me out and I needed his support. So I went on enduring what I felt was his contempt of people of my class , and he went on being sort of resigned to it all."

In order to fill her evenings, Dorothy took a course at the New School University in Exile, the history of the Progressive movement in America, given by Max Ascoli. Ascoli, she says, was fresh out of Italy, and while she couldn't understand a word he said, the course provided a reading list. She devoured the works of Lincoln Steffens and Frank Kent, the Baltimore *Sun* editor and author of *The Great Game of Politics*. An Ascoli lecture prevented her from dining with a man-about-town one night, but she agreed to meet him later at a party given by Harold Guinzberg, the founder of the Viking Press. When she arrived, her hostess asked if she had heard what had happened to her date. It seems that on Dorothy's turning him down for dinner, he had

Sitting in the front row at the dedication ceremonies for the 490-acre Mortimer L. Schiff Boy Scout Reservation at Mendham, New Jersey, are (from left): Felix M. Warburg, Mrs. Felix M. Warburg, Mrs. George Backer and John H. Schiff.

cocktails with another woman and died in her apartment.

"It scared hell out of me," Dorothy says. "But for the grace of God, he would have come to the Carlyle to pick me up for dinner and would have died there. It could have been misinterpreted, so I suppose I would have had to call Herbert Swope to keep it out of the papers."

This made her leery of having dates at night, and the fear of a man dying in her apartment is with her still. Should the reverse occur, she says, she hopes he could cope, adding that it would hardly be a matter of concern for her if he couldn't.

Politics came into Dorothy's life that summer through a letter addressed to Mrs. George Backer from Frances Perkins, Secretary of Labor in President Franklin D. Roosevelt's Cabinet, of whom she had never heard. She thinks it was intended for George's mother, but that didn't stop Dorothy from accepting the invitation to join a committee concerned with the operation of Ellis Island, where, among other immigrants, hordes of Eastern European Jews first experienced their new country. And so it was that she came to participate in the effort to alleviate the misery of a second generation of those "coreligionists" of Jacob's.

Her work on that committee led to a bipartisan one ostensibly
concerned with the unemployed, but which also used its ener-
gies in working for the reelection of President Franklin Delano
Roosevelt. Many New Deal women were on it, and Dorothy
found herself highly impressed by the work of the President's
wife, Eleanor, in trying to reduce the privation caused by the
Depression. In those grim and frightening times, it was more
than a question of merely trying to do something about the condition of the poor; it was a desperate attempt to find better ways
for the millions of the new poor to survive than by apple selling.

President Roosevelt seemed to Dorothy to have some answers,
and he was trying them with a courage and dedication which
persuaded her that the best chance for the country lay with the
Democratic Party. When Nancy Cook, vice-chairman of the
Democratic State Committee, kidded Dorothy about being a Republican, Mrs. Roosevelt put her arm around Dorothy and said,
"That's quite all right. I was brought up as a Republican too."

George Backer saw Dorothy begin to emerge as "a bit of a
public figure" when she took part in a Madison Square Garden
rally to boycott German-made goods. She wrote a letter to the
editor of the New York *Sun* refuting the charge that there were
no Jews of German descent at the rally, pointing out that she,
née Schiff, had attended. George explains that "she received numerous phone calls and letters of congratulation. Her efforts
symbolized the family's sense of responsibility and leadership,
but it was done to the horror of some of her relatives."

Dorothy adds, "I don't remember the congratulations, just Uncle Felix Warburg's disapproval. He sent for George and told
him so."

John Schiff gives George the credit—more accurately, the
blame—for Dorothy's desertion of the Republican Party. He felt
that she was taking some risks socially in crossing over, but that
her life was spent in taking risks. He added that although they
disagree on politics, "we've never insulted each other, which is
one reason we get along. The Democrats didn't ask for a contribution, just told her of all the interesting things she could do.
And then, sitting next to Mrs. Roosevelt at a lunch was pretty
heady wine for a young woman.

"I wasn't too worried about Dolly and didn't try to dissuade
her. But if she had joined the Communists, I would have been
concerned."

The luncheon given by Mrs. Roosevelt was for the purpose of setting up facilities to feed unemployed working girls at the Women's Trade Union League. Dorothy had joined the league's board of directors and thus came to know Rose Schneiderman, who, she says, was a "fiery Socialist and colleague of David Dubinsky, the International Ladies' Garment Workers Union head. The league was formed by former suffragists to train the girls so they could hold their own against the men at union meetings."

She describes the luncheon fare as "typical brownstone with jelly." The front hall table of the East Sixty-fifth Street house (which communicated with that of the mother of the President, Mrs. Sara Delano Roosevelt, next door) was untidy and piled high with odds and ends, Dorothy recalls. It spoke of the general busyness of the scene—much coming and going and incessant phone rings—and it complemented the activity of a rather harried hostess, who, Dorothy's diary notes:

> Is not as ugly as her photographs. She looks skinny at first but is really large from the chest down—a peculiar figure with stomach sticking out. She wore a dark skirt and homemade-looking blouse which bothered her a lot by sliding up from her skirt, and in speaking to us, she kept a hand inside the waistband.
>
> Nancy Cook, a radical and mannishly dressed with curly white hair, said, "Damn the rich—I hate them and hope they have all their money taken from them!" This had no effect on Mrs. Roosevelt; nor did Anna Boettiger (later Halsted), her daughter, who rushed in at the end of lunch saying, "Mother, I must talk to you and can't get an appointment to see you." Said Mrs. R., "Talk to Tommy [her secretary]; I'm sure she can fit you in."

When Nancy Cook added Dorothy's name to the list for Roosevelt, she made it not just Dorothy Backer, but Dorothy Schiff Backer. Dorothy was a little shocked, as she had scrupulously avoided use of the family name, both to get away from it and to avoid any possibility of its abuse, but in her new allegiance it didn't seem too large a sacrifice. Since then, she has had little reason to fear trading on it; that's for other Schiffs to worry about.

Later on Rose Schneiderman assigned Dorothy to the job of

Nancy Cook.

writing labor leaders asking them to speak at meetings, but there were no takers.

"I was appalled by this rejection," Dorothy says, "but Rose wasn't. She said, 'So now write to the second echelon.' "

Although spared that horror for a while, soon she was serving with so many organizations involved with the underprivileged and child welfare that her days and nights seemed an unending rush of getting from one meeting to another. If she didn't always understand the items on the agenda, at least she knew which meeting she was at, giving her an edge over some "do-gooders," as the *Daily News* called them. Her diary suggests she was having fun again, and although the work was not glamorous, she felt useful.

> Adele [her daughter] had an accident today in a taxi, which she was using because I had the car and chauffeur at an unemployment meeting. The child looked half dead, and never have I suffered so. We have brought her into a lousy existence, yet she is good and brave and I hope will have a happy life.

Lunched at the Colony Restaurant with all the social people and those who go to see them. Food is less good now, yet prices are no lower. One food break lately is that the man who supplies the house in the country says he would be pleased to donate groceries etc. for unemployed.

Attended an after-theater supper with journalists and writers—all so dull and unoriginal, attempting to be witty and not succeeding, and conversation mostly very coarse. It was a pretty good group—the Phil Barrys, Donald Ogden Stewarts, F. P. Adams, Russel Crouses, Harold Guinzberg and Dottie Parker—so it must have been something about me. They seemed so provincial compared to what I had known with Max.

During the summer Dorothy resumed commuting from Oyster Bay for her sessions with Dr. Sullivan, and George switched from the Democratic Party to the American Labor Party, then equivalent to the Liberal Party of today, the militant left wing not yet having taken over. Dorothy wanted to join, too, but George dissuaded her, saying, "We have too many Jews already." In the fall George and Dorothy moved to an apartment at 944 Fifth Avenue, which was big enough to accommodate their political gatherings. The other tenants may have raised their eyebrows at some of those attending, but not at one frequenter, the Brearley School doctor Benjamin Spock.

Dorothy speaks of her sessions with Dr. Sullivan as going "merrily along" in the fall of 1935, although she was aware of a growing dependence. She was impressed by his dedication to socialism more than ever as he talked about his life and associates, such as Dr. Karen Horney. He went into his work at St. Elizabeth's Hospital in Washington, D.C., too, and she didn't fail to note his anxiety about the difficulty in raising funds for research and training. After some thought, Dorothy told him she would like to make a contribution.

"He hesitated," she remembers. "Then he explained that it was absolutely not permissible for a patient to give money to anything a therapist was involved with, or words to that effect. He may have used the word 'ethical,' but I'm not sure.

"I said, 'Well, that's ridiculous; the money is needed badly, it will help a lot of people and I can afford it. It's wrong not to take it.' He was worried about taking it, but reluctantly he did let me send a check for fifteen thousand dollars. Of course, it was against his principles, and I was of two minds about it because I thought he might be right, but there are always exceptions to rules."

It is possible, Dorothy feels, that her having talked him into accepting the money might have shaken her confidence in him, but it was not enough to get in the way of their work. This had come to seem less a deep delving than a kind of supportive reference process for her. She had the feeling that he approved of her work in the Roosevelt campaign, and when she joined the Democratic Party in the fall, "he may have decided I wasn't hopeless after all."

Such was her insecurity that had she been asked for a contribution to the party, she would have thought that was why they wanted her. As it was, instead of making her all the poorer in spirit by seeing her as rich in money, they made her feel useful by appointing her New York State chairman of the campaign's radio committee of the Women's Division. Thus, she had not only her first title, but her first secretary. Her doubts about inexperience and lack of ability, which were waved away as modesty, didn't prevent her from discovering that the secretary didn't have much to offer either. However, Anna Boettiger, with whom Dorothy shared an office, made up for all of them.

One of Dorothy's jobs was seeing to it that broadcast announcements were sent to the vice chairmen of the state's sixty-two counties, so that groups could be gathered to listen. The chairmen, she mentions tartly, were all men while the vice-chairmen were women. Dorothy imagines that her fellow workers must have had some laughs about her efforts, but says, "It was fun being a member of the wedding. We'd all have dinner together after I offered a round of drinks sent upstairs—daiquiris or something like that. Only Anna and I took one usually."

Leading the campaign that summer was the party chairman and later Postmaster General, James A. Farley. He insisted that all letters be answered.

Ellin Berlin brought to her Irving Berlin's suggestion that he write the 1936 campaign song for the Democrats. Nancy Cook told Dorothy bluntly they preferred the 1932 theme song, "Happy Days Are Here Again," and Dorothy can't help thinking Berlin's turn toward the Republican Party was one result.

* * *

It was a surprise being consulted by Dr. Sullivan about his projected move uptown, but at the same time she was rather flattered. He settled for an East Sixty-fourth Street brownstone, which he remodeled, using what she felt was an unnecessarily severe modern decor. It didn't occur to her to wonder how all this was paid for, or why there was never a patient in his waiting room. She assumed that she was his only private patient and continued "babbling" to him daily of her life, political and social. If he felt they weren't getting anywhere, Dorothy says, he never mentioned it. All she knew was that she could cope and felt needed by those she respected. And that she had grown fond of the women working in the Women's Division. She enjoyed going to the 1936 National Democratic Convention in Philadelphia with them and then on to Hyde Park to be received by the President.

When Dorothy told Dr. Sullivan before the convention that she knew she wouldn't be able to say a thing to the President when they met at Hyde Park, he asked her if she had thought of saying nothing. She hadn't, and those who knew him could have assured her that the President was quite up to doing all the talking and enjoying it. Had Dorothy not been so moved by him at his 1933 inauguration, she might have been less petrified. George had been given a couple of grandstand tickets, and she sat shivering in the cold wind until, as she says, "I heard that glorious voice for the first time. I was thrilled and inspired as those words rang around the world, 'Let me assert my belief that the only thing we have to fear is fear itself—nameless, unreasoning, unjustified terror which paralyzes needed efforts to convert retreat into advance.' "

She was short on sleep when she arrived at Hyde Park, partly because of anticipation and the noise of empty bottles going out the Philadelphia hotel windows the night of the President's "Rendezvous with Destiny" acceptance speech. The jouncing of an upper berth on the Presidential train didn't help. There was a railroad siding on the bank of the Hudson River for delivering coal to the mansion of Mrs. Sara Delano Roosevelt, called the Summer White House, and once FDR became governor of New York he used the siding and was then driven up the private road to the great house.

The Presidential train, however, stopped at the Hyde Park station, and from there Dorothy was taken to the Val-Kill cottage of Nancy Cook and Marion Dickerman on the Roosevelt property across the main road. By then Eleanor Roosevelt had converted the furniture factory in which she had been a partner into a house for herself. Local people had been employed in duplicating regional items there, prized today less for their artistry than historical association with FDR.

After breakfast the group drove to the big house to meet the President, and Dorothy braced herself; it was too late to back out, yet she still hadn't thought of a thing to say. They found the President in front of the house in his Ford touring car, which was equipped with special manual controls for his use. Anna took Dorothy firmly by the hand and pulled her up to the car, saying, "Father, this is the Dorothy Backer we have been telling you about."

Dorothy remembers a broad grin in acknowledgment and with it a warmth that would from then on make her think of a sun-god. He held out his hand, shook hers heartily and said, "I've been hearing about you, Dorothy, and I'm so glad you are with us. I knew your father on the board of the Boy Scouts."

"I was so overawed," she says with wonder still. "Something happened in me I have never experienced before or since—my tongue literally clove to the roof of my mouth."

Anna took her back to the cottage for a swim in the pool, and after lunch Dorothy was startled to learn that the President had driven over and was asking for her.

"He was sitting by the pool, and when I appeared he said, 'Good. Sit next to me here.' I sat on the grass at his feet, only barely aware of his leg braces. I think I must have answered feebly a few of his remarks, but the effort was such I have no idea what I said. Certainly, nothing brilliant; I was still too petrified.

A line formed, and people came up to meet him for about an hour, as I sat there next to him. When I went back into the house after he left, I told my boss on the committee how terrible I felt it was of me to have been unable to have had a proper conversation. But she said it was good that I hadn't; people kept coming to him with petty complaints or to ask him for things.

Of course, I was still politically inexperienced and

naïve, but as I learned right away, I had made a very good beginning with him. In what became a kind of court relationship, I never did talk about myself; not a word. He wasn't interested in me but in having what he thought was a well-dressed young woman around with whom he could be comfortable and ramble on to. My clothes were New York designer things then, and he was amused by my John Fredericks hats, which I haven't worn for years. He didn't see many people who were well dressed, and the ones around him weren't even attractive. There just wasn't any competition, not that I was thinking of that.

There was a class thing, too. He was a snob—horrible word, and I wish I could think of a better one—and he liked women who were well bred and brought up. Ladies is the word, I guess. I was a rich kid of the right kind— not the robber baron type—and had been to the right schools. As to being Jewish, C. P. Snow wrote that once you reach a certain financial level, people don't think of you as anything but very rich. At thirty-three, I was twenty years younger than he—young enough to be attractive to . . . well, he liked the ladies."

Nancy Cook and the others were delighted by Dorothy's success, and it didn't take much convincing for her to know that it was not because she was such a "a great Republican catch." Something had happened that afternoon, and she knew she would be seeing him again. Although anxious to tell Dr. Sullivan of the encounter, it was not of her success that she spoke at their next session but of the President's "tremendous glowing self-confidence. He was radiant."

It was a kind of confidence Dorothy envied. When she agreed to make a speech on a national radio hookup at a hotel luncheon, the time had seemed a long way off. Suddenly, to her horror it wasn't. This shy and insecure woman, who had been unable even to announce to a roomful of women the amount her table had raised for a charitable cause, was caught by her commitment. Convinced she would never be able to pull the speech off, she went into something of a tailspin and did a lot of work on the problem with Dr. Sullivan.

By the time the day arrived she was surprised to find that she actually was able to get herself to the dreaded hotel. Then, to her astonishment, she was climbing through her speech, but it was as if it were being done by somebody else. It had been written by somebody else—Bessie Beattie—but edited by Dorothy, who wrote the last sentence. It, too, had had a lot of work, and it covered the rather unexpected distance between her embarrassing wealth and her newly developed social conscience.

My Republican friends say to me, "How can you, with your three children, work for the reelection of Mr. Roosevelt? Do you want them to inherit an enormous burden of debt and live in a land torn with class hatred?"

I don't believe in that enormous debt. Since Mr. Roosevelt came into office, both my broker's monthly statement and my safety-deposit box assure me that my children's security has materially increased. And as for class hatred, it grows out of unbearable inequalities—social neglect, joblessness, hunger and despair. More and more I feel how dependent we are, one on another. It is impossible for us or our children to be happy and safe unless women and children belonging to less fortunate groups can be happy and safe, too.

Exhilarated by the experience of speaking in public, Dorothy hurried uptown for her session. She was in a state of mixed anxiety and euphoria and abandoned the couch for a chair.

"I raced into his office and asked, 'How did I do?' He appeared not to know what I meant, and I said, 'But for weeks we've been working on my having to make this radio speech today, which I didn't think I could possibly do?' He asked how I felt about it, and how did it go? 'Well, I got through it,' I said. 'But you must have heard it?'

'No,' he said. 'It isn't my function to listen to you on the radio. Anyway, the electrician was here, but I never had any doubt that you would be all right.'

I couldn't believe it and said, 'You can listen to me for weeks worrying about this test, and then you don't even check to see if I got through it!' Again he said that he knew I'd get through it, but that wasn't enough for me. I knew better, but I still had to have total dedication; I had to be the only one. Then I said, 'You don't care and you're just not human. You're not interested in me, and I'm through with you!' I jumped up, ran out of there and never went back.

A few weeks later I received a long letter from him, saying that I had not completed my analysis and predicting what would happen to me. I laughed at it, thinking he had to say that. I thought that's his rationalization, a word I learned from him. But he was right; I did need help twenty years later. I never saw him again.

As for me, I was in the real world and had gone on to new interests. I didn't need a psychiatrist now; I had a President."

VI

"You don't say no to the President of the United States; as a patrician he was lord of the manor out of another century. Besides, I had nothing better to do."

Dorothy has given much thought to her relationship with FDR, and when asked how she thinks others would see it, she said, "I was on the edge of the ledge—always."

The answer may seem ambiguous, but it is given by one whose sense of self-esteem is so slight she could ask about Serge Obolensky, "Why me?" and of Beaverbrook and FDR say, "I couldn't believe it was happening to me." Such thoughts would not have occurred to these admirers, whose success owned much to their projecting self-confidence, but they may have found themselves wondering how they became attracted to this "willful woman."

Although Dorothy was often summoned to join the President for a Hyde Park weekend, she did not hear directly from that august presence. The invitations were relayed by FDR's personal secretary, Missy LeHand. The Presidential command sought Dorothy out even when she was away from home.

"Once I was at a Herbert Swope lunch party in Sands Point and impressed everybody by getting a call from the White House," she recalls. "Missy said the President would be in Hyde Park the following weekend and would be very happy if I could be up there in time for Saturday lunch at Mrs. Roosevelt's, meaning Granny's big house. It meant a long drive, but Higgins, my Irish chauffeur, was thrilled by these trips. The Irish were initially for Roosevelt."

Having delivered Dorothy to the big house, Higgins would

Missy LeHand and Grace Tully in 1934.

leave her bags at Val-Kill cottage and "disappear." Once, though, Dorothy says, she sat down at a long table at a Democratic Party picnic lunch given by Henry Morgenthau, and there he was across from her.

The cottage was still presided over by Nancy Cook, known as Nan to intimates, but as Nancy to Dorothy. The uncertainties of Dorothy's position in this Presidential group is reflected in the way she addressed its members. She called the President's mother Mrs. Roosevelt but always referred to her as Granny, to distinguish her from Eleanor. Dorothy called Eleanor Mrs. Roosevelt, too, but thought of her as Eleanor. FDR's "darling" for Eleanor could be as sarcastic as her "Franklin" for him was tentative. Outside the family only Eleanor's lawyer, Harry Hooker (FDR's close friend), and the head of Warm Springs, Basil O'Connor, still used his first name. He was Mr. President to Dorothy; when they were alone , he wasn't called anything.

FDR's Hyde Park visits, when Dorothy usually joined him, were scheduled about every month or six weeks. The visits usually followed a set pattern, beginning with Saturday lunch at "Granny's," which Dorothy remembers meant just the three of them except occasionally when they were joined by a relative or Missy LeHand.

"'Granny' sat at one end of the table and the President at the other with me on his right. It was very much her house, and she was very much the hostess—rather plump, not too discreet and frivolous. Also, she was in love with her son, and she watched him closely always. She approved of me, was very warm and affectionate and was quite open about me in front of him.

She told me once I was a 'lady'—that awful word—and 'the only person in Franklin's entourage that I like and can talk to.' She was aware of the Jewish thing, never failing to ask, "How are your aunt Mrs. Lehman and your aunt Mrs. Warburg?" I never told her that Mrs. Lehman, by whom she meant Mrs. Herbert Lehman, simply wasn't my aunt and that the Mrs. Warburg she knew (Mrs. Paul M.) was my Great-Aunt Nina. Her kind of person assumed all Jews of German descent were related. So I would let it go and say, 'Fine, thank you.'

I think she thought I was safe for her son because I didn't want anything and everyone else did. She might have worried if she thought I would hurt him politically. As to other designs he might have had on me, she wouldn't have cared. She loathed Eleanor and would have arranged things for him so he could have what he wanted. Her main concern was to get him to Hyde Park as often and for as long as possible, and I was a draw. In me he had a playmate who was willing to come up and see him there, which meant that *she* would see him, too.

He was very patient with her when she would say such things as, 'Franklin, why don't you like Mr. [J. P.] Morgan? I always thought he was such a nice man.'"

Granny's acceptance of Dorothy seems fuller than Dorothy's of her, but then she had heard Nancy Cook on the topic of Granny's spoiling of the Roosevelt children. Eleanor's way of disciplining them was to use the cold and silent treatment—not speaking for several days—which would be vitiated by "Granny's hugs, kisses and presents." The result was that Eleanor had

Mrs. James Roosevelt, mother of Franklin, with her son.

to deal with the intrusion by her mother-in-law in her relations with her husband and also her children. Dorothy has never forgotten one remark of Granny's. "Having heard that Dr. Holmes, father of Oliver Wendell Holmes, had once treated her for measles, I asked her what he was like. 'Well,' she answered, 'you see, we're not *booky* people.'"

A standard afternoon diversion for FDR was driving Dorothy in his V-8 Ford touring car equipped with manual controls. Its color, blue, was the same as his match folders, which bore a sloop outlined in gold with a large *R* in script on the mainsail. The matches themselves, also gold, lighted with less fuss than today's; they went well with his cigarette holder and its rakish angle. Yet, in spite of her fascination with his radiant personality, Dorothy could be just a little bored by these weekends.

"Hyde Park was for his relaxation, and there wasn't much to do except accompany him driving and swimming. This he did in an old-fashioned two-piece suit. He was rather lonesome there, his court preferring to be where the action was, and it was my function to amuse him. Nancy Cook cautioned me not to bring up worrisome topics, such as politics or later the war or anything sad.

He loved driving recklessly along his miles of wood roads, and whenever I would be slid across the front seat away from him, a strong right arm would pull me back. I was used to such roads, as my father had lots of bridle paths on which we used to ride, but I never did get used to his driving. It was done to scare people, and as a child might run away from its governess, he would give the Secret Service the slip. He loved trying to duck them when he would cross the main highway, where traffic was stopped for him, then speeding up on the other side.

The Secret Service didn't ride with us but followed in a sedan, and there was no escort in front of us. As much as possible they tried to be unobtrusive—and had their backs to us watching for possible trouble—and I managed to ignore them. His only interest in security was trying to duck it, which he thought a great joke, in spite of having been next to Mayor [Anton] Cermak of Chicago when he was assassinated. He had the same reckless courage as the Kennedys, but it never crossed my mind I might be shot, too, sitting so close to him.

All this driving about we did together must have been tough for Eleanor. She wasn't there much, and when she was, she was always busy doing things. I had a lot of respect for her and felt sorry for her having to be odd man out. After his dream house was built, he stopped by her house to tell her to send sandwiches and things up there for us. She complied, and while it embarrassed me, it didn't bother him a bit.

She had moved out of the Val-Kill cottage by then into the furniture factory next door because of the gossip about her living with a couple of women, but I think she was much too in love with him ever to have gone in for that; maybe so much in love that she, too, was glad he had somebody safe to play with. Still, it must have been irritating for her to see her good-looking husband driving about with a woman eighteen years younger. I guess she was used to it.

After all, she'd had a lot to get used to in her time with him. Much has been written of the Lucy Mercer affair, but she wasn't identified by name when I first heard of it from Nancy Cook. Her version as I remember differs from the others. One evening when we were alone in the cottage at Hyde Park during the President's second term, Nancy told me that he had once asked his wife for a divorce in order to marry. By way of reply, Eleanor had asked if he had told his mother. 'Not yet,' he said. Nancy went on to say that Eleanor, in view of their having five children, then asked him to wait a year, at the end of which time if he still wanted a divorce, she would give it to him. During that year he came down with polio, she said, and the lady married 'some socialite from Newport.'

I never saw Lucy Mercer at Hyde Park, the White House or Warm Springs, although I have read she was there at his death. My theory is that he wanted to run away from the conflict—that between duty and desire—and his legs resolved it for him by becoming useless. He does seem to have been caught between two strong women always; first between Granny and Eleanor and then between Lucy and Eleanor, reinforced for once by Granny.

In the evenings again there were mostly just the three of us, and after dinner we would sit around together in the library. He would be at a bridge table working on his stamp collection, and although later I was collecting stamps of famous women with their biographies to educate myself, I thought his steaming stamps to cut the glue was pretty pathetic. His mother would talk plaintively about her friends who complained about the New Deal, and he would explain issues to her patiently.

One evening we talked of heroes, dead ones. Mine were Thomas Jefferson and Benjamin Franklin; liberal friends of mine speak of Ben Franklin as just a salesman. As for Jefferson, the President—mine, that is—used to say he didn't know why people were always quoting Jefferson. He claimed he himself said things which were a lot better. The President had a couple of heroes, too—Woodrow Wilson and his wife's uncle, Teddy Roosevelt, who had given her away when they were married. In his competitive way, the President never forgot the way the guests at the reception surrounded *that* Roosevelt, not bothering with *this* one.

Because I wasn't good at small talk, he would say, 'What's the matter—cat got your tongue?' He, of course, talked a great deal—mostly anecdotes. He liked a response from his audience, and when he told one of his funny stories—they were for the most part country wit—he would look at you suddenly to see your reaction. He must have been awfully bored with me as I never said much or joked with him. I did ask questions occasionally, and he tried out ideas on me sometimes.

I think I was more serious than he would have liked, I was so concerned about the one-third of us ill clad, ill housed and ill fed. He never really talked about those things, being more concerned about votes.

Once when we were talking of India and its poor, I realized that although he had heard of Gandhi, Nehru was an altogether new name to him, and he said lightly, 'He can't be much if I haven't heard of him.' Nehru's autobiography was out by then, and I told him that he was quoted both in it and in Nehru's speeches, 'so he knows about *you*, at least.' The President threw his head back in that way he did when having a good laugh and said, 'Then he must be a good man.'

On election night, 1936, the President's family and court were there at the big house for the returns as usual; the victory was historic, only two states being lost. Fannie Hurst, who as one of Eleanor's group had been invited, went up to the President's mother and asked how she felt about it. She answered, 'I expected that of Franklin. I hope he will continue to be a good President and a good boy.' She turned her back on Fannie Hurst to talk to me about my shoes. They were open-toed, quite new then, but a style I have worn ever since. For some reason the President was fascinated by them, too; I don't mean that he had a foot fetish. George said that *he* did, but I'd never heard of it before.

It's odd to remember that it was my brother John's concern about what 'that man' was doing to our income and his saying that I'd better look into it that was responsible for getting me involved in politics and later with the President. We never did discuss money, by the way; everyone knew FDR's money was Granny's, although it was never mentioned. I was never asked for a campaign contribution, which I suppose must have been a decision of Nancy Cook's; I was too important in other ways, I guess.

George was overwhelmed by the President, and it was he who really sold me on him. George saw it all in a sort of *droit du seigneur* way, his wife being tapped by the lord of the manor. He was proud of it, and it gave him tremendous prestige with his friends. Alexander Woollcott, for the first time impressed by me, tried to get into the act by having himself invited to the White House by Mrs. Roosevelt. Those thirty-six million votes, or whatever it was, and the power it meant dazzled George.

George would be asked occasionally to large gatherings for party workers, and if the President was more than dimly aware of him, he probably sized up the situation and decided to pay no attention to it. The President, after all, hadn't been part of a full marriage since his wife found out about Lucy Mercer. As to the reaction of my friends, they were always saying, 'Tell what happened; what did he say?' I would just repeat funny stories, trying to play it down.

Apparently, I was considered very sexy in those days, and he probably saw me as a sex object. This was a warm, sexy guy who was in an isolated position and was looking for a turn-on and companionship, too. In a rather sweet way he was fairly bold, and everything about his body— except his legs—was so strong.

His tremendous self-confidence and security of self would rub off on me, and in his presence my depression would lift. I never saw him depressed; he was an optimist, and there wasn't a neurotic element in him. He never drained me emotionally; in fact, it was just the opposite. He gave to me out of himself and I don't think he was ever aware of it. For me there was always that charm, warmth, radiance. . . ."

Asked if George's being so impressed by her relationship with FDR worried her in terms of their marriage, Dorothy's answer was immediate: "A lot." For George it was more than having a wife who impressed his friends by the connection. He was able to feel that, however peripherally, he was making an impression on history. FDR was much more than just the founder of the New Deal. A master of political timing, he was the symbol of hope for the nation, even if Al Smith had said, when asked to support FDR in his campaign for governor of New York, "Frank just doesn't have the character for a job this big."

But a Groton formmate of FDR felt himself doubly injured— his stock brokerage business was ruined, and he thought FDR was a traitor to his class. He then expressed amazement at the 1936 victory. "I can't understand this thing about Frank," he said. "He never amounted to much at school."

In discussing Dorothy's widened and influential associations, George wasn't bashful about his contribution to her success, asking, "Who the hell did she know? Harpo Marx and Woollcott and so forth were my friends, not hers. She didn't introduce me to her friends because she didn't have any outside the Dick Hall world. I mean, I knew Irving Berlin before she did, and it was I who introduced her to the Bill Paleys."

He went on to recall: "There was a New York financier named George Blumenthal, who was president of Mount Sinai Hospital. He had this enormous house on Park at Sixty-ninth Street. The design was Venetian, so Venetian there was no electricity on the first two floors. It had only two bedrooms, which I commented on as we walked around it, and our host said he wasn't in competition with hotels.

"When he opened a door on this huge linen closet, Dolly at once started going through the things at a great clip. I was rather embarrassed and, when we left, asked, 'For goodness sake, what was all that about?' she said, 'You know, he's a very old man, and before long those linens are going to be for sale. Didn't you see the initials? G. B.'"

In Dorothy's view George was undergoing a major personality change at this time, and it was one she did not understand. Typically, she tends to blame herself for it. She says it took a few years for her to realize both that she was too much for him and that he wasn't enough for her.

"I mean socially, not sexually. Gradually, he became completely different. He seemed affected and began speaking with an English accent. His close friend Samuel Chotzinoff, with whom he wrote a play, said, 'What the hell's the matter with George—where did he get that accent?'

"I said, 'You've been such good friends for so long, tell him.' He said he couldn't risk the friendship and that I was the one to do it. But how could I? You can't tell your husband he's acting like a phony, can you?"

On reflection, Dorothy wonders if George's accent was an unconscious attempt to associate himself with the British types she had met with Beaverbrook.

A view of the Backer marriage about that time is contained in a letter to Dorothy from S. N. Behrman, who included in it a scene that Robert E. Sherwood has called the greatest marriage story ever told. He, Behrman, suggested that the pauses in dialogue be articulated, as in the work of Harold Pinter.

SCENE: *A hot Sunday afternoon in my room in your Oyster Bay palazzo. I decided to go down to the drawing room to perhaps pick up a magazine or a book. Once I got there I saw you and George on the veranda. You were sewing; George was reading something. I drew closer; I wanted to eavesdrop. I was just about to give up when you saved me. You said languidly:*
DOLLY: I think I'm going to Europe.
(Long pause. Finally)
GEORGE: When?
DOLLY: I think in September.
(Enormous pause. Then)
GEORGE: Well, bring me back some shirts.

Politics, a common interest, helped the shaky marriage survive a few years longer. George was appointed to the City Council term of Charney Vladeck, who died in office. Vladeck was a

great leader of social reform who saw himself as a bridge between the Upper and Lower East Side. He was beloved by Dorothy, who speaks of his "charismatic personality and enormous
integrity. He said, 'You can compromise on principle but not on
personality.'"

*Dorothy with Mayor
Fiorello LaGuardia.*

George later ran unsuccessfully for Congress, while Dorothy
busied herself with new duties when Mayor Fiorello LaGuardia
appointed her to the Board of Child Welfare. She had some time
for once, having resigned from the Mount Sinai Hospital board
when its interns tried to form a union against the wishes of the
rest of the board. Dorothy was involved with the provision of
financial assistance to single parents with dependent children
under sixteen. Professional social workers dealt directly with the
cases, to Dorothy's annoyance. As a believer in direct communication she felt that she might have been effective in reaching cases others couldn't.

The job meant a couple of new experiences for Dorothy—riding the subway and standing up to a boss. "The Little Flower,"
she says, "was a short, stout, choleric man with much energy
and strength. His attitude toward women was odd; they were not

George Backer (candidate of the American Labor Party from the Seventeenth Congressional District) shakes the hand of Democratic nominee for member of the New York State Constitutional Convention, Dorothy Schiff Backer.

to wear lipstick or nail polish. I said I'd be damned if I would change my ways, and I didn't."

This stand won the approval of Robert Moses, who dominated the public works programs and interparty politics of both New York State and City for over forty years. During that reign he was the bender of the wills of six governors and five mayors to his own—for the benefit, as he liked to point out, even of the unborn—and he told Dorothy that the only way to handle a bully is to bully him back, and this she did. In 1938, when she ran as a Nassau County delegate to the New York State Constitutional Convention against this monster builder, she led her ticket, though she lost to Moses. It was during this campaign that she gave a lawn party at Old Fields for fellow party workers and overheard them referring to the formal garden and extensive lawn admiringly as "a nice yard."

The summonses from Missy LeHand were not always convenient, but it never occurred to Dorothy to fail to oblige. FDR was the President, and he was not to be denied. Besides, she was still bemused by having been picked by him, and yes, there was the envy and admiration of others, too. But Dorothy was never quite sure of her position with this bringer of hope to millions. She says that he always seemed comfortable with her, even if she wasn't with him, and she would leave reassured, marveling that a man with such enormous burdens never displayed a sense of stress. Stress did affect Miss LeHand, however; increasingly withdrawn in her White House quarters, she suffered a nervous breakdown after repeated nightmares in which FDR was assassinated.

In May, 1937, Dorothy received a summons for a Hyde Park weekend which promised to be a little livelier than usual. In honor of the biographer Emil Ludwig, a press picnic was scheduled for Friday night and a luncheon on Saturday. The picnic was held at the Val-Kill cottage pool, and Dorothy observed the easy, charming way FDR dealt with his guests, his ability to ask the right questions, come up with the jokes and stories to make a point and transfer his enjoyment to the others. Most of the working press were already on his side, of course, but the majority of their publishers and some of the editors were not.

At the big house luncheon, Dorothy recorded:

> The President, on whose left I sat, talked sailing to Jimmy [FDR's eldest son and White House aide], who was on my left. Sam Rosenman [Presidential counsel] said he was doing it to avoid serious topics, and maybe he was right; soon the President was chatting away gaily to me.
>
> Secretary of the Treasury [Henry J.] Morgenthau said he had been having trouble remembering what day of the week it was, which seemed odd for a man supposed to keep track of our money.
>
> The President was very anecdotal for the benefit of Ludwig and very proud of his architectural ability as demonstrated by the Val-Kill cottage. He ate heartily, although trying to diet, and fell for several pancakes rolled with cinnamon and sugar. Ludwig said it was obvious he was no dictator, as he looked too happy and had but one phone on his desk and no bells. He was also impressed by the lack of soldiers with bayonets and the simple dress of the guests. A tramp, who had been picked up by Mrs. Roosevelt [Eleanor] some time ago, was there with her and seemed a nice young man.
>
> After asking if I had been to South America, the President, who spoke French and German, talked of his trip there the previous fall with great enthusiasm. He added that he hoped on retirement at the end of his second term in 1941 to be granted the

same privilege as Grant, a trip around the world. Although he was informal and charming, the other guests seemed strained and awed, even Sam. So did I, I guess.

After lunch there was a fair at which the President had promised to speak, and he announced that not only did he not know what to wear, but he didn't know what to say, having nothing prepared. Speech writers did this for him, but he would edit their drafts to make them readable and speakable, using his own words and making them very much his. He told one speech writer in my presence to take out the word "adult," saying he could never say it "because it sounds too much like adultery."

His extemporaneous speaking was terrible; I heard him make a speech at a nearby school dedication, and he sounded like a bright child trying to make a grown-up speech. At least it was short—he hated anything long and claimed that no speech should last more than twenty minutes.

On the way back from the fair he went to inspect a new post office in Poughkeepsie. He was not at all pleased by what he saw, and as soon as he arrived at the big house he called the appropriate authorities with detailed instructions about what should be done. Then, wearily, he told me it was just another case of someone not doing what he was told.

He had joked with his wife about mutual relatives that day. She seemed quite cheerful, and later on I was made very happy by Harry Hopkins. He told me that only he and I had ever managed to act as a bridge between these opposing forces, saying that we were able to deal with and were trusted by both camps. This meant a lot to me. In his second campaign it always seemed that if an area needed rain, he brought some, and if sun, then that.

So thoroughly was Dorothy accepted that during that summer she was to find herself in a Hyde Park involvement which was to mean far more than mere command appearances. She and others were aboard the Presidential yacht *Sequoia* on the Hudson, and after lunch the President asked her to join him under the fantail awning. They chatted for a bit while he was sketching a map. Then, casually, he said, "Dorothy, I'm thinking of buying a farm of ninety acres adjoining my land. Won't you take on half of it?"

In describing her reaction, Dorothy shrinks and pales, as she

FDR in the front seat, Dorothy in the back (center) at Hyde Park, returning from speaking at a school dedication.

does when facing a possible impending financial problem at the *Post*. With a bewildered shake of her head, she says she was appalled by the thought.

"I still had that monster house in Oyster Bay, and the last thing I needed was forty-five acres of land next to his. I couldn't

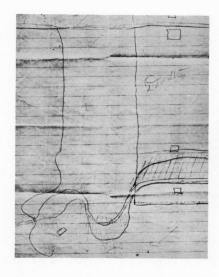

The map FDR drew on September 12, 1937 of the land he wanted Dorothy to buy at Hyde Park.

believe he was serious, although I knew he was always trying to get congenial people up there so there would be someone to see when he retired and wrote his memoirs. He loved buying Hyde Park land. It didn't make any sense for me, so I asked what I would do with it.

" 'Why, you would build a house on it,' he said. 'I'll talk to Henry Toombs [FDR's cousin, who designed much of Warm Springs]. He'll design it for you.'

"I was astounded, but I could understand his needing my help because he couldn't afford the land. So I told him that, well, I would think about it."

Rather than do so, however, Dorothy put the matter out of her mind and before long was even more astounded when the President wrote that his lawyer had closed the deal. He asked the favor of her check for $9,000, a favor Dorothy was in no hurry to oblige. This wasn't a matter of saying no to a President; it was money. Finally, a worried Rosenman came to see her, saying that the President had yet to receive the check. Dorothy's expression as she describes the visit is the one worn when that prediction of a financial problem turns out to be true. " 'Well, Sam,' I said, 'I really didn't take it that seriously.' "

"But *he* did," Rosenman replied. "He's very serious about it, and when the President of the United States wants his money, well, you send it to him."

Dorothy, not surprisingly, did now oblige, and in trying to forget the matter, she was helped by the fact that there was no further talk of building. Indeed, the land was considered unfit for building by Toombs; aside from being undesirable esthetically, it was in a depression and both boggy and subject to flooding. The President insisted that these problems could be overcome by proper drainage and that there was nothing to it, but Toombs objected that experts claimed it would cost a fortune.

"The President argued that experts don't know anything," Dorothy recalls, "but that he did."

To this day Dorothy isn't sure why she let herself be talked into land she didn't want, but she suspects one reason may be that she was dealing with a spoiled man, one "who wanted this thing terrifically, so you give what he wants. Which is more than I ever achieved.

"Of course," she says, "his paralysis was never mentioned, and seeing him at big public meetings, one forgot about it. He would be wearing braces and could stand, but at Hyde Park he didn't use them much. Either he'd be carried by the Secret Service, who made a sort of seat by crossing their hands, or he'd be in a wheelchair.

"He would ask me to walk alongside the chair, and at first I couldn't look and would turn my face away. Sometimes he would ask me to push him about in it, and this was sort of a shocker for me. I had pushed my children occasionally, but here was this great, strong radiant sun-god, the answer to the prayers of millions, seeming the child I had pushed in the park. It was . . . well, confusing for me. Embarrassing, too."

By the time Dorothy visited him at Warm Springs, Georgia, a few weeks before Christmas, 1938, she no longer felt ill at ease. As usual, she had to make her own travel arrangements, and it never occurred to her to wonder why it wasn't done for her. She now suspects he was afraid to have it known that it was always at his invitation that they met.

In order to catch her Warm Springs train, Dorothy was obliged to leave a dinner in New York for Mayor LaGuardia early. Her excuse was of such validity it more than made up for her absence. George was delighted by her trip to Warm Springs, even if he didn't bother to see her off, but once on the train Dorothy began to have doubts about the undertaking. Although she was going there to be with the President, she would be staying not at the Little White House but with Henry Toombs and, at that, in his rumpus room. He was to meet her at a stop outside

Atlanta, and alone that night on the train, she found herself undergoing an anxiety attack.

"I was afraid I might not be met down there in strange Georgia, where I'd never been, and I'd be lost in the darkness. I thought, 'I just can't take this.' Somehow, there I was on the platform with my bags and then I *really* got ready to panic; there wasn't anyone to meet me.

Henry arrived probably much sooner than it seemed, but I didn't really recover until I saw the President in the morning. The minute I set eyes on him I was all right; he was the sun-god again, and every bit of anxiety dropped away. As a joke, he was called the great white father, this marvelous, unneurotic and confident man, and he really was that for me.

It threw me a bit to see him in the pool with all those other cripples, but his doctor took me for a drive and explained that it was better that way, that together they didn't feel so inferior physically. I had wondered if the President was still potent and the doctor said, 'Don't forget, only his legs are paralyzed.' "

The President asked Dorothy to join his train on the way back north, and since again the arrangements were left to her, she shared a section with Doris Fleeson, national columnist for the New York *Daily News*. There was a stop at Chapel Hill, where FDR gave a rousing speech at the University of North Carolina on a national radio hookup.

"You have heard for six years that I was about to plunge the nation into war, that I was driving the nation into bankruptcy and that I breakfasted every morning on 'grilled millionaire.'

"Actually, I am an exceedingly mild-mannered person—a practitioner of peace, a believer in the capitalistic system and for my breakfast a devotee of scrambled eggs."

As the journey was resumed that evening, Dorothy was in the press car enjoying herself when she received a summons.

"That little black valet Duffy whispered to me that the President wished to see me. I followed him through what seemed an endless succession of cars, with the eyes of officials and the press upon me, to the Presidential car at the end of the train. FDR was alone near the rear platform and asked me to sit next to him. Duffy disappeared, in spite of the fact that the President was without a drink. He seemed powerless to get one, and after he had rung several times, William C. Bullitt, ambassador to Russia, came in to say hello. He was flabbergasted that this history-making President of such a powerful nation couldn't get a drink on his own train.

It was ridiculous, of course, and although he did finally get a martini, it took awhile. He wasn't a heavy drinker, incidentally—a couple of cocktails before dinner from a silver shaker with much talk while he performed the ritual. I don't remember wine or liqueurs; his wife was pretty much a teetotaler, having had a father and brother who were alcoholics. During Prohibition she didn't permit liquor in the house, but I suspect he may have had something stashed away in a desk drawer and that the boys drank in their bedrooms. By the time I came along there had been repeal and things were pretty relaxed.

Bill Bullitt didn't stay long; he went back to join the fun and drinking in the front compartment. I felt so sorry for the President, left all alone like that. Although I'd already had dinner, I stayed with him and had cocktails all over again before a second dinner in the forward compartment. Each time the train slowed at a crossing, he would order, 'Everybody wave,' and demonstrated by flapping his arms like wings. I did not.

He kept asking how I had liked the speech, wanting to know what I thought of each point he had made. I kept saying it had all been great, and it was. He was like an actor in his dressing room taking off his makeup; the excitement and applause were still with him. He needed people to unwind with, but all he had was me.

Much later I found John Charles Daly in the press car. He was a radio newscaster and would be the first with the news of the President's death at Warm Springs, April 12, 1945. I sat up with him for what little was left of the night talking, I was so excited. Doris, of course, was amazed when I joined her at breakfast. She said, 'How could you sit up all night with a *radio* man?'"

Dorothy is pretty objective about the men around FDR. She was not impressed, saying of Justice Felix Frankfurter, "His humor was not on a level with his brilliance, Harry Hopkins was the social worker he really was, but sick and cadaverous, and Sam Rosenman let himself be treated almost as a law clerk." She notes that the President had nicknames for most of them; Hopkins, for instance, being Harry the Hophead and Rosenman being Sammy the Rose, but that she was always Dorothy. She liked Hopkins, feels he was the most influential at that time and refers to him as "an angry, driven man." She says that he was the type that leaders such as FDR too often kill off with work and responsibility.

Dorothy is also objective about the President. It seemed to her that he was less a creator of ideas than an appreciator of those of others, which he would seize upon if they could be put to political use. She is not sure that he always knew quite what he was doing, being influenced by such people as Eleanor's old-style socialist friends. As a man of action he worked in terms of the moment, rather than as a long-range thinker, and while not patient as a listener, he was a good milker of brains. He tended to set one member of his staff against another, and his agreeing with all of them meant that none was ever quite sure where he stood. Dorothy adds:

"He just didn't like saying no, and as a practical politician he didn't want to get too involved. He needed tremendously to be admired, to please and to succeed. He thought appointing Joe Kennedy to the court of St. James's, putting an Irishman there, the greatest joke in the world. Not only did he feel the British were always putting us down, but Joe wasn't backing him as he had once. That bothered me; it was done in the wrong way and for the wrong reasons.

And then he was given to tricky ideas, such as the Supreme Court packing plan; he thought it a great joke on those nine old men. Although the plot was serious, dead serious, his enjoyment of it was obvious.

The night before it was announced, I went to the White House for what was supposed to be a fun dinner in the family dining room, just eight of us. I had attended a large formal one the night before at which the President had been his charming self, but this one was just the Frankfurters, Missy, the President, the Jacksons and Harry Hopkins and me. I wore my beaded Empire yellow dress.

Felix came in with a red, white, and blue American flag tie on—much laughter. They thought it was the funniest thing they had ever seen, the great Justice Frankfurter. It was the kind of joke the President loved, but then he was always reducing everything to its lowest common denominator."

FDR's relations with his children were rather remote, Dorothy says, and at this time he was not even very close to Anna. He saw much of his son, Jimmy, owing to his being an aide, and Jimmy's wife, Betsy (now Mrs. Jock Whitney), was a favorite. Dorothy thinks Betsy had fallen for him and says that it was a big joke around the White House. She remembers Nancy Cook saying, "She used to bring him orange juice every five minutes, even if he didn't want it."

"What he wanted very much," Dorothy says, "was to be loved by everyone and he wouldn't have dreamed of trying to turn her off."

The President had spoken to Dorothy of his need for a simple cottage at Hyde Park where he could get away from the activity of the big house and in which he would be able to write after his retirement. He drew up a design with Henry Toombs for not much more than a lean-to, but in the manner of Old Fields, it ended up as a nine-room house boasting a forty-foot living room with an eighteen-foot peaked ceiling. Since its panoramic site was on one of the highest hills in Dutchess County, about three miles from the big house, he named it Hilltop House. However, the press, who headquartered at a hotel in Poughkeepsie and were permitted on the growing Roosevelt acres only by invitation, called it the Dream House, a name FDR disliked but which, in spite of his frequent corrections, stuck.

"The day he and I staked out the site," Dorothy remembers, "there was to have been just the usual Secret Service men along. When we left the big house, Betsy turned up and the President told her, 'Hop in.' At the site she suggested some rhododendrons, but he said, 'No! They remind me of funerals.'"

FDR couldn't bear talk of suffering or sickness, Dorothy says. Topics which were sad were out, too; when she showed him a portfolio of Rembrandt illustrations which she had brought him from Holland, when she was looking for tile for his hearth, as soon as he came to the well-known "Lesson in Anatomy" he closed the book and laid it down. Death simply wasn't mentioned in the presence of this great leader, who spoke those words for which he is probably better known than for his public works programs, "The only thing we have to fear is fear itself."

Many who knew FDR well have spoken of his almost boylike enthusiasm and pleasure in his accomplishments. Dorothy recalls the pride with which he escorted her on a tour of the Dream House.

> "The Secret Service were standing on the terrace with their backs to the french windows, oblivious as usual. He wheeled himself into the bedroom, and there was this double bed. And I said, nervously, it's very nice. And we went back in the living room, and had some drinks, ginger ale or something ghastly. He was so proud of his design and everything about the house, but I was scared.
>
> It was one of those times when I was worried about Mrs. Roosevelt and what the President really wanted. I guess I went on seeing him because, as with that check, you don't say no to the President of the United States; as a patrician he was lord of the manor out of another century. Besides, I had nothing better to do."

VII

"A lot of my life has been a search for love—to love and be loved. The men I was in love with were in love with someone else, and the men who were in love with me were a nuisance."

Dorothy was soon to have something better to do. Ownership of the New York *Post* would mean a fundamental change in her life, one that would please both FDR and Beaverbrook. Indeed, each would be credited with this new direction for Dorothy, but the change was really brought about by her handling of a situation presented by another.

George Backer had committed himself to the acquisition of the *Post*, and Dorothy felt obliged to honor it. Several liberals (including FDR at one time) had owned stock in the paper, which had changed over the years from the Tory philosophy of founder Alexander Hamilton to Whig under William Cullen Bryant in 1829. Bryant's son-in-law, Parke Godwin, who was with it for almost forty-five years, broadened the editorial view from antislavery into other areas. Carl Schurz, as editor, was also a strong influence, as were two owners, Henry Villard and his son, Oswald Garrison Villard.

The younger Villard took on an editor, Edwin Godkin, and with him a weekly, the *Nation*, which he retained after disposing of the *Post* to Curtis interests. Then J. David Stern, whose papers included the Philadelphia *Record*, bought the *Post* in the early 1930s and dropped the word "Evening" from its masthead.

An Albany reporter for the paper, who had met Dorothy when she had been lobbying for social legislation, first spoke to George about the *Post*. "He knew me when I was a councilman and asked me to talk to Stern, saying he had to give up the paper, which would leave nobody for this left-of-center constituency.

"I was much taken with newspapers as a vehicle of information, and I saw Stern several times. He explained the financial situation to me a little disingenuously, I'm afraid; it seemed it would only take a few hundred thousand dollars and that in a year I could make it profitable. I didn't have any money—and here is where it hurts—so I told Dolly about it on account of her having money. She, a wonderful sport, said sure. . . ."

George's "wonderful sport" takes a different view of the acquisition.

"George had been told that the *Post* was going down the drain but could be saved. I told him that it was out of the question—it was ridiculous even to think of. But he kept talking to Stern, with whom he used to play chess, and I would hear that not only was the *Post* the only evening paper for the President, it was the oldest paper in the country. If it folded, one thousand jobs would go and so on.

Although everyone said no—accountants, Herbert Swope, lawyers—George insisted a couple of hundred thousand dollars would take it out of the red. The next thing I knew, he told me his honor was involved; he had made a commitment. Stern had borrowed money to keep it going for a few more months, and I was told that all that was required to save it was payment of its debts and meeting future ones until it was carrying itself.

I had no idea what I was getting into or why I was getting it just for its debts. Eventually I found out that if Stern had shut it down, he would have had to pay severance to the employees under the Newspaper Guild contract; I had never heard of that. This would have amounted to two or three million dollars, and so they tried unloading it on everyone, and no one would touch it except George—which meant me. Stern wrote a book saying he got a check for five hundred thousand dollars for the stock, which is not true; I got the controlling stock for nothing.

Stern and others transferred their interest in the *Post,* then at 75 West Street, in June 1939. The presses were in the basement, offices were on the next three floors, and a two-story penthouse was on top of the building. I didn't do a tour then, but when I did, I didn't even realize the presses were pretty obsolete. The city room looked bigger than the one we have now, and while there has been talk of messy washrooms, the ladies' room didn't seem too bad. I guess I'm really not very conscious of my surroundings, and at that point I was too worried about paying the bills.

The signing was done in the penthouse living room on the sixteenth floor, a huge paneled room with fireplace. Stern used the penthouse for advertiser parties; it had been installed by the Curtis family, who lived in Philadelphia, as a *pied-à-terre*. In addition to the living room on that floor there was a large bathroom and double bedroom. The seventeenth floor had a dining room, pantry, kitchen and servants' rooms. One reached these two floors by transferring on the fifteenth floor to a little pushbutton elevator, which took me awhile to trust.

Everyone was very gay at the signing, cracking jokes and so forth, except me. I kept wondering what I was getting into. Stern, having unloaded his white elephant and gotten rid of creditors by telling them they would be taken care of by us, was happy as could be. After the signing there was no celebration for me; I went back uptown to the children. I had only been needed for my signature."

In picking up the *Post*, Dorothy also picked up the titles of vice-president and director; George became editor, president and treasurer. Except for writing checks, she stayed out of things. People thought George had bought the paper, and since he came to Dorothy almost monthly for a hundred thousand or so ("I don't know how poor George could do it, but he did"), Dorothy grew increasingly worried both about the money and him. She didn't think of herself as a newspaper owner, she says.

"I was just a woman who had gotten sucked into another sort of monstrous country house. All George's schemes looked rosy at first, he being such a soft sell, but only the *Dead End* investment paid off. At least the losses weren't as bad as they might have been; one was for a cancer cure a doctor with an office near the Colony Restaurant came up with; all it needed, George said, was a little money. After I had put in twenty-five thousand dollars, the wise types pulled out secretly, leaving me with sheep glands."

Soon after the acquisition, George rescinded a 10 percent cut in wages without telling Dorothy, which, while it may have endeared him to the employees, didn't do much for her view of him. Also, the Newspaper Guild ignored his claim to union membership, claiming that he was merely a management spokesman. He was so hurt he refused to meet with them in the future.

"I worked very hard," George said of this trying period, "and I had loyal support from the staff, all of whom were very nice. I got rid of the editor Stern left, as I wanted the editorial policy to be what *I* thought was right."

John Schiff, Dorothy's brother, was concerned about her investment and advised her to do with the *Post* as stable owners do: decide how much money she wanted to pour into it and make that her limit. (He himself was about to dispose of 932 Fifth Avenue and most of his father's art collection and library.)

Dorothy's worry about the *Post* was relieved a little by FDR's continuing approval. His greeting for her became "How's the pape?" and those who didn't think George was running it went right on thinking the President had persuaded her to take it on.

"I never asked his [the President's] advice about anything, but he was always giving it," she says. "He was really a frustrated editor and maintained that only twenty-five percent of the people read editorials. Of course, he overlooked the fact that those are the ones who influence others. He resented the one-party press—only two or three dailies in the whole country were liberal enough to be for him—and he was always making cracks about it. In terms of the vote it didn't matter much, and besides, he had most of the columnists and writers."

In spite of the *Post*'s giving them an interest in common, the Hyde Park visits didn't get any easier for her. On one she found herself unusually anxious because she had to work her way through a large crowd without escort to get to his car. He had told her to attend a school dedication speech, and she asked how she was to get through the police lines. He said, "Oh, you'll find a way." She did, by explaining shakingly that the President had told her to go to his car. As soon as he joined her in it, her anxiety disappeared.

He kept bringing up the topic of her acreage at Hyde Park also, but on one occasion, in the Dream House living room,

Mrs. Felix Warburg (Aunt Frieda) with John Schiff in 1939. Portraits behind them are of Jacob Schiff and his wife, Theresa.

abruptly changed the subject and instead asked, almost casually, if she thought he should run for a third term.

"It was a ghastly question, and I told him I thought he should do what he wanted to do," Dorothy remembers. "He looked off at the woods, past the Secret Service men outside, and was quiet for some time. Finally, I asked, 'What do you want to do?' He said, 'I don't know, but many people think I should.' Now I know, of course, he wanted to."

Part of Dorothy's shock in being asked her opinion was the result of the President's having always felt free to advise her unasked but never seeking her advice. She says the only man she ever knew as free with unsolicited advice was Bernard Baruch, whom Dorothy's grandfather, the imaginative financier, Jacob, had called a speculator.

"My father had to be sneaky about poker playing and womanizing with Bernie," Dorothy says. "Bernie was fascinated by him because my father insisted on doing his own unpacking so he could find things" when he came to Hobcaw, the Baruch plantation in South Carolina.

During the war Baruch's relations with the President became somewhat strained, owing to the former's advice that the most qualified men should be selected for government posts regardless of political affiliation. The fact that he wrote and made public a commendatory letter to William Randolph Hearst didn't help, the President objecting to Dorothy that Hearst was "associated with the worst elements in the country." FDR attributed Baruch's unsavory counsel to his declining health, emphasizing the fact that after an operation Baruch had lost the use of his legs temporarily, Dorothy notes.

> "I thought it peculiar the President would make such a point of it, in view of his own handicap. He was always interested in the women Bernie surrounded himself with, calling them 'the most beautiful ever.' When I mentioned a new nurse, the President said at once, 'I bet she's pretty.'
>
> Everyone thought Bernie was Sephardic, which he didn't mind their thinking, but he wasn't. He had all sorts of economic ideas and was always looking for ears. I was amused when, at seventy plus, he asked me to the races after checking to be sure George wouldn't be jealous. Bernie could be a bore at times, but I learned a lot."

In one of their more relaxed moments in FDR's study at the big house, the President pointed out to Dorothy that her experience was largely limited to New York, as his had been before he had gotten into national politics. He felt that she should be doing something useful on a broader scale, such as the specialized education of farm women. He seemed a little vague, Dorothy says, and so she came up with something more concrete.

> "'There is another job I would much rather have,' I said. 'While I could never replace Missy [Missy LeHand had recently died], there are parts of her job I think I could do.'
>
> Very quickly and agitatedly he waved the thought aside, whispering, 'You better not let Grace hear you say that.' As it happened, Grace Tully, the second secretary,

En route to Florida.
November 28, 1937

Dear Dorothy:

Henry Hackett has sent me the enclosed
description of the rear line of your new
property.

Translating the various distances and
directions into plain english, it means that
the line runs through the narrow strip of
woods fields and follows, part of the way, the old
stone wall in the woods.

Always sincerely yours,

[signature: Franklin D. Roosevelt]

Mrs. George Backer, Jr.,
c/o Miss Nancy Cook,
Hyde Park,
New York.

December 23, 1937.

Dear Mrs. Backer Dorothy,

I enclose a note from Henry
Hackett in regard to the deed. If you
would be good enough to send him your
check for $9,000, he will be able to close
the whole transaction and have the deed
recorded in your name.

Best wishes of the Christmas
Season.

Very sincerely yours,

[signature: Franklin D. Roosevelt]

Mrs. George Backer,
944 Fifth Avenue,
New York City,
New York.

passed the window just then. After she disappeared, the President said she was upset because he had continued to dictate speech drafts to Missy until she became incapacitated. My guess now is that it was another case of his being afraid of gossip. I was getting to be a problem."

One evening in New York, Sam Rosenman consulted with Dorothy about her working in the administration. Much of their conversation was concerned with Rosenman's jealousy of Harry Hopkins, who he felt had prevented him from receiving a Washington post. He was also critical of Averell Harriman, which Dorothy put down to the fact that Hopkins and Harriman were close. She adds that "Sam had been the boy about the house up in Albany, but Harry was *it* in Washington." She reassured Rosenman that FDR was a great believer in him, but she wasn't able to see herself working with farm women.

Dorothy was no longer able to avoid building a house in Hyde Park on the strength of the land's being unusable, for the President had exchanged her boggy plot for acreage on high ground adjacent to the Dream House. Pressure to build kept increasing. The design was ready, FDR had chosen the site, Anna Rosenberg told Dorothy she was delaying construction, and Sam Rosenman used his "you can't say no to a President" approach. Finally, exhausted, Dorothy agreed, insisting that the house be as small as possible—two bedrooms, one bath. For once, she had

April 5, 1938.

Dear Dorothy:-

While at Warm Springs I saw the preliminary sketches for my proposed cottage on top
of the hill and Henry Toombs told me he was sending you preliminary sketches for your cottage this
week. It is my thought that if the two, which
will be very similar in specifications, could be
opened to bidders at the same time, we might both
get lower prices if one contractor did both jobs
simultaneously.

I told Henry that if you and I could
both approve the general plans by April twenty-
fifth, he could complete the builder's plans and
specifications by June first and submit them to
bidders. Bids would be received by June twentieth
and if any of them are satisfactory, the contracts
could be entered into within a very few days. That
means that actual work could be begun by early July
and both cottages would be under roof before cold
weather, and the interiors could be completed late
in the autumn and early winter.

A schedule such as this would give both
you and me a chance to watch the building from
time to time during the summer, and, incidentally,
I think we would both save money.

Will you thank George for his mighty
nice note of March thirtieth, which has just come
to me?

Always sincerely,

Mrs. George Backer,
944 Fifth Avenue,
New York, N. Y.

---

her way, even if by the time it was done the Red House boasted a
butler's pantry.

Dorothy comforted herself by recognizing that the new house
would eliminate the President's calling for her at Nancy Cook's
cottage all the time as might a high school boy his date, sitting in
his car and blowing the horn. It would give him a place to drive
to, and anyway, she had been practically ordered to build it. She
had become very good at doing what she was told by the President, who, she says, "in his spoiled child way didn't get mad or
anything; he just expected people to do what he told them."

Dorothy had put Old Fields on the market, but for some time
there were no takers; even if there hadn't been both a manpower
and gasoline shortage because of the war, the country had not
succeeded in climbing out of the Depression. While Dorothy
wasn't aware of it, her decision to rid herself of the place affected her growing disillusionment with her marriage, a disillusionment reinforced by continuing financial demands of the *Post*.
She sometimes saw advertisers. George's concern seemed limited to its editorial policy. His charm was now diluted by failure
in Dorothy's eyes, and to this was added a new element: mis-
trust.

The President and Dorothy were on the Dream House terrace one Saturday afternoon when Eleanor, who was supposed to be spending the weekend at Alexander Woollcott's in the company of George, arrived unannounced with a basket of fruit. Dorothy recalls:

"I was appalled. The President, who always joked with her, said a little sarcastically, 'Why darling, where did you pop up from? You were the last person I expected to see this afternoon.' As he laughed, she said in her high voice, 'Well, I heard you and Dorothy were up here and I just thought you might want some sustenance.' On my saying that I had understood she was at Alec's, she said she'd been unable to go at the last moment. 'And now, I must race off.' Then she put the basket down and really did.

When I got back to Oyster Bay, I asked George how his weekend had been 'Marvelous,' he said. 'Mrs. Roosevelt is just wonderful.' I wasn't trying to entrap him—honestly—but I had to tell him. 'George,' I said, 'she wasn't there. I saw her.' Things like that never bothered him. He said, 'That's right; she couldn't come at the last minute.'

As to what Mrs. Roosevelt was really doing taking us by surprise that afternoon, I suspect that it may have been a sign of approval of me and at the same time confirming her claim on him. I still think she was in love with him in spite of everything, and after his death she asked me to dinner so she could talk about him. She sounded as if they'd never had anything but a happy marriage, saying, 'Do you remember, Dorothy, how he loved doing such-and-such? And how much he enjoyed this-and-that?' It was all said without jealousy, venom or anything like that.

At the time, though, the situation was made to seem even more impossible than it had. I felt a failure with him; here was this warm, sexy guy in an isolated position looking for companionship and affection. He wanted me to make bright, witty talk and tell him all the Long Island gossip, but I didn't know any and wasn't inventive enough to make it up. I think I was scared most of the time, too on guard. I didn't do the best possible job, but as well as I could at that stage of my life.

Before long I began to wonder if he was really of first magnitude and if it wasn't merely the sun-god quality which gave people confidence. His conversation was mostly trivial, there were all those juvenile stories being repeated endlessly, and he wasn't well informed on anything except naval history and current political issues which are dead now. I missed the intellectual and sophisticated world of Max that I had known in London.

Although I was still very inexperienced, I knew a lot about older men and how lost they were with their vast needs nobody listened to. The President seemed just another one sometimes. Certainly, he didn't compare well with Max, that barefoot boy from Canada, who was not a so-called gentleman—quote, unquote. Sure, the President was a country squire and an American gentleman, but for me the barefoot boy was about a million times more interesting."

In her restlessness Dorothy found herself wondering about Sir Leslie Hore-Belisha. As British War Minister he was much in the news and had begun to look even more like Prime Minister material than had Max. Friends had brought word of him, saying that he had been so hurt by Dorothy's rejection he couldn't speak of her. This troubled her, of course, making her wish again she had been more gentle in turning him down.

"Part of that rejection was due to Max's having pushed him at me. When I saw him in New York just before the war, he wasn't quite as funny-looking as he had been; I had met many worse-looking people by then. I even wondered how I would do as a Prime Minister's lady; the thought was rather fun. I always did have the common touch sort of thing, but there was the problem of being such a bad hostess. Anyway, Leslie turned out to be no Disraeli."

Dorothy had yet to find suitable use for herself or, indeed, to learn that it was not to be found through men.

Part of Dorothy's restlessness in the FDR relationship reflected dissatisfaction with her role as a mother. She was conscientious, responsible and highly concerned about her children, but she was prey to the uneasy feeling that something was missing. She went to considerable effort to include them in her activities.

Dorothy's daughter Adele Sweet remembers meeting the President for the first time when she was about twelve. Such was her expectation of greatness, she thought she would find a heroic presence, larger than life. Instead, she remembers a man who was playful, even boyish.

"He was just huge in his impact on me. He loved driving that special car of his and used to ask me to spot stone walls he was trying to locate as boundary markers. Once as his car crawled up a hill on one of those wood roads while I looked for the ubiquitous stone wall, the escort cars stalled. He gunned ours ahead, lost them and roared with that laugh of his, glorying in it.

"I had a pretty clear view of his relationship with Mother, and it didn't particularly impress me. I was never with him alone; she was always along. The President was very physical, which may be why I was never made aware of his handicap."

Adele also remembers the day when the President was shown the completed Red House by Dorothy. His tour was interrupted by the arrival of Mrs. Roosevelt, who promptly took up with him the fact that Senator Burton K. Wheeler was not being given a chance to air his political and national views. An argument ensued, and when Mrs. Roosevelt said it was a great mistake not to hear all sides in a democracy, the President replied that it didn't apply in a time of war. She objected that the country was not at war, but he said that while not declared, the truth was that we were at war.

According to Adele, the scene ended with his teasing Eleanor when she said wearily that there was really no such thing as true democracy. "You just don't believe in representative government, that's all," he said.

The President was pleased by the Red House and claimed some design credit. A lady at a big house luncheon one day mentioned to Dorothy that she had heard Old Fields was on the market and wondered what its architectural period was.

"Is it Louis Quatorze or Quinze?" she asked.

Laughing, the President interrupted. "What is the style of your Hyde Park house, Dorothy?"

"Franklin the First," she answered.

Old Fields found a buyer shortly after the fall of France: Madame Jacques Balsan, formerly Consuelo Vanderbilt, then the Duchess of Marlborough. She acquired it for about a tenth of what it had cost Dorothy. She bought only 100 acres of the land

and took great interest in the interior of the house, which she transformed from eighteenth-century English to period French. Dorothy says, "She was hung up on the French. One item Madame Balsan did not change was the pay phone in the servants' quarters."

Dorothy has no regrets about the sale, saying that the agent told her "it was all he could get and if I wanted to sell, I'd better grab it. I was very glad to unload it." On her final visit Dorothy had a discussion with Colonel Balsan regarding the chandeliers, which she wished to keep. He pointed out that as fixtures they went with the house, a fact she had not known. Nor had she realized that she couldn't retain the Chinese Chippendale wallpaper she had bought in London, even though the new owner didn't want it and sold it through a dealer to a future ambassador to the Court of St. James's, Walter Annenberg. Dorothy recently mentioned her relief in no longer having a staff to run and referred to work schedules that were prepared for her for each position. Asked who took care of the stairs, the upstairs or downstairs maid, Dorothy smiled. "I had them meet halfway."

In speaking of John's razing Northwood after the war and replacing it with a Normandy-style manor, Dorothy says that at least her houses are still around. She admits Old Fields was beautiful ("It's nice I've built something beautiful that still stands"), even if she had never wanted it, and that the Red House is attractive, too. Her staff problems there were minor, in that a couple took care of things, a Mr. and Mrs. Bie.

"Mr. Bie, who had a withered arm, was a carpenter, I don't quite know how, and Mrs. Bie was a great, big, good-looking Scandinavian. She had taken care of the Dream House for the President and had been a second cook in the Vanderbilt house nearby. The President didn't know she could cook. She told me that she could have cooked a much better dinner for the King and Queen of England when they came to Hyde Park and that it had been a lousy meal with duck soup and duck for the main course. She could have done everything for him, but because she was married to a carpenter, he saw her only as Mrs. Carpenter, not Mrs. Cook. That's the way he was; he categorized people. She came to work for me after he died.

She was a country woman and absolutely marvelous.

The Red House at Hyde Park.

She brought her chickens with her, so any time you wanted one, she would go out and wring a neck. I didn't really use the house until 1943, giving it to Sam Rosenman the first summer and Jim Forrestal the next, while I rented Alfred Vanderbilt's house in Sands Point for summer use. That made it nice for George, as his croquet friends were all about.

My timing on the Red House was off. I didn't build it when the President wanted me to, and by the time I did, it was too late. By then, I think, he may have given up on me. He wanted the house to be built, of course, and to have me in it, but it was all for him. Once I saw this, I was no longer the child and he the father. Somehow, next I seemed to have become the provider, though not a mother figure. Before long I was kidding him about a new girl he was supposed to be very keen about, Princess Marta of Norway. He said that was nonsense; King Haakon, an old friend of Uncle Teddy's, had asked him to take care of her when she came here. Of course, I didn't know then he was still seeing Lucy Mercer, who, being married, had to keep in the background."

The only one of Dorothy's children who seems to have a really warm feeling about the Red House is her youngest, Sarah-Ann Kramarsky, also called Sally. Sarah-Ann hadn't quite reached

Sarah-Ann and Dorothy.

her teens by the time it was finished, and while she didn't spend more than a few summers and occasional weekends spring and fall there, it provided in its simplicity a homier feeling than Old Fields or the rented Vanderbilt house at Sands Point. Its atmosphere may be one reason that Sarah-Ann is more a domestic type than her half siblings and, unlike them, has never been divorced. She is married to Werner Kramarsky, New York State commissioner of human rights, is prettily attractive in a dark, Dresden-doll way and is immersed in politics. She sees much of her mother, of whom she is less in awe than the others, and combines the most interesting aspects of two worlds, each in their season—New York liberalism and East Hampton vacationing.

"My earliest memory of my mother is her appearing in blue and looking divine when she would come in to say goodnight," Sarah-Ann says. "At the Red House there was the neighbor, who was always trying to get free of the Secret Service. He was good at giving children's parties, which was marvelous for friends who came up and discovered that one so important could talk about things for children, such as Flexible Flyers. But he didn't

have the impressive prophetlike air of Weizmann, whom I saw
with my father."

While the President was free enough with his unsolicited
advice on these Hyde Park weekends, Dorothy did not discuss
her personal or professional problems with him. She had lost
$2,000,000 in the *Post*'s first two years and remembers that al-
though George was still delighted by the editorial side of things,
he seemed less and less able to cope with the business end. Dorothy began to see George as something of a *Luftmensch*, by
which she means one who is insubstantial. As the distance between them widened, their views of the *Post* became increasingly at odds.

This is apparent in an interview she gave the *Herald Tribune*,
which quoted her as wishing to make it a more popular and less
intellectual a paper. She added that she was drawn to the tabloid
form and had been thinking of doing a column. The *Post*'s feature editor, Theodore O. Thackrey, had an immediate reaction,
and it was one which would change the course of both his and
his employer's lives.

"I didn't know him, but he telephoned me and asked
for an appointment. He discussed the column idea and
was pretty bitchy about it, then asked what my qualifica-
tions were. Like all of them on the *Post*, he thought
George owned it and that I was one of those wives no one
knew what to do with. They were newspapermen but re-
markably naïve; they didn't know the facts.

After I told him of my experience in social work and
politics, he thought I *should* write a column. And he
thought a lot of other things, such as buying columns,
having a woman's page and so forth. His ideas clicked
with me and led to a plan for saving the paper. No one
else had any ideas, the *Post* was going down the drain
rapidly, and with George everything was terrible. Ted
was confident about his newspaper competence, and
quite rightly.

He was a strong and positive person. Women went for
him, but I don't think I did particularly. He really wasn't
my type, being sort of snaggle-toothed, and I think his
judgment wasn't great. He had been editor of the Cleveland *Press* at twenty-three and when Roy Howard bought

the *Telegram*, he brought him to New York; then Roy tried him on a Buffalo paper. I didn't know this until Roy told me years later; he had hired Ted because he thought he was brilliant. He told Ted he didn't want a yes-man and Ted took that to mean he should always say no and fought him on everything.

Finally, Ted ended up on the Shanghai *Post*. A lot of journalists in the Far East—old China hands—acted as spies for the British in the thirties, although Ted has denied he was one of them. He was a fighter, had been a flier in the First World War and was wild. After he saw things happening—the Japanese killing people at the racetrack—he wanted to get out and wrote a New York *Post* editor whom he had once hired. He was offered a job which turned out to be one so minor he thought it insulting and sadistic on the part of the editor. Once Ted got power, the editor left."

Ted Thackrey is a rather cadaverous, harried man with gray hair, heavy glasses and a chain smoker's throaty voice. He is now handling public relations for a social agency, and it is clear that he is still very much committed to the human cause. His recollection of his first meeting with Dorothy differs from hers. He says it took place when he resigned from the New York *Post* to become managing editor of the Washington *Post*.

"She came in to the city room and said if I were free for lunch, she would like to have a conversation with me about staying on. This was the first time I ever saw her, and she was unique in my experience. She was pleasant, dedicated to saving the *Post*, or deciding that it could not make it, and wanted rather desperately to find somebody who had been in the business long enough to identify what and where its weaknesses were.

"I was not at all aware of Dorothy as a woman or of her background and family, although I became increasingly aware as we began to do a series of revolutionary things with the *Post*. I think she was influenced by a whole circle of friends which grew up around the Backers, but owning a newspaper was increasingly alarming. It was losing well over one hundred thousand a year. She obviously liked the idea of having an organ that suited her socially and gave her a professional status which she had not. It was a very expensive hobby.

"She offered me the job of executive editor, a created post, and

George got sicker and sicker. The impression he made on the staff was that of an extraordinarily decent gentleman with a kindly, somewhat philosophical manner and a series of concepts of what a newspaper ought to be. It was an ideal patterned on a somewhat more liberal version, editorially, of the New York *Times* in combination with aspects of the *New Republic* and the *Nation*, a kind of gentleman's product. He was well intentioned, had virtually no interest in news coverage or advertising and business, but was more efficient than I'd expect from a man who had no experience as an executive at all—you know, literally none!"

The more Dorothy thought about Ted's ideas, the better they seemed. Soon she was reading books about newspaper publishing and editing, then began frequently dropping by the *Post* where she would sit with editors to learn something of their functions.

George resisted the idea of popularizing the paper, which he saw as vulgarization. Dorothy thinks that as a liberal he was uncomfortable having to represent management with labor unions and that what was needed was a publisher who was fascinated by advertising and administration, yet could function as a hard-hitting, city-room kind of editor. What was not needed was "a gentle soul who was worried about his friends' opinions."

An example of her doubts about George occurred the day she was showing an officer of the League of Women Voters around the *Post* plant. She encountered George in the hall and, seeing that he had forgotten to shave, was so ashamed of him she couldn't bring herself to introduce him. She led her guest past him in silence, thinking how impossible it would have been for her brother, John, to appear at his office unshaved.

On the night of Pearl Harbor, George stayed uptown to work on editorials, while Dorothy went down to the *Post* to help get the early edition out. "Working all night with Ted was pretty exciting. Stories kept coming in fast on top of us, and I worked to try to get the woman's angle. I came up with some pretty good stuff, too."

That sense of excitement returns to Dorothy as she describes the scene, and it is obvious she felt right about herself in a deep, intense way; she had discovered the joy of working with another and of belonging.

Dorothy had earlier talked George into engaging a general

manager to take on the business end, but the net effect was merely to add another executive salary. Circulation on the *Post* had dropped from 250,000 when she took it over to 190,000, and it gave every indication of continuing downward. It had been built partly on contests which were wearing thin, but not as thin as George's patience with them; you don't influence opinion with contests. Along with the loss of circulation, of course, went a drop in revenue.

George was still optimistic. "We were reaching an audience which the New York *Sun*, the New York *Times* and even the *Daily News* couldn't—a sort of intellectual lower-income middle class. In a time when the grandsons of the great newspaper publishers—the Pulitzers, Howards and the rest—were going down like ninepins, the *Post* survived. It fitted our readers and going to tabloid helped; that I credit Thackrey with. But nevertheless, he was Dolly's biggest error."

Dorothy gives Ted credit for much more than the tabloid form, as do others. Between Dorothy and Ted the *Post* would survive, but they wouldn't see its survival together. Dorothy recalls:

"George didn't really want the paper anymore, and he was sick besides. I said, 'Let me go down,' but he said, 'Let's just throw it in the river.' I told him I'd like to see what I could do with it, but he objected. 'I don't want to be married to a career woman. If you go down there, I'm going home to my mother.' I went down on Monday morning and took over. And George did go home to his mother—that very day.

It was quite an experience, showing up to take over a paper I owned but had turned over to others. Of course, Ted was there, and I inherited a male secretary who was very nice. He told me what to do, but I didn't pay any attention to him. When he came and said he wanted to quit, that was all right. I was doing things my way, and before long others were, too. I didn't even know I had a way until then.

Ted and I really worked together well at the office, and it carried over into after hours, too. He never seemed to go home, and it was hard to say where work stopped and fun began, except . . . well, he was such a take-charge person and that was rather nice for a change."

"It was Dolly's money," George has explained. "I just happened to be the beard. It ended up with my becoming sick, which I suppose was a blessing in disguise. I had opposed Hamilton Fish on radio by favoring our going to war for moral reasons, in addition to having written a front-page editorial for which I was picketed by the Communists. In our debate he said that it was all very well for me to talk of going to war because I was thirty-six and didn't have to. I said I would enlist as a private soldier the day the United States declared war, and when that day came, I had to rush it or Fish would have had my hide.

"I was thrown out because I had tuberculosis, of which I'd never had even a clue, and after we parted, I went to Saranac and didn't see her for months. Dolly may have decided on divorce before then, but I didn't see it coming; I never think of those things, and I'd never been divorced. I was a little devastated and remember saying to Bill Paley, 'It's a bad indication; it shows I did not succeed.' He, having been divorced, had another point of view. 'You're a goddamned fool! That's not the way it is; it just didn't work, and that's it.'

"I do think that in a sense I consider the failure mine. Certainly, I wasn't adding anything to her life, but while this may be male chauvinist, I doubt if I had really been doing my part in that marriage, Dolly would have divorced me. I don't know—I mean, these imponderables about being in love and all that. . . . The thing I was terrified about was losing contact with my child.

"I am very grateful to Dolly; she was always wonderful when I ran for office or wrote a show. I would be very pleased to do anything for her, but there is nothing I can do for her; she doesn't need my wisdom, such as it may be."

Dorothy's attitude toward George is less sentimental than his about her, but it is perceptive.

"Once the Army rejected George, he must have thought about my rejection. He came to see me to say he thought he might be able to be with a career woman after all. He wondered if maybe we could stay together, and I asked for what reason. He said he thought he could be useful as an escort, and when I wanted to know how he felt about me, he said, 'Don't be silly.' I wanted him to tell me he loved me, and I suppose if he had, we would have stayed together. But he didn't, and that was that.

The marriage should never have taken place. He was terribly jealous, irrationally suspicious of me. I was too much—much too much—and he wasn't enough. I don't mean sexually. Jeannie Campbell, who has been around, called him the most fascinating man she had ever met, and my friend Alicia Patterson told me she practically had an orgasm every time he came into the room. She made a date with him after our divorce, and he forgot to show up—typically George. He always had answers to everything, usually wrong, but he was afraid of women. And that may have been his lure for them.

The reason I was too much, I have begun to realize, is that he thought he had married above himself socially. That may be why he became his worst with me, putting on the dog and the accent.

I think the marriage sort of knocked him out, really. He was thirty when we married, he didn't want to marry anyone, and he wasn't someone who should have married then. His friends still say, 'You shouldn't have done that to George,' and they are right. It was a failure, that marriage, and it was my fault he was pushed into it. I only hope he didn't suffer too much."

Nevada again was the scene of its legal dissolution, and this time Dorothy went to a Carson City ranch. As for the children, George's daughter, Sarah-Ann, nine at the time of the divorce (1943), was naturally the most affected. Her comment is brief and to the point. "I'd had little contact with my father. I was stunned, thinking we were out there for a cure, but it didn't change my life in any way."

From Morti Hall one gets the impression he didn't see George as up to his mother on any level, although he found him amusing. What seems to have most interested him about George was that the senior Mrs. Backer gave her son an allowance (as did FDR's mother him), a support Dorothy says ceased on their marriage. Adele appears equally unmoved by the divorce, speaking of her relationship with George as having been passive. "He was clever, but ineffectual, and didn't seem to have a point of view about anything I did. He wasn't someone whose approval was important or whose disapproval was felt. He was a guest in the house."

A high point of the Nevada sojourn for Dorothy was the visit paid to the ranch by Eleanor Roosevelt. Mrs. Roosevelt had come out to see Trude Pratt, who was also getting a divorce—Trude would later marry Joseph P. Lash. This informal visit of Eleanor Roosevelt's gave Dorothy an opportunity to know her in a way she never could have at Hyde Park, and she discovered that Eleanor represented much of what she aspired to be. Dorothy speaks movingly of Eleanor's unrequited love for FDR, a kind of hurt to which she, Dorothy, was really a stranger.

A man new to her, Dorothy recognizes, has figured in all her divorces. By the time she has obtained her decree, however, the man is no longer new and doubt arises.

> "When I came home, there was Ted on the platform to greet me and I thought, 'Ick!' I heard alarm signals, but he'd got a divorce, too. Besides, there weren't any other men in my life then except the President. Ted was opposed to him; he thought my association with him was bad for the independence of the *Post*. I think Ted and I both had doubts, but I didn't talk to anyone about it; I had left Dr. Sullivan in '36, and this was '43. It's acceptable for a man to marry out of his social world, but not for the woman.
>
> One quality of Ted's absolutely floored me. It may have something to do with his having been a fighter pilot, but he was reckless—absolutely reckless. One evening we were walking down Rector Street, and two drunks were in a fight. As a joke I said, 'You ought to separate them.' My God, he ran over to them and got his face all bloodied up! He was that kind of guy—if two dogs were in a fight, he would be in the middle. When I took him to Alicia's for tennis, he was so competitive he played until his feet bled—just wouldn't give in. Of course, he didn't care about having anything that fitted properly."

What did fit Ted properly was the *Post*, even better than his relationship with Dorothy. Of this she says, "If I had stopped our affair, I couldn't have worked with him—having a dead body around. I needed him as an executive, just as he may have wanted me because of his job."

A *Post* employee senior in both position and years of service who has a vivid recollection of Ted's situation on the paper is Paul Sann, executive editor, now the top man on the news side.

Paul Sann.

The George Backer period he calls "a dilettante operation with editorial meetings, no one in charge and nothing happening—a pure scramble. Our circulation was way down and when Dolly asked the five or six top editors to present memos on what they would do to improve the paper, the best was Ted's. It exhibited a large vision of the *Post*, and if there had been no memo suggesting a viable operation, I think she might have thrown up her hands and gotten rid of it. Ted, who had made it to Shanghai and back without going to alimony jail, was coming back from the grave. It was a shot at the big league; he saw that in her eyes."

Ted remembers the first time he saw Dorothy not as the publisher but as a woman was on Pearl Harbor night; he says her work was professional, and he admired her dedication. The shift from the working relationship to the personal is hard for him to pinpoint, and he sees it as an outgrowth of her being without an escort and confidant—"George was not available, and I was handy."

The *Post* and Ted slowly moved Dorothy away from her close relationship to FDR. She had in any case been increasingly aware of the war's effect on him. In view of this strain added to failing health, his self-control was remarkable. She says:

"This may have been due to has having suffered polio. Although he must have been in real pain often, he never showed it any more than he did anger or depression. But he did take glee in doing things to irritate others who irritated him. It was a way of getting back at them, and this he was very good at.

Because he took an eighteenth-century patriot's view of the American Revolution, he often complained that British Cabinet ministers had a way of putting down their American opposite numbers. He was uncomfortable with Churchill, but Randolph Churchill later told me that his father always deferred to the President and really loved him. The President was provincial compared to the cosmopolitan Churchill and felt terribly inferior in spite of commanding so much more power. Of course, in addition to being intellectually superior, Churchill exhausted him by keeping him up late at night with his verbal pyrotechnics and brandy. Churchill knew more about even Civil War battles than the President and in literature would quote such writers as Swinburne, while the President could think only of Longfellow.

The President kept looking for little ways to put down the British for overemphasizing formality and titles, which he thought were a great joke. This I thought was cheap and childish; we were in a war, and it seemed petty.

Ludicrous as it may seem, he thought he and Stalin spoke the same language. The President thought he was great, was crazy about him. He said that they were brothers in being for the common man and that they spoke the same language. Now it seems idiotic, but probably gave him relief from the feeling of inferiority he had about Churchill. I used to hear endlessly that the two of them would gang up on this ghastly Churchill, who was so superior. It was always Uncle Joe and I this, and Uncle Joe and I that. . . . I never heard the President talk about anyone else that way. It was as if they were two naughty boys ganging up on teacher.

I guess I was sympathetic because of having been petrified of Churchill when I met him at Max's in London; he just sat there grunting and looking me over. He didn't appear exactly charmed, but maybe he was worried about money; he always needed it and borrowed some."

Reflecting on Dorothy's association with FDR, Max Lerner, columnist, teacher and writer with over twenty years of association with Dorothy, says, "Dolly knew Roosevelt intimately. I imagine he saw her for his political self-interest, as well as for his sexual interest. When the two come together, that's wonderful—it's the perfect setup!"

The "perfect setup" for Dorothy by this time meant having to deal with Ted's resistance to the relationship, and she began to realize that Ted was something of a take-over man in addition to being a take-charge one. Although she was resigned to the disintegration of her association with FDR, it worried her that she had never been able to find her position within it.

> "I never felt I belonged; it was rather an *Alice in Wonderland* thing, and I had no sense of identity. I had never felt I belonged in Max Beaverbrook's milieu either, although I liked his intellectual world, but with the President there were all those juvenile anecdotes. I don't think he ever wanted to get deeply involved; that might have meant some emotional scenes. So it was all rather boring, these endless hours with him, and I don't think I understood our relationship. In fact, I don't think I had the slightest idea of what it was all about.
>
> The sun-god quality wasn't working for me all of a sudden; I knew that I should love him or be in love with him, and I wasn't either. By the first I mean a deep, long-lasting relationship and by the second, more of a brief infatuation.
>
> I had known too many of these hunting and fishing types, but I went for the oddballs. I was fond of him and flattered, and it was nice impressing people, I guess, but they enjoyed it more than I did. It was a frustrating relationship, and I felt a failure.
>
> The trouble was that what I really wanted to be with him was an invisible presence, able to observe and record all the things going on around without having to take part in them. I didn't like having things expected of me, being an actor in the play. I wanted to be a member of the audience—an anonymous one—and to observe the production and learn from it, rather than experience it.
>
> At first I was flattered when Ted told me the press thought I was the mistress of the President. I asked what

In the early years as executive at the Post.

evidence they had, and he answered, 'Well, you're always up there with him and in that house with him.' Then he wanted to know if I was going to let this be my record in life—a President's mistress—and I said, 'Of course not; I'm better than that.'

I don't know what the word is for my marrying Ted, but there must be one for a woman who marries a man because he is so good at making arrangements and taking care of things. But I do know, of course; it's dependence. He said he didn't have much except that no one had ever loved me as much as he did; I think he was anxious to hold the publisher. We had been together for two years—working and the other—and he was strong and insistent. There wasn't another man in my life then, so, much against my better judgment and maybe his. . . .

It was the middle of summer, 1943, when we were married; the West Street office would do, I thought. I wore a gray dress and picked Judge Sam Rosenman to do it, God knows why. He was a friend of George's, but only too willing to perform the ceremony, and he made a nice little speech. Some of my girlfriends from the old days came, and so did Sarah-Ann; Adele stayed in Nevada, taking flying lessons, and Morti was in training camp. Sam brought a message from the President—something about he didn't need to wish me luck on my wedding day since I must know how by now.

We were back in the office the next morning, and that night we drove to Lake Placid. Ted put a bottle of whiskey on the bureau—a very unglamorous start for our marriage.

I think I remember the sound of that bottle being put on the bureau, and I think it said I was giving up on something. A lot of my life has been a search for love—to love and to be loved. The men I was in love with were in love with someone else, and the men who were in love with me were a nuisance. My mother used to say when something nice happened to me, 'Dolly, you don't deserve it.' I thought she was probably right. And so I have given that side of me to things—my newspaper, really. I had to; I was too much."

VIII

"I think Ted was hurt more than I was. I never felt bitter or anything like that, and he contributed a great deal to the New York *Post*."

Most newlyweds, even veteran ones, speak of coming home from a honeymoon, not being "back in the office." Dorothy's choice of words neatly defines the essential nature of the Thackrey union—less a relationship than a joint occupation. The home they came back to was Ted's ground-floor apartment at 9 East Tenth Street ("really not bad either, or was it 10 East Ninth Street?")

Ted saw Dorothy as an Upper East Side type and felt that since she had always lived there, it must continue to be her world. She had already been typecast by her new, take-charge spouse, who had found them an East Side penthouse through the *Post* real estate advertising department. Rented in his name, it offered terraces on four sides, giving Ted ample scope for his landscaping bent. "He had good taste," Dorothy says, "and had all kinds of things built at enormous expense. They have long since fallen apart and disappeared—pools, paths and such—but he was very creative."

In addition to room for creative expression, the apartment provided room for Dorothy's children, a French governess, and three Scottish servants. There was ample room for entertaining also, but this was limited almost entirely to *Post* executives. Business entertaining, devoted largely to advertising accounts, was done at the office. Except for Dorothy's children, the paper was the main topic of conversation for the Thackreys; they experienced the cultural life of New York only through the *Post*'s news columns, reviews and advertising. The Thackreys did not need films, plays, operas, ballets, concerts, exhibitions or lectures. They had the *Post*.

Eventually and under pressure Dorothy would make Ted, by then editor, copublisher. In return, she made herself coeditor. The line of distinction between their lives and that of the paper appears so faint there could almost be said to be none.

Had it not been for Ted's Upper East Side fixation, they could almost as well have lived at the *Post*. The view from its duplex apartment was even better than the one uptown, but West Street was short on the ambiance expected by one of Dorothy's background. Former *Post* writer Susan Szekely, now free-lancing as Susan Edmiston, remembers office conditions in terms of plumbing. "I passed the men's room each day coming in. It was foul-smelling, and in the grime on the wall was a legend never wiped off in my five years, 'philthy.' "

Dorothy, when asked about such conditions, is mildly amused. "I've heard about those men's rooms but was never in them. Early in the century newspapermen used to be considered pretty rough types and were low on the social ladder. Although dedicated, they were terribly underpaid and turned to drink, most of them. As strong individualists they thought other things more important than cleanliness."

Such matters were not a problem in the duplex converted to executive offices. She had the dark paneled living room stained honey color and the upholstered furniture covered in a crewel pattern. She had as little time to enjoy the view from the eight tall windows as she did the fireplace.

"I was afraid my office would be ivory tower," she told an interviewer. "And it is ivory tower."

The concept has not influenced Dorothy's thinking or reacting, however. Her manner can be regal, even imperious, yet she is not haughty. Her curiosity, which is all-embracing, has saved her. In reaction to the garden staff at Old Fields, for instance, she took a course in ornamental horticulture and plant propagation ("they gave me an A!"). And in spite of having always had a staff, she has taken courses in cooking. Indeed, she says she did all the cooking at the Red House in Hyde Park before Mrs. Bie.

Ted Thackrey and Dorothy in the Post *offices at West Street, 1945.*

"I would work with *The Joy of Cooking* by my side and Ted saying, 'Why are you so slow?' He'd never known a woman who didn't know how to cook. I can follow directions, but I'm not imaginative, which is why I wished there were books telling one how to cut up an onion and to carve.

Cookbooks assume you know a lot of things about celery, for instance—whether to cut it and how to wash it. I finally learned to cut off the tip and wash the stalk with a little wire brush, and I've watched celery being chopped the way you're supposed to—zip, zip, zip—but I can't do it. And I've tried holding a piece of bread in my mouth when cutting up an onion, too.

Before we had Mrs. Bie, Ted would invite people working on the place and tell me to fix lunch for twelve. I would say, 'Fine,' then painfully try to make something or other. He could do everything; he told me he and his brothers had been brought up in poor circumstances in one of those two Kansas Cities—the wrong one, he said—

and they didn't have a flush toilet. His father had died long since, and his mother, whom I never met, was a hardworking woman who ran a boardinghouse.

Ted was a big project man, always building or repairing something on the place. I had suggested he paint some unfinished furniture one day because I thought he wanted to. He did start to in the garage but became infuriated with me; apparently he hated doing it. Such things didn't make for gracious country living exactly, nor did the rationing due to the war. We did know a big, fat man who was involved with the black market, I think, but our life was quiet. Sarah-Ann and the other children would appear occasionally, and Ted had a friend who lived in Rye—a very nice man with a little black mustache—and we would see Elliott Roosevelt and his then wife, Faye Emerson, sometimes. Not much social life, was it?

Town or country, we had lunch and dinner together alone mostly and Ted would read to me—I asked for the *Spectator* papers and Dr. Holmes. I liked it because I had my needlepoint, but I didn't always listen carefully. He taught me how to play chess, which I was bad at and found required a great deal of concentration. It wasn't relaxing, but Ted was patient with me, and I think he understood me better than I understood myself. He didn't want to make too large a change in my life, which he thought provincial, and felt I'd better live as I always had.

He was very kind at first and tried to help people. I was so neurotic I'd given up trying to drive, and once coming to New York, he made me drive the car; I didn't want to, but he forced me. When we got into city traffic, he made me go on, saying, 'You can do it.' I drove down Riverside Drive somehow, terrified, but I never did it again. Of course, he was fearless, but it was dangerous.

Ted knocked himself out trying to get Sarah-Ann's love; he knew she was very important to me. He would always have something in his pocket for her, a little present, and she would have to guess which pocket it was in. And he could be thoughtful, such as giving me flowers, not that I knew how he paid for them. As for Sarah-Ann's love, he didn't succeed."

Ted "respected and admired" Dorothy's brother, John, but John, who understood her marriage to George Backer well enough—"a good talker and writer with great charm"—was baffled by Ted. "I don't know why the hell she married him," John says. "I guess he appealed to her as part of the paper."

Ted seems to have made little impression on Dorothy's son, Morti Hall, and a not very favorable one on their Hyde Park neighbor. The Thackreys saw little of the President; his wedding message to Dorothy via Judge Rosenman was hardly a blessing, and Ted's reaction to FDR's desire to have her working with farm women didn't help either. "What do you want to worry about little pigs for?" he asked. "You have a newspaper."

Dorothy says that Ted, who tended to be jealous, feared FDR's political influence over the *Post*. As for the sun-god himself, however unlikely it may seem, Franklin Delano Roosevelt, President of the most powerful nation in the world and on its way to victory, may have been hurt by the marriage of this "willful woman," though Dorothy says one "couldn't hurt Franklin Roosevelt." When an invitation to a Saturday luncheon arrived from the White House in the fall of 1943, several months after the wedding, in a telegram signed by Eleanor, Dorothy accepted not to the White House but to Mrs. Roosevelt's cottage. Eleanor had told Dorothy earlier that she planned to be in Hyde Park that weekend. Dorothy says that the invitation was unusual for her in that it was extended on behalf of both the Roosevelts and came from Mrs. Roosevelt instead of the President. Dorothy wrote a memo about it, one of her first.

> Early that Saturday morning I received a phone call at the Red House from Hacky, the chief White House operator, saying that Grace Tully, the President's secretary, wanted to speak to me. Hacky and I, being old friends, chatted for a bit while waiting, then she said, "Grace will speak to you now." I waited more than a minute in silence—no Grace. Hacky came on again, sounding embarrassed, and said Grace had been called away, but she knew the call was to find out if we were coming to lunch. When I told her I already had accepted, she said hurriedly, "Oh, I see. *She* must have received it, but the telegram came from Grace." I was amused, because I now knew the telegram had actually come from the President rather than Mrs.

Roosevelt, and that something was up. He never would have is-
sued the invitation for purely social reasons.

Ted and I arrived fifteen minutes late, having walked and not
knowing the shortcut through the woods, and found the guests
assembled behind Mrs. Roosevelt's cottage. The President was
seated at a card table between his sister-in-law, Mrs. "Rosie"
Roosevelt, and Princess Juliana of the Netherlands. At an adjoining table were seated her two older daughters with their
governess, and a little distance away was her eight-month-old
baby daughter, playing in her pen. Other people present sat on
logs or on the ground. Among them were Mrs. Roosevelt, of
course, her secretary, Malvina Thompson, Grace Tully, Mrs.
FDR, Jr., and a friend of hers, whose name I did not get, Marion Dickerman and Nancy Cook and a Poughkeepsie businessman with his son, a marine just out of the hospital, who
had some grievance which Mrs. Roosevelt was trying to
straighten out.

I went right up to the President to say how do you do. I
thought his greeting was most impersonal, on the cold side, because at previous meeting he always kissed me and was most
warm. We retired, after having been introduced to the princess,
to the log where the others were eating, and as usual, Mrs. Roosevelt served and stirred, the food consisting of delicious fish
chowder in large paper cardboard containers, hot dogs, very
bad spaghetti, tomato and lettuce salad, coffee, apple pie,
cheese and fruit.

After lunch the children made popcorn which even the baby
ate. I remarked to the princess that her baby was the best-
behaved little boy that I had ever seen, playing quietly for two
hours in his pen without crying. She said quite coldly, "She is
a girl, not a boy." I remembered all the excitement when the
child was born in Canada and the desire of the crown prince
and princess to have an heir and thought I had certainly put my
foot in it. The princess looks like a nice, shabby housewife, no
makeup, straggly blond hair devoid of a permanent wave,
while the children's governess looks like a princess.

Mrs. Roosevelt told us in great detail of her trip through the
Pacific, all of the while seated on the ground; fortunately the
day was warm and fine. The previous Sunday we met her on a
walk and were persuaded to sit in the middle of a cornfield
with an icy wind blowing while she told us of her trip. All of a
sudden she said, "I know the President wants to talk with you,
so come on over and sit with him." She led us to him, and he

told us that when he had his first meeting with Queen Wilhelmina, he had been scared to death. However, he found that "the old lady was most genial and easy to talk to. I don't know why I call her an 'old lady'; she's only one year older than I am." He said that it was later reported to him that she had been equally scared to meet the President of the United States, and I remarked that people were always scared of each other unnecessarily; labor was scared of employers and employers of labor.

The queen told him that in Holland it was possible to borrow for a long term at a very low rate of interest, and he proudly said that it was his bill at Albany, when he was a state senator, that reduced interest rates in New York State. He then repeated a story about Lindbergh's father, who was at one time a Congressman, pointing out that it shed some light on the Lone Eagle's character. Because one phrase in his own bill had been amended, Lindbergh, Senior, had refused to vote for the entire bill. I said, "You mean he wouldn't take half a loaf?" The President laughed and changed the subject.

Then he told us of a luncheon with Adolph Ochs, the publisher of the New York *Times*, in which he said, "Your editorials are a luxury, aren't they, and don't accomplish much." Ochs said it was worth it to him because he loved them, even though only 8 percent of the readers look at them. The President has often told me this story; I think he likes to kid himself that editorials aren't important and don't influence anybody. I said, "This minority of readers consists of leaders in many fields—teachers, ministers, heads of unions—and they spread editorial ideas through their groups." The President smiled and again changed the subject.

We discussed Captain Patterson and the *Daily News*. He said that Lord Beaverbrook, the last time he was in this country, after seeing Patterson, had returned to the President and, describing Patterson, knocked on his forehead with his finger. The President added that Patterson had been that way since he had joined the Church, which amused us. A few days previously the President had stated that the battle for Rome was a crusade to free the Pope.

His next remark may have been directed at the *Post*, which had accused the government of miserable handling of the news. He said he was having an awful time with Churchill; he was constantly violating their agreement on not giving out news personally. He said, "When I talk with him, I speak to

him about it but never put anything in writing." Then with obvious satisfaction he told us that he was the only person who
dared to kid Churchill and in the middle of a long speech
would interrupt him, saying, "Well, so what, Winston?"

Then he said, very casually, as though he thought it a matter
of minor importance, "I would like to see—what's his
name—a—Sam—on your paper." "Oh, you mean Sam Grafton." "Yes, tell him to come and see me." (Sam, our editorial
writer, has been seeing Willkie and is quite enthusiastic about
him.) I said, "Well, Mr. President, Sam has tried to see you for
quite a while but has been unable to make an appointment."
"Why, that's ridiculous; just tell him to call Steve Early and
stay after a press conference." Two days later, in a telephone
conversation with Trude Pratt, she told me that the President
told her twice that same weekend that he was very serious
about wanting to see Sam, and she had the feeling that this was
supposed to be relayed to me.

Dorothy, in recalling that she was with FDR for the election
returns in 1936 and 1940 at the big house in Hyde Park, sees his
first term as the most effective, the second and third and fourth
increasingly less. His mother's death in September, 1941, had so
severe an impact, Sam Rosenman told her, the President "went
into a complete collapse and couldn't do anything for days."
Dorothy adds that in the third and fourth terms "he was having
trouble with Stalin but didn't find out that maybe he'd been had
at Yalta."

The next and last time she saw him was at a big house dinner
on Labor Day weekend, 1944. She says that he looked bad, was
eating only soft cereal, his speech dragged, and his coordination
had slowed. He explained the baby food was due to tooth trouble, but she wondered if he'd had a stroke. In his last campaign
it was explained that his slurred speech was due to warming up
with whiskey after driving in an open car in the rain. The condition was serious enough for him to go to Bernie Baruch's plantation, Hobcaw, in South Carolina, for recuperation. FDR didn't
really like his host, Dorothy explains, as both he and Eleanor
thought Baruch too conservative, but he was a source of campaign funding.

For all the distance from her Hyde Park neighbor, Dorothy
was still interested enough to want to go to San Francisco for

FDR's formal opening of the UN in early 1945. However, word came from the White House that her attendance would be difficult to arrange. It didn't occur to her to go on her own or as a member of the press, and the reason, she realizes, was that it had been her need of FDR and his welcoming kiss on her cheek which had made it possible for her to make her own travel arrangements on other occasions.

The news of his death in April that year reached Dorothy from a surprising source, considering she is a newspaper publisher. Sarah-Ann, then eleven, had been in bed with a temperature and on Dorothy's return from the office, called out, "Mother, the President is dead."

Dorothy says she couldn't believe it.

> "I called the office to ask why I hadn't been told and they said, as they always do, 'We thought you knew.' Everyone was in a state of shock, and I was stunned, but the show had to go on.
>
> I wrote the lead paragraphs for the editorial in the office, and Ted had it framed; he must have liked it. I was surprised and pleased as I'd rather have my work liked than me. And Ted, after all, was a professional. He and I went to the funeral, where there was an awful lot of standing around. I really had no emotional reaction; the President had been sick and wasn't having any fun.
>
> As a man, I wouldn't know how to judge him. As a President, he was always *the* President in a way that neither Jack Kennedy nor the others were. He just *was* the President."

Late in 1944, Dorothy, an RH negative blood type, developed symptoms of miscarriage in the third month. "The obstetrician I had with Sarah-Ann had disappeared," she recalls, "and this one said of the symptoms, 'Well, you don't want to have this child anyway, so why worry about it?' I remember being shocked, then wondering if I did want it. It ended with my being rushed to the hospital in the middle of the night."

It doesn't seem likely that a successful pregnancy would have done much to change the nature of the Thackrey marriage, for the *Post* was so much the basis of their relationship there was room for little else in their lives. While Dorothy didn't have to

FDR's interment at Hyde Park. The Thackreys can just be seen, to the right beyond the flowers and in front of the cadets from West Point.

marry Ted to use him as the *Post*'s savior, the fact that she did gave him an authority and reassurance which made the restructuring of the paper easier. Dorothy and Ted together as copublisher and coeditor provided a good balance of money and expertise, which, in combination with commitment, was unbeatble.

"I didn't have that much faith in myself to really think I could pull it out. I stayed with the paper because I couldn't face going back to the nothing I had before—copying verses from Shakespeare and stuff at the New

York Society Library after the children had gone to school and committee work which was really fund raising. It all seemed just marking time.

Operating a newspaper is like running a small dictatorship. I have tremendous admiration for the boys and girls who do the reporting. They have physical courage, in which I am lacking, and a total disregard for personal safety.

I'm fortunate in having average tastes—neither highbrow nor lowbrow—and although I'm interested in serious reading, I love gossip, scandal and human interest."

In an effort to increase circulation, the *Post* bought the Bronx *Home News* in 1946 at a cost of $1,950,000. Its circulation, which Dorothy hadn't realized was so conservative, was then 114,000 readers. Ted thought it a good buy.

"Dorothy bought the idea without great resistance," Ted says, "but by this time it was not a question of throwing good money after bad, the losses had been so reduced. My thesis was that despite our progress, it would take five or six years of reduced losses to get our advertising rates up to the point of real profitability, whereas with this investment—about the same amount—we could wipe out our deficit.

"As to my being responsible for saving the *Post*, I wouldn't want to denigrate the contribution made by the staff, from the city room right through the organization. Practically nobody was brought in from the outside; we stayed away from so-called experts. At this point no one was advising Dorothy, and I don't want to seem in any way to minimize her courage and contribution. In that early period it was not difficult to work with her, possibly because she still did not feel quite strong and experienced enough, and we had no confrontations. Occasionally, we had differences of opinion as to the best way of arriving at desired ends.

"As each experiment worked, losses were reduced, and we were brought nearer the goal of having a self-sustaining thing. There was a period, in trying to find out how to make the thing work, in which Dorothy thought she either ought to sell out to Marshall Field or buy his *PM*, and I advised against taking it strongly, as it was a duplication of circulation.

"I had no resentment of Dorothy, as a woman, being the boss, and I think I studiously attempted to block out later any evidence in myself of hostility. In the end—I trust this doesn't sound patronizing in any way—my impression of her was as the product of a very unhappy and uncertain childhood, the epitome of what you might call the poor little rich girl."

The Thackreys needed to make the *Post* a success for the sake of their marriage. Ted's first revolutionary change was the tabloid format; then he went ahead with the three-year plan he had designed. Ted found Dorothy "very cooperative and with the open eagerness of somebody who wants to find out about a subject on which she is not well informed."

With her concurrence, he added numerous features. Soon there were forty columnists (most left-wing), a syndication service, a foreign bureau and a Paris edition in competition with the Paris *Herald* ("It didn't survive," Dorothy says). There were some major changes in executive personnel too, but there were no wholesale personnel changes; with the Newspaper Guild contract there couldn't be.

Paul Sann, now the executive editor, who has been with the *Post* since the thirties, was one of those advanced from within. He went along with many of the early changes brought about by Ted, whom he speaks of as "lifted out of exile and taken upstairs to the top job." Paul was a believer in the format and the Saturday magazine, but he can't forgive those forty columns, which displaced the news and even began on page one. He has a very vivid recollection of Dorothy at the office.

"She came on with an abundance of the necessary humility and respect, as if she were dropping in on a brain surgeon at work. We could see that she was totally inexperienced, except for ownership; she was just uptown somewhere and knew nothing about newspapers. She was in awe of the talents of some of us who had dirty fingernails and had been up and down in the sewers. She'd say, 'Oh, is that how it's done? I thought you'd have to. . . .' She conceded to you in everything you knew she didn't know and with her impeccable manners, she was a kind of acolyte—only, it didn't last. She wasn't as good-looking as she is now, not that she's changed much—maybe a little fuller in the face, and brunette instead of gray-haired."

After the Bronx *Home News* acquisition, Ted began thinking of further expansion but not in those areas where Dorothy saw a future.

The Thackreys admire the first tabloid edition of the Post.

"Ted was terribly anti-radio and -television, as were many old-time newspapermen. Although TV was by then in existence, we never looked at it and seldom used the radio either. I knew they were the future, but he wanted to buy more papers—in places like Binghamton, New York, Chicago and San Francisco. We had a terrific set-to, and finally he said, 'Okay, so you want a radio station.' Then he went haywire; we had one, two, three stations and two television stations. He got stuck with WLIB in New York—it began losing money terrifically—so I took it over and got it breaking even.

Then he decided it needed night broadcasting hours— it was a daytime station—but we couldn't have that because a Westinghouse station in Fort Wayne, Indiana, was on the same wavelength. That company's head was subpoenaed at Ted's insistence to testify before the FCC in Washington. My brother, John, as a Kuhn, Loeb partner, Westinghouse's bankers, called me to see if it really was necessary. John was upset. During the case, which incidentally we lost, I learned that our little station's overhead was as much as a major station's, and I said to

Ted, 'This is ridiculous, the way it's being run.' He blew his top at me, so I managed it myself until the losses were cut and I could unload it.

Television was just being born, and he rushed me out to California, where there were five channels available, to testify at a hearing. The networks had three of them, but the other two were to be given to local people. To everyone's surprise, I was allotted a wavelength; the FCC lawyers were liberals and loved what I stood for. It had to be built from scratch and never had a chance, as it was an independent competing against the networks. A lot of money went down the drain, which was supplied by a radio station we had in Hollywood, KLAC, substantially in the black, and to which I sent Morti. He advised selling the TV station, which I did, and eventually got rid of a San Francisco radio station, KYA, as well. These things meant quite a lot of fights with Ted about money.

Papers for sale kept coming up, such as the San Francisco *Chronicle,* which actually never was sold. I first met Adlai Stevenson through negotiations for the Chicago *Daily News,* which the widow of a Republican Secretary of the Army, Frank Knox, wanted to sell. Adlai, who wasn't governor yet, came to see me and said that it was ridiculous for us to be competing for the *News*; he represented a liberal local group, and we shouldn't be bidding against each other. I told him I hadn't known that and, of course, we would pull out. When I told Ted, he was furious, asking why we should bow to them. Neither of us got it; it was sold to a Republican.

The Binghamton paper was another we looked at. The *Daily News* founder, Captain Joseph Patterson, told me acquisitions were distracting, and J. David Stern asked me why on earth I wanted a paper that had no influence and was in a place like Binghamton. When I asked Ted that, again he was furious, but this time I didn't go ahead. I didn't pursue the project. There were a couple of projects I got us into which lost money—a liberal magazine and a book through Marion Dickerman that was going to be a best-seller but wasn't.

The Bronx *Home News* had also meant a fight; Newhouse was competing for it. After the *Post* bought it, he told me we kept bidding much more than we needed to and had paid too much. This I told Ted, and he was not pleased."

Ted and Dorothy also disagreed about Ted's political line in the paper. Dorothy was not a Zionist but was in favor of the partition of Palestine. It seemed then the only answer for most refugees from the Nazis, and she couldn't imagine a better way to provide it than by Israel, since a majority seemed to want to go there and could not enter Western nations. Wistfully, she adds that if only they could have come to New York, it would certainly have made for more *Post* readers. Her belief in the justice of Israel as a solution didn't extend to Ted's involvement with the Irgunists, however.

"I don't think Dolly was nearly as aware as I was of the political direction of the paper," Paul says. "Thackrey was very close to the Irgunists and Menachem Begin. They were a must—conferences, interviews—but we were pushing their cause instead of covering it. I was against those bastards—I don't knock them now they got a stake—but they were very, very suspect to me. I knew some of them; they were creepy. They had an inordinate access to our columns."

Dorothy, it is clear, was not wholly unaware of the way her paper's columns were being used.

"These terrorists and other pressure groups would come to Ted in the office. I think it was a psychological thing; he was jealous, wanted his own thing, and walked right into their hands. I didn't know they were terrorists until I found out from one of our reporters, Fern Eckman, but of course the Haganah were more moderate. Ted was apolitical originally, and in becoming far left, he may not have understood he was in the hands of fellow travelers.

The Palestinian leaders I knew were of a different order, such as Weizmann. George fell madly for him, and while I knew him fairly well, he didn't affect me as he did most women; they were crazy about him. He had a wonderful, very sophisticated wife who didn't speak Hebrew, which made a problem with Ben-Gurion. I knew him pretty well, too; he was more of a David Dubinsky type—very bright and affectionate. Once when he was here raising funds for Israel, he said, 'I would rather kiss you than ask you for money.'

When I knew Golda Meir her name was Goldie Myerson. I liked her but never thought she liked me much;

Lillian Wald didn't either. They thought I was a rich kid and not serious. Henrietta Szold, who was of German Jewish descent and started Hadassah, was the first of the early Zionist leaders I met. I was in my teens and told her that I wanted to dedicate myself to Palestine. She asked me what I could do and I said I could sew. She didn't seem to think that would be useful."

In speaking of his conviction that there had to be a homeland for the Jews, Ted becomes almost wrathful and gives something of the feeling of an Old Testament prophet. He says that although he had reached the point of believing that the world needed fewer languages and fewer distinctions based on religion or race, he was staggered by the tragedy of a homeless people being "unable to find any place even to exist. They were identified as something nobody could quite define; what is a Jew?

"We as the United States of America were not willing to throw open immigration and other barriers and say for God's sake come home. No other places were willing to, yet these people had to have some identifiable place as a home. It became an absolute imperative to beat the drums, not against hostile opposition but against uneasiness. Yet there was a fear that Dorothy and the newspaper would be identified as Jew-oriented—absolute anathema!"

This is not a fear that Dorothy acknowledges, but there was one view of Ted's then that Dorothy agreed with strongly—his opinion of President Truman. While they had been impressed with his managing to break out of the Kansas City Pendergast group and by his fight against the Ku Klux Klan, his attitude during a visit Ted paid him at the White House stunned them. Ted explains: "Almost immediately in the conversation he said, 'Now, Thackrey, if only the goddamn New York Jews would just shut their goddamn mouths and quit hollering.'" Dorothy remembers Ted told her Truman also included the New York Irish in his condemnation. "'They're screwing up the situation, and I could get along with them, if they would just get together and decide what the hell they want. They're all over the lot, the goddamn Jews, and here you are, not even a Jew, representing the spearhead that's causing all kinds of hell.'

"I had to say, 'Well, Mr. President, you make it impossible for

Harry S. Truman, Dorothy Schiff and James Farley.

me to continue this conversation. I've got to assume by "goddamn New York Jews" you must mean my wife, who is a Jew. I know you better than to believe that you are consciously anti-Semitic, but I consider it absolutely outrageous.' Immediately, I went to his press secretary and the chairman of the Democratic National Committee. I told them I'd had this absolutely terrible conversation with the President and suggested he be advised more clearly on such matters."

Paul Sann was disturbed by the *Post*'s increasingly leftist views. He says, "When Thackrey embraced Henry Wallace, around 1948, he lost a hell of a lot of us in the city room. We were violently anti-Stalinist, anti-American Labor Party, which was a captive, and even more violently anti-Wallace. Some of us drew up a petition demanding that our disassociation from what the paper was saying be published."

So, to the tensions in the marriage which first had expression in the abrasive imbalance of money, basic matters of political philosophy were now added. Those affected the Thackreys' future as much as the future of the paper, and in 1948 they had public expression in a series of columns, entitled "Appeal to Reason." A parenthetical note in the paper explained that they were "A series of exchanges between the Co-Publishers and Co-Editors of the New York Post Home News [as it was known briefly] arising from a difference of opinion on the candidacy of Henry Wallace for President."

Ted wrote: "I say a vote for Mr. Wallace is the ONLY way to let the major candidates know that there IS a progressive force alive in this country that must be reckoned with—and that we are sick of being told that democracy can live only by becoming more totalitarian!"

In response, Dorothy S. Thackrey wrote:

> I have great sympathy with the many fine people, new voters, members of minority groups, or old stock Americans, includ-ing Mr. Wallace, who have become more and more horrified with the turn world events have taken. . . . I implore them in spite of all this not to lose faith in democracy. . . . I implore them to stop flirting with Communist totalitarianism. . . . I implore them to throw every ounce of their strength . . . into building democracy at home and abroad, because more and more democracy is the only effective way of defeating reaction, no matter what its form.

The "Appeal to Reason" columns excited considerable won-derment and comment, even to a piece in *Editor & Publisher* which underlined their "take-your-choice editorials" and noted: "At the office the couple have divided their duties. She devotes almost full time to her radio interests. . . . He runs the Post Home News. Whenever she has suggestions for the paper, she funnels them to him via memos. Many a day passes without either Thackrey entering the next office. . . ."

Though areas of general disagreement seemed to multiply al-most on their own, the Thackreys reached one decision harmoni-ously—selling the Red House at Hyde Park. Dorothy gave vari-ous reasons for the disposition in a letter to Eleanor Roosevelt, but she now offers a simpler and more accurate one. Just as she once explained her remaining with FDR because she had nothing else going, she says as casually of leaving Hyde Park, "After all, the President wasn't around anymore."

Another reason, of course, was the Thackreys' social isolation there. The Condé Nast house Dorothy bought at Sands Point offered for a neighbor her old friend Alicia Patterson, and life

VAL-KILL COTTAGE
HYDE PARK, DUTCHESS CO.
NEW YORK

July 9, 1947

Dear Dorothy:

The rumors that always fly around have
it that you want to sell your land. I
feel very badly about it because I had
hoped that as time went on, we would have
more opportunity to see each other.

However, if you are going to sell your
property, I shall appreciate your
letting me know as Elliott has some
friends who might consider taking a
part of the land if the price is not
too high.

If you come up here, do please let me
know. We will all be away from July
15th, for about a month.

Affectionately,

Eleanor Roosevelt

July 15, 1947.

Mrs. Eleanor Roosevelt
Val-Kill Cottage
Hyde Park, Dutchess County
New York

Dear Mrs. Roosevelt:

This time the rumors are correct. We are heartbroken that we have
had to put our place on the market due to the fact that it is not
within commuting distance of New York and both Ted and our son-in-
law must be in town this summer.

Our daughter Adele now has two babies, so we have bought a place
in Sands Point. We really wanted to rent, but were unable to do
so and were forced to buy a house on the Sound. It was a real
wrench to leave our darling house in Hyde Park, as you will
realise.

Mr. Hatfield in Poughkeepsie is the agent handling the property.
He believes that we should try to sell the place as a whole rather
than piecemeal. However, if Elliott wants details, I am certain
that Mr. Hatfield will tell him about it.

I do hope that when you are on Long Island for sessions of the
United Nations we can lure you to our house for a meal, at least.
We shall get in touch with you when you return in August.

Affectionately,

DST:mi

there involved Ted in a different part of Dorothy's past, to the point that he invited Dick Hall for dinner.

"I guess Ted was trying to help him. Anyway, Dick, who came with a wife, seemed to be getting old, but that didn't prevent his playing footsie with me under the table. I don't think Ted felt so sorry for him after that evening.

Being so different in background, Ted and I had no friends in common. He was shrewd about my continuing to see my kind of people, though.

Although Ted spent money lavishly, it was not on himself—he never had a suit that cost more than thirty dollars—and it must have been embarrassing for him to come to me every month for money to keep the *Post* going. It was still in the red, but nothing like what it was in George's time.

Maybe I was underpaying Ted, but the thirty-five thousand dollars he set for himself was a lot in those days. Out of it he took care of the apartment rent of five hundred dollars a month and, I suppose, his income tax. I paid for the servants, food and stuff, and when it became obvious he was hard up, I was worried.

The whole thing must have been making Ted very nervous. At first he was nice to people, and he was fond of me—later, less so."

Ted speaks with regret of the growing disintegration of the relationship and with a sense of puzzlement, too. He has a warm smile for Dorothy's children, saying, "I felt very close to Morti and Adele. He was growing up with the same difficulties that Dorothy herself had experienced—not conscious of being loved by a mother, as an orphan and encumbrance. Adele was less so, being determined to take what friendship she could find and to make sure that her children didn't suffer this kind of disaffection. With Sarah-Ann, being much younger, there was a different relationship; she had more access to her father."

At one point in their efforts to get the *Post* in the black, Dorothy looked at the competition with an eye to merger. A liberal afternoon daily, *PM*, seemed a likely possibility. It had been founded in 1940 by millionaire liberals, including Jock Whitney and Marshall Field, and so pure was their dedication to the cause, *PM* at first took no advertising. It was a decision of which Dorothy would never be guilty.

"When Marshall Field took it over from the others, Ralph Ingersoll was the editor. Ted fought the merger idea as hard as he could; he was afraid we would be taken over, I guess. Marshall and I tried to get together several times—he and I could have gotten on beautifully—but he was dominated by others, among whom was Dr. Zilboorg, the noted analyst. Marshall had problems but was immensely rich. *PM* never had as much circulation as we did; they were more left-wing and were always being smeared, which took the heat off us. They had a lot of Communists on their staff and we had some, too, all protected on the Guild contract. They didn't realize until near the end when they took advertising what a big reader feature it is, no matter how idealistic you are.

Finally, Marshall came to me and would have given it to us just not to fold it, but Ted said, 'Why get mixed up with them?' It shows that Marshall and I were rather weak—we weren't sure enough of our abilities—and we let ourselves be dominated by people who had a lot to lose. Ted was certain that they wouldn't survive, and he was right."

The 1948 Democratic National Convention in Philadelphia exacerbated the Thackreys' tensions. According to Dorothy, a lot of people dropped in at their hotel suite the first evening, among them Alicia Patterson, Chester Bowles and Randolph Churchill. She thought Ted was behaving strangely, and he complained that she knew everyone there and he didn't know anyone.

"He got sore," Dorothy remembers, "and said, 'I'm getting out of here.' He later joined the Wallace drive, which everyone knew was Communist-controlled, where he was made much of and felt happy."

Wholly opposed to the regular Democratic candidate, Harry Truman, Dorothy finally came out for the Republican, Thomas Dewey, a difficult endorsement for a liberal, even though he was a liberal Republican and carried New York state, although Truman won the election. As if to emphasize the distance between her and Ted made obvious by the convention, Dorothy joined Alicia Patterson on a trip to Paris for a UN session after the elec-

On board ship en route to Paris, a cigarette holder characteristically clenched in her teeth in a fashion reminiscent of FDR.

tion. The voyage gave her ample time to sort out her thoughts on the marriage, and Alicia was available as a consultant. She lost no time in telling Dorothy that "no one had given a member of the working press as great a break as I had given Ted and that he was treating me like a dog; that it was absolutely terrible and I shouldn't put up with it. She was very strong and it began to worry me. I thought, 'Gee, maybe she's right.'"

At the end of the UN meeting, Alicia flew home, but Dorothy, ever leery of flying, went to London to await her sailing. A mining engineer, whom she had known since she was eighteen but who was really more a friend of Alicia's and had crossed with them, called her at Claridge's. It was not a huge surprise.

"He had an unbelievable Welsh name and was married to a rather well-known artist. They lived pretty separate lives, though they shared an apartment and belonged to the Algonquin group—very convenient. He and some others, like Willia Rhinelander Stewart, had a lot of fun. A womanizer, he was amusing and gay, but sixty to my forty-five. I remember being shocked when he confided to me that he was pretty upset, just having had that birthday. I thought it was pretty old, too.

Since he was going back on the *Queen Mary,* too, he suggested we share a table. When I got to the dock, there was this attractive guy on deck with a slouch hat over one eye, drunk like everybody else and terribly glad to see me. It was a very gay crossing—fun and drinks—and although we never dreamed we'd be involved with each other, that's the way it started."

Dorothy arrived home in a snowstorm just before Christmas, and Ted had a surprise for her which was no Yuletide present and created its own storm. It was a leftist attack on conservative policy around the world which Dorothy found so bitter she couldn't finish reading it; Ted had to read it to her. She says it was in such bad taste for the season she insisted it was unprintable, and it never ran. "He was unhappy and miserable, and so was I," she says. "He went downstairs, terribly angry, and I followed to say, 'Ted, I'll give you the paper; just get out of here.' He said, 'That's very generous of you. Thank you.' Then he packed a bag and left."

An agreement was worked out through lawyers, Dorothy says, under which Ted was given "control and management" of the *Post,* only limiting his authority to incur liabilities or debts, to pledge or dispose of assets, or to increase salaries or grant other compensation. In addition, it was agreed that "there will be no material change in the liberal policies of the newspaper or the practices relative to its operations."

Dorothy put further distance between herself and Ted by going to California, but it wasn't so simple to put the paper behind her; bleak reports of its financial problems pursued her. And although Ted continued to function at the paper that January, 1949, it was "obviously under increasingly difficult circumstances." He adds: "The situation between us was never really quite the same from that point on. As to any offer to turn the *Post* over to me altogether as a gift, that's not so."

Dorothy returned from California in March to discover the bleak reports had become, in effect, dire predictions. She now saw that transference of control does not mean release from responsibility; only disposition of ownership accomplishes that.

Still, coming up were some bright moments with her Welsh "fun man."

"He and his wife had a civilized arrangement; if he had affairs, which he was rumored to be having all the time, it would not be with anyone in their set. She wanted to do my portrait, so I went to her studio with the dress she told me to bring. She looked at me, then couldn't paint me and I knew why—she knew. She was upset, I guess. . . . Anyway, to my horror, a few weeks later she died.

My 'fun man' was the son of an upstate minister, and we used to spend weekends in Manhasset—New Year's Eve and stuff—and it was fun. We went out west together, too. A lot of things were happening that winter; Randolph Churchill, who had given a cocktail party for me in London, stayed in the apartment. Fortunately, he was on the wagon.

I got fed up with my 'fun man' eventually; there was nothing but talk, talk and jokes about sex. He liked to write alternate limerick lines, but the level was too low. I thought really, I can't go on with it. I had been reading Plato and one afternoon came to a passage advising that one should dispose of companions who pulled one down. I went over to his house that night for dinner, told him I didn't think it should go on, and gave him back his dead wife's big gold cigarette case.

When I came home, I read more Plato; he went on to say to consider carefully before acting. A few weeks later my 'fun man' married—this always happens. She had been a great friend of his wife's and had an English title, but it didn't last long. Quite a few years later he was in the hospital with a stroke or something, and Babe Paley said I should go see him. By then, though, other things were happening, and I never did. He was bright and wrote a couple of quite good books about mining in Cuba and Latin America—a typical minister's son. Come to think of it—Max was a minister's son, too."

Randolph Churchill, a man of varied talents, more than paid his way as Dorothy's guest that winter. Not only did he persuade her that the living-room lamps could be controlled by a single switch at little cost, disputing the experts' opinion that it was a major undertaking, but he also told her that if he were running a

Randolph Churchill.

liberal paper—"God forbid!"—he would bring in James A. Wechsler, then a Washington correspondent for the *Post*, as editor. Dorothy is always attentive to advice when offered by men of conviction. Jimmy, who had been a leader of the anti-Communists of the Newspaper Guild unit at *PM*, is now the *Post*'s editorial page editor and also writes a daily column.

Increasingly, it was pointed out to Dorothy that as the *Post*'s sole owner she was ultimately responsible and that destructive forces were threatening its future.

"The paper was very close to dying," Paul Sann says. "The accounts receivable had been factored, about one step ahead of the sheriff, and there was legitimate distress over the payroll, week to week.

"Dolly had to make a decision whether to get this guy the hell out and then do you fold it or take one more shot with another editor or set of editors and see if we could keep it going. She invited me to write a memo, which was history repeating itself, and I argued very strenuously that this paper had every goddamn right to stay in the field and could do pretty well. I had

been hampered as city editor about how you cover news—play
it, makeup and so forth. And how you don't use all the space for
the causes."

Fears over the paper's increasingly leftist policies were expressed, and in addition, Dorothy was advised that a half million dollars' worth of working capital was required. She did not
feel she should put up such a sum; she had been meeting the
deficits and need for capital financing for ten years, and that
seemed enough. In casting about for someone to come to the rescue, she turned to Averell Harriman. He heard her out politely,
including her offer of subordinating her investment to his if he
joined in the venture, and declined the opportunity. He then
offered to explain to her how she could borrow against her trust.

"I thanked him for the offer, and I, too, declined. Even
as I did so, I realized what had happened; I wasn't rich
compared to him, but in trying to sell him, I had sold myself. I could see I was going to put up the money, and I
knew, too, that I wasn't about to borrow against trust
funds to do it.

As to Ted, I didn't know what to do. He had departed
from liberal positions. He was opposed to the Marshall
Plan and the Atlantic Pact. There were problems with the
Guild, too, and finally there was nothing for it but a meeting with our lawyers. There was a legal settlement of everything in April, 1949, and Ted left the *Post*.

When Ted started a morning tabloid, the *Compass,* I
took back my maiden name—so as to avoid confusion. I
called my brother, John, first for permission; I was nameless. John was nice about it.

I think Ted was hurt more than I was. I never felt bitter
or anything like that, and he contributed a great deal to
the New York *Post.*"

The qualities with which Dorothy credits Ted as a newspaper
executive weren't enough to keep the *Compass* going. The attempt is a good example of that courage of Ted's which Dorothy
says she admired. "Ted always had answers," she goes on, "always knowing what to do, and I relied on it. He was very quick,
and while he might be critical of his staff within the organization, on the outside he always defended them."

Ted, in taking a long view of Dorothy, goes back to her childhood, saying, "I suspect if Dorothy had been a child of moderately successful parents, she could have developed into a fairly competent, interested, modern-day housewife concerned primarily with her children and their education. My prognosis for her having a happy life is not very good. I see her as a woman who is consciously trying, often successfully, to be a useful contributing member of society. She has my compassion, if that doesn't sound patronizing, and God knows I wish her well."

IX

_____

"It's hard to run the paper without making enemies."

Having served her time, Dorothy was as ready for executive responsibility as she would ever be. It was 1950, the _Post_ was all hers, and from now on it would be her primary commitment. This dedication, plus the fact she was accountable only to herself, gave her an edge over other publishers. And she would need it.

She continued the innovations which had proved themselves, while cutting costs and changing editorial emphasis. News columns were confined to news, editorializing was confined to the page meant for it, and columnists were changed to gain a wider spectrum. While she worked in consultation with others in both her roles, Dorothy didn't forget the lessons learned from Ted.

"The first one I didn't need to be taught—no sacred cows. A sacred cow, of course, is one whom you do not criticize; a good example was J. Edgar Hoover, who was very sacred to most publishers. I have hit—that's the wrong word—been critical of friends and refused to support or endorse them in elections. There's always a lot of pressure by big names to protect this one and that one; the Kennedys were always calling up to keep things out of the paper. Although they gave up on me early, they still called downstairs.

Then there are those who were social friends, such as a woman who was heading up a hospital fund drive in which lottery tickets—hundred-dollar ones—were being sold illegally. A charwoman picked up a ticket off the floor which happened to be a winner, and my friend called me after she had called the six or seven other publishers there were then to kill the story. It was a very worthwhile hospital, and she said it would absolutely ruin them if it were printed—the purse was huge—and I told her if the city room didn't have it, I wouldn't give it to them, but that if they did, there wasn't anything I could do. It wasn't printed anywhere, and I don't think we had it, but it's always worried me. I have been in publishers' houses and heard them get calls from friends—millionaires and socialites with children in trouble—and agree to keep things out of the paper, but I have never done that.

Ted cared a lot about organization and taught me about the hierarchy—not going over people's heads. I never call our reporters or work directly with them, always going through their editors; I always ask whichever editor it is to be present when I see a reporter. I follow the same policy in other departments, and it can save a lot of trouble

The publisher's office at West Street featured the same partner's desk Dorothy uses today.

in an organization. Ted tried not to have teacher's pets, that's also important. I controlled the women's pages after George left and would have those editors up for lunch in my office once a week. Ted put a stop to it, didn't like it at all. The others didn't get to see me this way and decide things together, and he got rid of most of the women's page editors. Of course, he was a big teacher's pet himself, I guess.

He was a believer in jurisdiction, as am I. Each employee must have his own area, and as Bill Paley said, 'If only my executives could say they don't know the answer and would get back to me, instead of pretending.'

Another lesson was giving praise before blame. When Ted picked up the phone and would say something nice to one of our people, I knew the second remark would be, 'I think we could have done a little better on this, that or the other thing.' I became suspicious of that and never learned to do it, but when I'm sending down a memo on the Saturday magazine, occasionally I try to pick out the good things first. Mostly, though, I don't; I just let them go by and pick out the bad things.

Although Paul Sann has suggested giving a bonus to people who have done particularly well, I don't. I'm afraid even now to send a memo saying something was good, because I expect one back saying, 'Okay. A hundred bucks for him.' I have complimented writers, but I'm not willing to give money prizes. It isn't that demand for a bonus that stops me from giving kind words; it's just not in me. They weren't given to me as a child, and any words I did receive were not ones of praise.

Does it worry me not to give kind words to employees? No, not a bit. Which is a reminder of another lesson from Ted; any time there was badmouthing he would say, 'Clap a suit on them.' And sue, I have. The only thing is, it's expensive."

One lesson Dorothy didn't learn from Ted or anyone else is how to live alone. This she has been doing for years, and she does it gracefully, if not gratefully. In spite of her activity, she is essentially a solitary—in the scene but not of it. A participant, she is also an observer—watching, listening, wondering. . . .

Among the men there would continue to be in her life was one more husband. Of course, there was a divorce to obtain from

Ted (again out west and in July, but at Averell Harriman's Sun Valley house).

The *Post*'s needs were preeminent now. One of Dorothy's main concerns as publisher is advertising—how to get it and how to keep it. She credits Mrs. Ogden Reid, doyenne of the *Herald Tribune*, with teaching her about advertisers. Mrs. Reid, according to Dorothy, called New York merchants the world's most difficult and powerful people and warned that, if permitted, they would walk all over a neophyte.

"She scared me," Dorothy goes on. "You would never think that such a tiny, pretty woman had been a suffragette. But she was very strong, and I decided the best way to get advertising was first to build our circulation."

In selling space Dorothy never talks about the paper and knows nothing about such mundane matters as rates; these are not upstairs matters. As always before a meeting with people she doesn't know, she checks the clips in the *Post* morgue to learn as much about them as she can, particularly their interests, and concentrates on them. "And that's what I talk about, be it a sport, pet charity or art collecting."

Getting an advertising account is one thing Dorothy works hard for, but keeping one is a challenge she will do even more for. She lunched with one prospect and got the account, only to lose it after she refused to have a date with him the next time he came to town.

Another account was dealt with successfully, however. This corporate head was a national hero whom Dorothy had persuaded to advertise in the *Post*. She never forgot their evening, which started at a dinner in his honor at 21.

"I was so thrilled we had this advertiser, but then a sad thing happened. He was human, as my second analyst said of herself, but I never should have let him come up for a nightcap. He was a reactionary—very conservative—but how was I to know that this hero, whom I was so impressed with, would become just a pathetic old guy and get drunk? And that he would crawl around on the floor saying, 'Mommy, Mommy, I love you.'

It was awful, dreadful, and I felt terribly sorry for him. Also, I was afraid I would lose the account. I guess he vaguely remembered what happened that night in this

penthouse the next morning and didn't dare cancel the
account; he was too important to. Anyway, I got him out
before dawn, never saw him again, and we still have the
account."

Advertisers have avoided the *Post* in reaction to editorial
stands, according to Dorothy, but not recently. Her view is if the
paper offers the kind of circulation the advertiser wants, the account will remain. She adds that managing editors are careful
with stories involving local accounts. There have been times
when space salesmen have said that such-and-such an account
could not be sold because of editorial positions in opposition to
account thinking. While over the years there has been more pressure from the right than from the left, Dorothy is used to both.
Recently, she was threatened with the loss of an account owing
to the *Post*'s endorsement of Ramsey Clark for the Senate, while
other advertisers objected to a front-page headline proclaiming
the seriousness of the economic crisis. This, it was maintained,
is not the way to sell goods; instead, it encourages customers to
save. Such pressures do worry Dorothy—she is not one to take
loss of advertising linage lightly—but the quality of the paper
comes first. It is not a stand always easy to stay with, not with
her eye for the bottom line on the weekly financial reports.

By the Christmas after Ted's departure the *Post* was doing
much better, owing to Ted's economies and restored advertiser
confidence. Once again Dorothy's money had saved it, just as
her tight control on overhead, ability to ask advice and disregard
it sometimes, and a willingness to take risks would put it in the
black ("some years, very much so"). She knew her job, her market and her limits.

In spite of having proved herself, Dorothy found herself in a
depression that Christmas. She was not entirely surprised as this
time of year has been a difficult one for her since childhood,
when she would be asked what her presents were. In addition,
for her it means "duty giving"—checks for people at the *Post*,
the apartment building and "everywhere else—it's a horror.
Then there are the 'Merry Christmas' greetings to be exchanged,
but lately 'Happy Holiday' has taken over."

Such routines weren't bothering Dorothy on this bleak Yuletide; something far more fundamental and serious was.

"It was a case of being adrift on Christmas Eve. I was alone in the apartment—the older children were in California, and Sarah-Ann, sixteen, was at a party—and I was not only reminded of the break with Ted, but there had just been one with somebody else. It was dark outside. I was utterly alone and quite desperate. I thought, 'Who in my past can I get in touch with? Who is a true friend and really cares?'

I could have called Ellin Berlin; she phoned me one evening around that time and we talked for a while. I was in bed reading, and about ten minutes later she called again and asked, touchingly, if I were all right. I wasn't, being unhappy about something or other, but said, of course, I was all right. She said she was glad—just wanted to be sure—and as we hung up, I thought why wasn't I able to say to her, 'No, Ellin, I'm not all right. I'm absolutely desperate'? She, of course, would have tried to help but how? Besides, I don't like asking for help.

On that Christmas Eve, though, I did think of someone who cared—Bastien [the Vicomte Sebastien Foy had been Morti Schiff's racing stable manager and her beau]. His father had died, so he was the Comte Foy, and I thought I might reach him through his Paris club, the Travelers. My father had also belonged to it.

It meant activity—you know, getting the overseas operator, and it took up some time—but the call didn't go through, and I never did reach him. I think I may have had a drink or two, and I remember feeling almost suicidal. I put in a bad hour and then decided this night was no different from other nights; rather as they ask at the Seder, 'Why is this night different from other nights?' I decided it wasn't Christmas Eve but just a night—any night—and I got through that desperate time. I went to bed and read, telling myself to be a big girl."

Trying to make the paper succeed, where others had failed, was her greatest challenge. Dorothy likes to quote the "original Rothschild," who said he owed his success to his lieutenants. She always adds, "But, of course, he picked them." One could say the same to some extent of her success at the *Post*.

One successful lieutenant is editor Jimmy Wechsler, about whom there is still something of the bow-tied radical. He is

James Wechsler.

small enough physically to have said of Abe Beame, "This is one mayor I won't be looked down on by." Unlike those on the news side, he relates to Dorothy on a peer level, which may be due to the fact that while theoretically there is no difference in status between the news and editorial sides of any paper, decisions of the former tend to be more for the day, while those of the latter involve stands that are expected to be around longer.

Wechsler's move to the Washington bureau of the *Post* from that of *PM* was in 1946, he explains. "I had been fighting with so-called Stalinists on *PM*, and while I saw Ted sort of falling into their hands, we had very pleasant social relations the few times I had seen him in Washington. My most vivid memory of him is the night of the '48 election when we met at Wallace's headquarters. I had been given the grim task of covering Wallace, and one of his characters had even taken a punch at me for my lack of enthusiasm for the campaign.

"I remember saying to Ted that I thought he had been journalistically sound in giving the Wallace campaign full coverage, but that he had made a terrible mistake in supporting Wallace himself. Ted was a sort of dashing guy with, as someone said, a hundred ideas a day, of which one was always good. But he got involved in politics of the left, a world he didn't understand and that I'd grown up in, and I had a sadness for his predicament. By the time I was moved to New York he was no longer in the building.

"Dolly came to Washington at the time the stresses on the *Post* were growing, and we had a friendly conversation. A few months later Paul Sann and I, who were old friends, talked over the situation. I suggested we see her together, and to put it totally modestly, we proposed she let us become the new executives of the paper. I remember her smiling whimsically and saying, 'No. But I do have a lot of problems here, and I think in about ten years you two might be ready.' In May of that year I was asked to come to New York as chief editorial writer, which I was for about a month, then suddenly discovered I was editor. I guess it was partly because I used to finish the editorials too early, and I think she began to wonder what I was doing the rest of the day."

Jimmy explains that when Dorothy made him editor of the *Post* in May, 1949, she told him he could pick his executives but urged him to take time over it. He felt that owing to the internal uneasiness on the paper, it should be done right away and picked Paul Sann as his top associate.

"Dolly and I wanted to give a new tone and to be more objective on the issues of the left and the Middle East, in which Ted had been so frenetically involved. These changed from his flirtation with the Stalinists to our view that Hiss was not an innocent victim, and I think it startled some of our readers.

"The flirtation with the Stalinists under Ted was over. We began to do investigative reporting, which wasn't being done by other papers in that period, including civil rights stuff in the South—Ted Poston was an outstanding reporter and our only black—and later, a lot on the whole McCarthy movement.

Dorothy stood behind her new editorial team and their investigative stories even when the subject was a man she knew and admired, Robert Moses.

"Although Bob Moses was a hard man for most people to get along with, I liked him. Even now, when I remember running against him for the Constitutional Convention and seeing my name opposite his on the ballot, I think, 'My God!' He was a loner—well educated, a skeptic and an idealist. At one time I saw a lot of him and his first wife at Herbert Bayard Swope's, who was crazy about him. Mrs. Moses, a tiny woman in contrast to Bob's great height, was bright and claimed that the idea of Jones Beach was hers; she had pushed him into it, yet never got credit for it, she said.

The *Post* and Bob Moses were a David and Goliath affair, that's how large he seemed when we ran stories about him. These attacks on Bob appalled me since he was a friend, but as long as they had the facts right, I couldn't interfere.

Bob said it wasn't the Title I stories he minded but the ill-mannered way the questions were put, especially by Bill Haddad.

Bob was no man to attack; he was as much a hero as J. Edgar Hoover. I was under pressure from Bob's friends and mine to go easy, and when Bob went over the editors' heads to complain to me, I could only be polite and ask why he didn't answer the questions we put.

If you're a Bill Haddad, who worked on these pieces, you don't know these people, but to me they are friends, and attacking them is really tough. Things like this were always happening, which is one reason running a paper is so hard.

The respect of my staff is important to me, and the no-sacred-cow thing is vital, but when reporters have something about their friends, they are the first ones to play it down. I'm proud of the *Post* exposés, but it's hard to run the paper without making enemies.

Bob, after all, was a superior man, and I think was terribly hurt by us. Eventually, Bobby Kennedy raided Bill Haddad from us, and I was very shocked. Politicians are good at attracting people and subverting editors, or they wouldn't be elected. Roosevelt and Kennedy were, for instance, while Nixon wasn't. As for me, a publisher has to grow scar tissue, and I have.

When a friend's son, an addict, committed suicide, we put it in the wood (top headline, page one), which Joe Lash thought an outrage. My friend didn't, understanding it was a big story. Joan Payson, owner of the Mets, Jock's sister, was once very upset by our attacks on New York's Cliveden set but forgave me."

Dorothy's admiration for men who get things done was to have more intimate expression through an introduction which took place in April, 1951. In fact, although she didn't realize it at the time, this man would become a major part of her, and, to a lesser degree, of the *Post.* This future mainstay was Rudolf G. Sonneborn.

Dorothy met the man who would be her fourth husband through the *Post.* On one of the rare occasions in which she has violated her credo about being unapproachable about killing stories, a syndicate manager came to see her on behalf of a member of a family then the subject of a series to ask her to kill a chapter dealing with a major scandal. The emissary was successful, and the story being an old one, one of the family, who later became an ambassador, expressed his gratitude by taking Dorothy to dinner. He happened to mention that the Rudolf Sonneborns were separated and was as surprised that Dorothy didn't know them as she was that she was expected to.

"He said it was amazing I hadn't even heard of Rudolf and described him as an enormously attractive man, very handsome, and a leading Zionist. I wasn't part of that group, and although there weren't many German Jews who were Zionists, Rudolf came from Baltimore, where there were. Then, in April, a dinner was given by still another member of that family, and while I wasn't sure it wasn't a setup, there was Rudolf. Although I'd heard he was so marvelous, I didn't think he was attractive-looking that night.

He was talking to another man at the buffet, and when I spoke to him to tell him that I'd heard about him, he didn't realize who I was. I said, 'I hear you're very interested in Israel.' Then he lit up and asked if I'd been there. I said I hadn't.

'I'm going in June,' he said. 'Why don't you come?'

'I will,' I said, and he laughed.

I knew my friend Alicia Patterson was very sold on Israel, like so many people who were not Jewish. She thought it was marvelous and exciting—flowers in the desert—but she'd never been there. The next day I called a friend of George Backer, who was a very forceful promoter of Zionism—he was always calling me for money for things—and asked him about Rudolf. 'Are you inter-

Alicia Patterson (Mrs. Harry Guggenheim).

ested in Rudolf Sonneborn?' he said. 'Well, I'll ask you to dinner.'

The three of us went to dinner at some joint on West Fifty-ninth Street across from the park, and halfway through dinner this friend of George's got up. He said he had an appointment and had to leave, which left me alone with Rudolf, who looked better than before—much more attractive. After dinner he suggested we take a walk and we headed for Fifth Avenue. In front of the Sherry Netherland, which was run by Serge Obolensky, whom I hadn't seen for years, he said he lived there and wouldn't I come up for a drink. 'Sure,' I said.

I was amazed at his luxurious apartment—way up high, a huge living room overlooking a marvelous view, a big bedroom and a marble bath—it just spelled millions of dollars. Immediately he made a pass, I evaded it, we talked, he took me home, and then I was having an affair with him.

Rudolf had had a thing with Jessie Royce Landis, but I

was never involved with actors; the playwrights I knew thought them vain and a lot of other things. But the men I did become involved with, some of them, were equally bad—had other faults.

Rudolf had been made much of by women, and his first marriage didn't take place until he was in his late forties. His father had emigrated from Germany to Baltimore and become a clothing manufacturer. Later there was a successful oil products company, which Rudolf joined. I was quite fascinated at what I was told about Rudolf's father, who was a frustrated intellectual, and his mother was charming. Rudolf, an only son, was very attentive to her.

He was a man of character with an excellent reputation in the community—far above average. Alicia thought he was great and said, 'Don't let this slip through your fingers.' Morti liked him, too—they talked about money all the time—and called him 'smooth as silk.' People thought he was older than me—he looked for some reason fifteen or twenty years so—but he was only five years older. He took me to a Passover service in which the rabbi castigated evildoers, but it didn't mean much to me. I guess I was bored. Rudolf was a Rock of Ages type.

His schedule for the Israel trip meant a couple of weeks in London and Paris that July, 1951, and I told him I had friends there. Alicia was so thrilled about the idea, and I decided to go with him. We went by boat, in separate cabins and fifty/fifty. In London he prevailed on me to go to the Dorchester, where he always stayed, instead of Claridge's, which I preferred. He was quite strong, and we had a suite of two bedrooms and a living room, where all his English Zionists came to see him.

I was seeing my old friends and took him to a ball Max Beaverbrook gave for his granddaughter, Jeannie Campbell. Seeing him again in his own setting, I realized I was free of him at last. It was exactly twenty years after I had become so involved, and I saw . . . I just wasn't up to handling a man of so many demands, and besides, I had some of my own by then. Max had sounded a little surprised by my asking to bring a friend that evening, but Rudolf handled himself really quite well. I was impressed.

We visited Leslie Hore-Belisha at his country place, near Devonport, and he asked me if Rudolf and I were 'together,' which must have been obvious. Leslie was much more attractive than I remembered. He had married an American Mortimer, who was attractive but not pretty, and who he said married him because she loved his farm. In World War II he was there and heard the Nazi Lord Haw-Haw on the BBC boast that he would bomb it. Leslie had been Secretary of State for War and no sooner went out the door than a bomb came down, hitting the barn, not the house.

The Hore-Belishas were later divorced, and he was elevated to the peerage. When he died in 1957 at Rheims while making a speech after a tour of the champagne cellars, I wondered again how it would have been had he—or for that matter, Max—become Prime Minister and I was his wife. Except for wartime England and the entertaining problem, I still think it might have been fun."

Dorothy was worried about having to fly to Israel. At the end of the trip, Dorothy asked her companion what she owed him for hotels in Israel and plane tickets. She says he laughed, insisting he hadn't kept an account, but she paid him anyway.

"In Jerusalem we stayed at the King David Hotel, in which there was a shortage of bathrooms. Rudolf took the only room available with one which I had been about to take. I was furious, but he said I could walk through his room, and this sort of amused me. He was quite forceful and quite spoiled, besides. Anyway, I was stuck there because I didn't dare fly back alone—it takes someone I can trust to protect me—and I was there for two months, while he took care of his Zionist matters.

I was surprised by the physical aspects of Israel; it looked very much like the desert of all my divorces, and I didn't see any of those flowers Alicia had raved about. It was grimmer than I expected, with all kinds of hardships like rationing, not that there being no fats bothered me. It was very hot, but the minute I clapped my eyes on a kibbutz I wanted to stay. I felt secure; everyone had a function, although it was hard work, picking up stones with your hands. I was terrifically impressed with the dedication and selflessness, and the communal life, poor as it was, appealed to me.

When I told Rudolf I wanted to stay there and quoted a phrase from the New Testament which he didn't know—

Dorothy and Rudolf Sonneborn.

'Give all that thou hast to the poor and follow me'—he said, 'Don't be idiotic. They don't need you, and you wouldn't like it after a while. The whole idea is ridiculous.'

I liked the community of European intellectuals and the commitment of the government officials, too. Ben-Gurion, who was Prime Minister and looked like any Jewish labor leader, was lots of fun. He didn't get along well with Chaim Weizmann, who was aloof and an intellectual, but he had a marvelous, very sophisticated wife named Vera—worldly-wise, like a French wife. Golda Meir was an earth mother and cooked dinner for us."

During the next couple of years after their return Dorothy saw Rudolf regularly, mostly on weekends at his place near Danbury. He is a tall man of dignified mien and very well dressed. These interludes were a welcome change from her heavy days at the *Post.* She had relinquished her title of coeditor with the withdrawal of Ted, replacing it with the simpler but more absolute rank of publisher, and she was involved in editorial decisions. The boundaries between publisher and editor are apt to be flexible, and when the publisher is the sole owner, they can be pretty intensive roles. It has always mattered to Dorothy what the *Post* says and how it is said, since the paper reflects her own curiosity and thinking. And it matters scarcely less how her money, which has made its survival possible, is spent.

Jimmy Wechsler still expresses surprise at what he calls "Dolly's place in history." "I've always thought that if one had said in '49 that she was going to be the only survivor in the afternoon field in New York, Lloyds of London would have given you a thousand to one against it. There was a very real question of whether the paper was going to survive; after the demise of *PM* and the *Compass,* everyone was talking about it being the next headed for the cemetery.

"One of the more astonishing sessions we had that first year or so was when a Jimmy Roosevelt divorce story broke. She came down to my office and said, 'I want to talk to you about this. It's the most human story of the day and should have been on page one; I think you were protecting the Roosevelts.' I began to glimpse her emergence as a person with her own sense of journalism. Dolly and I hadn't known this about each other, but we shared the view that we wanted a liberal paper with a large degree of humor and interest, which would include sex as a major phase of the human condition. Eventually, we began to be a little ambivalent about the last, maybe having gone too far in that direction. She finally asked me if I were ashamed of being editor of this newspaper, and I could answer no, I really wasn't. We had a problem of survival and basically what we were doing was right, even if there were some things which were undistinguished."

A mid-1950 memo to Jimmy Wechsler stated her policy pretty concisely. She wrote that the paper must not cater:

> to ignorance, superstition, myths, bigotry and narrow-mindedness, prejudice and all the things it is the business of liberals to fight. We must not overprotect ourselves, our readers or our children; the disillusionment always comes finally, and is devastating.
>
> The *Post,* with some truth, has been charged for years with unjournalistic lack of objectivity. I think we agree that we are more interested in putting out a good, independent newspaper than in becoming a party organ. The *Post* must grow up, lose

its naïveté and recognize that it stands alone, free and independent to print the facts, letting the chips fall, etc.

You and I may, as we have in the past, be tempted to forget this. You must hit me over the head when I want to compromise more than I should. And you know I'll wallop you because you are one of the very few people I have known who can take it.

My concern with immediate results in circulation is a factor, and one of which I am not ashamed, but I don't think it's the only one. Perhaps I have become more ruthless, due to past idols whose feet usually wound up by kicking me or the newspaper. I really don't give a damn at this point whether the name (at issue) is Roosevelt, Stevenson, Wechsler or Schiff, as long as it isn't the *Post.*

One *Post* effort which was distinguished, however, was several courageous series attacking some of the strongest conservative figures in the nation's history. Starting with Jack Lait and Lee Mortimer (a libel suit brought by them was thrown out of court), the *Post* took on Walter Winchell (who replied with regular and vicious Sunday night radio attacks on both the paper and Jimmy Wechsler) and eventually the king of innuendo himself, Senator Joe McCarthy. The result was a campaign against the paper in the best Goebbels tradition, and by April, 1953, Jimmy was summoned for an appearance before McCarthy's Permanent Subcommittee on Investigations ostensibly on the basis of evidence brought back from an inspection of U.S. Information Service libraries abroad by G. David Schine and Roy Cohn. They cited a work of Jimmy's on John L. Lewis.

Jimmy says that it's hard to re-create the tensions and ugliness of that period. "The paper was under tremendous fire, and there may well have been moments when Dolly said, 'Why the hell did I ever hire him?' I probably underestimated the stress she was under, and I'm sure there were advertisers she had trouble with. I think I have a greater lust for combat than she has—I guess it was easier for me to deal with these attacks—yet she went to Washington with me to consult Senator Stuart Symington, who was a committee member and an old Palm Beach family friend, Dorothy has since explained, adding that the Senator called *her.*

"The role she occupied was equivalent to what Kay Graham went through in the Watergate period, only in a sense even more; Dolly was taking a terrible beating and partly because of my early history. I had been in the Young Communist League in the thirties, was subsequently a leading anti-Communist in the Newspaper Guild and advised in the formation of Americans for Democratic Action. Of course, my appearance before the committee was an absurdity—an intimidatory operation in which Roy Cohn was out to get the paper as an example to others—and my book on Lewis included large amounts of anti-Communist passages. Poor Leonard Lyons came to me, saying that McCarthy would lay off me if the paper dropped its attacks. It wasn't much of an offer.

"I had two long sessions before the committee, and it came down to the issue of my giving names. Finally, McCarthy agreed not to make them public if I would give them, and I spoke to Dolly. She said, 'It's between you and your conscience.' That point has troubled me a good deal, but the names were quite well known, and even Roy Cohn complained I hadn't given them anything they didn't know. We got support from newspaper editors and a long editorial in the *Times* and survived to do a series on J. Edgar Hoover, long dead now with McCarthy."

This survival did something for Dorothy in a personal way; she had met the enemy—as big a one as even *she* had a right to expect—and not been found wanting. Her steadfastness under pressure did much to enhance her reputation and even tempered the harshness of adversaries. Things were going well for her; the *Post* continued in the black and was less of a manifesto and more of a newspaper. While there were marital problems for her Hall children, her personal life was just about where she wanted it; she was involved, respected—yes, and feared—and by some large names, both trusted and revered. Popular affection was in short supply, but then it hadn't been courted.

Those were productive years, too. Dorothy's ability to meet figures of importance with pretty much the same manner of aloofness and interest she uses in all her dealings gave her an opportunity to ask questions which have been called startling. It occurred to her that expanding her memos into a weekly column might bring her more readers. Her first column appeared on September 30, 1951. The columns brought in considerable mail, most of it favorable, and launched Dorothy as something of a personality rather than a name on the masthead. Their range was wide, and to the comment of the *New Yorker's* late A. J. Liebling

From left: Sarah-Ann Backer, Dorothy, Michael Gray (eleven), his mother Adele Hall Gray and Morti Hall.

that the letter was "a cross between Msgr. Sheen and W. R. Hearst, Jr.," Dorothy replied, "They, too, have a large readership." The one which follows is typical.

Dear Reader: One advantage of being a newspaper publisher is that it gives you an excuse for calling on people who, normally, might not care to see you, or whom, on the other hand, you might not care to meet.

In the latter category falls a certain "Prime Minister"—not a P.M. in the usual sense of the title, however, like Churchill or Ben-Gurion, both of whom I have met—but a man who has often been referred to as the Prime Minister of the Underworld: the gentleman known as Frank Costello, now under indictment for contempt of the Senate.

My visit to Costello came about in this way: In 1950, I spent Decoration Day weekend with my friend Alicia Patterson, publisher of *Newsday,* a very successful Long Island daily tabloid newspaper, at her home in Sands Point, Long Island.

One morning, Alicia told me that she and one of her photographers had an appointment that afternoon to take pictures of

Frank Costello at his house, which was also in Sands Point.
"Would you like to come along?" said Alicia. I hesitated for a
moment, wondering whether I should go to see a man of whom
we at the *Post* took such a dim view, and had attacked so often.
Also it entered my mind that, for the same reason, I might not
be a welcome guest *chez* Costello.

But my curiosity got the better of me, and my duty as a newspaperwoman to investigate everything that might be interesting was rationalization enough to overcome any scruples.

After lunch we drove the short distance that divides the rack-
eteer's weekend retreat from those of the more respectable millionaires which line the waterfront of that neighborhood.

From the outside, which is all I saw of it, Costello's place is a
comfortable-looking brick house like dozens of others one sees
in the suburbs, surrounded by an acre or two of landscaped
grounds.

We drove up, were greeted by Mr. and Mrs. Costello, who
ushered us to a terrace at the back of the house. We were asked
to sit down and were offered drinks from the bar.

At first Costello didn't realize who I was—but shortly afterward caught on to the fact that I was the publisher of the newspaper which had probably campaigned more strenuously
against him than any other in the city. The minute he became
aware of my identity, he moved over to take a seat next to me.
Costello is a heavyset, tough-looking man. As you know, he
speaks in a husky voice, not always ungrammatically. He put
himself out to be charming to me and seemed to bear me no ill
will.

I asked him how he felt about all the stories we had printed
exposing his unsavory activities. Costello replied that he didn't
mind any of them except one in which he said *Post* reporter
Bob Spivack had claimed that he had indirectly been offered a
bribe of $1,500 to lay off Costello. This, the gambler said, was
not true. (For Christmas, in 1947, Costello sent Spivack a case
of scotch. Bob wrote Costello, telling him that someday he
might want to write something nice about him and he wouldn't
want him to think it was on account of the scotch, so would he
please send for it. Costello did.)

Mrs. Costello is a plump, dark, rather pretty woman. She was
most amiable and explained to me that the house was only used
weekends. She looked like a person who enjoyed her food and I
had a feeling that she was probably a wonderful Italian cook.
(Cooking is a subject in which I am very interested.) When I

asked her about this, she replied in a quite uppity tone: "The maid does that."

I tried another tack: "What is your husband's favorite dish?"

Her reply was quick and cute: "I am!" she said confidently.

I have been told that Costello suffers from stomach ulcers, is being psychoanalyzed, wants to be respectable now.

I saw Frank Costello once again, under very different circumstances. Last March I had a front-row seat in the jury box in the courtroom in which the Kefauver hearings were being held.

No longer was Costello the relaxed, husky, urbane host he had been that lovely afternoon under the flowering fruit tree in the garden of his country place.

This time, only a year later, I saw a different person: the perspiring, croaking, unwilling witness called before the pitiless glare of public opinion.

"Bearing in mind all that you have gained and received in wealth, what have you ever done for your country as a good citizen?" the former immigrant boy was asked.

"Paid my tax," the rich gangster rasped.

I laughed, but I knew the sin was not Costello's alone. Aren't we, the so-called respectable citizens, also to blame when so many of our energetic, underprivileged boys go wrong in our big cities? Aren't too many of us satisfied that we have paid our debt to society when, after taking advantage of every loophole in the law and perhaps even bribing an underpaid official, we send our checks to the Bureau of Internal Revenue?

Jimmy Wechsler says that the story of Dorothy's life in the years of his association with her "is the growth of her self-assurance. It would be hard to recognize the woman I went to work for in terms of her confidence . . . she was certainly a person who, in my judgment, had enormous insecurity. She was prone to let things happen, giving everyone their heads to a certain degree."

Others echo this feeling about Dorothy then, but in view of the tone of the memo on her visit to President Harry S. Truman at the White House in May, 1952, one has to wonder if she didn't have more confidence than was apparent.

The President said newspaper criticism didn't bother him, that all the great Presidents—Jefferson, Lincoln—had had a

bad press. He didn't care what editorials said about him because nobody reads them, anyway.

I was told afterwards that the President had been very
pleased with our meeting, but I must say I was not. To me, he
does not seem one of our great Presidents and I am glad I did
not support him, in view of the Hiroshima decision.

That same year she had dinner with Bernard Baruch, who had
rejected the privilege of underwriting the *Post* at the same time
Averell Harriman did. Again one wonders about any lack of self-
assurance. The memo reads:

> As usual, when I dined alone with him, a butler and second
> man served dinner. He told me he had been awfully sick and
> went into some rather repulsive detail. Dressed in a wine-col-
> ored velvet suit, he had a bourbon on the rocks before dinner
> and spoke of General and Mrs. Marshall, who had just spent
> the night with him before sailing for Europe. The general told
> him that when he went to a San Francisco bank to cash a check,
> he was asked for identification because nobody knew who he
> was. BB was the only person to see him off on the boat and, al-
> though he suggested that they be photographed together, there
> was no photographer.
>
> Bernie said his wife had been the most wonderful woman in
> the world because she never criticized him. "Everything I did
> was fine—she always said that I knew best." I knew he had
> stepped out a good deal while he was married, and when I
> asked him why he had never remarried, he said that he had
> been sixty-nine when his wife died and that was too old for a
> woman. He added that he had been studying women for almost
> eighty years and he still didn't know much about them.

Dorothy found enough assurance to take on the country's most
powerful prelate, too—New York's archbishop, Francis Cardinal Spellman. She was running in the primary for state commit-
teewoman and also wanted the cardinal's influence in connection with an important advertiser. Her lunch at the archdiocesan
house in early 1952 marked the end of a contretemps which had
arisen half a dozen years before over a *Post* editorial criticizing
him for having attacked Eleanor Roosevelt. She noted in a
memo:

The Cardinal is short and plump and doesn't give the impression of being a cultured man. His grammar is not too good, but he is most agreeable and easy to talk to.

During lunch, Monsignor [Fulton] Sheen said that he had been told in Italy that the Americans had taught the poor Italians to love the Russians during the war, and he said this with utter contempt and hatred. The Cardinal asked me what I thought Roosevelt would feel if he came back to earth today, then made a vitriolic attack on his Yalta Conference.

On the subject of the Russians, one of the priests at the table said, "The enemy of our enemy is not our friend."

By now Dorothy was being taken seriously as a political influence. However she has not supported any political campaigns financially since she has run the *Post*. Nor, she says with a sign of relief, has she been a joiner; it just isn't the function of a newspaper publisher. This memo of a phone conversation in midsummer, 1952, shows the kind of political role she was playing.

I called Wilson Wyatt [campaign manager for Adlai Stevenson's Presidential campaign] yesterday to discuss the selection of a U.S. Senatorial candidate on the Democratic ticket. He repeated the reasons Harriman had already given me for his lack of desire to make the race. I told him that possibly if Harriman were assured that he had no chance of becoming Secretary of State, he would run [he had lost his bid for the Presidential nomination at the convention].

He asked me what I would do if I were Adlai. I said I thought the fair thing was to put Harriman out of his agony, that the risk would be, of course, that Harriman would not contribute financially to the campaign. I said I didn't think Harriman had any real following except that he could be elected in New York State, if he ran for Senator.

Pursuing this concern about Harriman, she met with him at his house following an evening TV appearance he had made with John Foster Dulles.

Harriman seemed pleased at the tremendous backing the *Post* has been giving him, but he said to be a junior Senator for

three years, after all of his worldwide experience, would be un-
thinkable and would make him unavailable for any office Stevenson might offer him after election. He seemed convinced
that he would get some office in the new administration, if not
Secretary of State, and said he was the only person who was
qualified.

I told him that I am convinced that Stevenson will carry New
York State [he lost by nearly 900,000] even if Wagner runs for
the Senate; however, it would help to have a strong Democratic
Senatorial candidate. I was amused when Wyatt said, "You are
the first honest person I have talked to. Everyone else insists
the Senate will be lost unless Harriman runs."

The tipoff came to what was going on in Harriman's mind
when he said that Stevenson would have to appoint him to
some important international job, possibly not Secretary of
State, because the pressure on him would be so great. He said
that he had a lot of support all over the country including the
farmers. It seemed to me that he was unutterably naïve. Boys
like Averell, who have always bought everything they wanted,
never learn that you cannot always start at the top. He gave
money to both parties in the Willkie campaign and saw nothing
wrong with it, which shocked me, and he advanced Carmine
De Sapio beyond anything he expected to be national commit-
teeman. Though Carmine is a good friend of mine, I'm told he
never got free of the Mafia and can't.

I felt sorry for Averell, who is one of the most charming men
I have ever met, but decided he didn't have much political
sense and it might be as well to let him go his own way. His
wife, Marie, who has enormous influence on him, is terribly
bored, she told me, by having to listen to his hourlong
speeches.

Dorothy's life had opened up a great deal by the summer of
1953, and as it did so Rudolf Sonneborn continued to offer both
support and reassurance. He was a good listener, tactful with
suggestions, and was secure enough to give her the room she
needed. Yet she was again about to make a major change not by
decision but by acquiescence.

"It was July, and Rudolf and I were out in California
on our vacations; I had gone out to see Morti and Adele
and he had come along. We had separate rooms in a marvelous hotel—the Bel-Air something—outside Beverly

Hills. Rudolf was still married, and since his wife, who was much younger than he, was in an institution, it took seven years—or maybe it's five—to get a divorce.

I didn't know the question of marriage was going to come up, but one morning he said a doctor was coming to take blood tests for it. I said, 'But how can we? You're married.' 'Not anymore,' he said. 'Here are the papers.' It turns out he'd made a deal with her; she had flown to Mexico with doctor and nurses and gotten the divorce in one day. He was now free, this man of character, who was strong and protective. He was in love with me, and that's always nice. Only, I should have loved him.

So I called Morti and said, 'He wants to get married right away.' He said, 'What do you want me to do—throw him out? I will, if that's what you want.' 'No,' I said. 'It's not that, exactly. But what do you think?' He said, 'Well, I told you.' So I married Rudolf."

Included in the press coverage, complete with picture of the groom, was mention in Dorothy's column, by then appearing three times a week.

In case you missed the item when it was printed on August 19—the name of the (I hope) lucky man is Rudolf G. Sonneborn. Rudolf was born in Baltimore. He is tall, gray-haired and very handsome, with a beautiful speaking voice. To top it all, although the head of a large oil refining and chemical business and a director of a bank, Rudolf is a liberal Democrat!

My husband is very modern in his attitude toward careers for women. He reads the New York *Post* avidly and considers its continuance as the city's only crusading liberal newspaper to be of such vital importance that he is willing to have his wife retain her maiden name professionally and to continue to devote the major portion of her time to its publication.

Among those who kept their fingers crossed about the new marriage was Dorothy herself. She says that there were some problems about money; in spite of Rudolf's having made his own—several million—"he didn't want to pay for things. Even when we were married, he wanted to go fifty-fifty on the hotel bill and I said, 'Goddammit, on our honeymoon *you* can pay. After that, I'll go fifty-fifty.'"

Mr. and Mrs. Rudolf Sonneborn on the day after their wedding in California.

John Schiff saw the marriage as a reaction on Dorothy's part, saying of Rudolf that "he is a charming man—intelligent and very able. He was probably the first of her husbands who insisted on paying the rent for the apartment; the others were more than willing to take a free ride."

Dorothy explains, "Actually Rudolf didn't carry the apartment expense; he owned the weekend house in Danbury." George Backer also thought highly of Rudolf. He remembered that Dorothy had called, asking if he "knew a fellow named Rudolf Sonneborn. I told her he was a very nice fellow, an estimable man.

"'But,' she said, 'what's he like?' and I tried again, saying he was rich, good-looking and a respected member of the community. 'That isn't what I asked you. What about him?' I said, 'Well, if you want the truth, Dolly, he's a little heavy.' 'Thank you,' she said. 'I'm going to marry him.'"

Dorothy explains that she didn't call George for a Rudolf reference—"I wouldn't have dreamed of it; I called George's wife to ask if I could bring Rudolf to a party for a visiting Israeli. George said I couldn't, but I went anyway because it was business."

Dorothy says in those days she had never thought about the possibility of living long term with a man without marrying him eventually. It did occur to her, however, that it can take a long time to realize that you can live alone, and from this she had gone the next step: that for some it is the only way to live. If nothing else, such a life eliminates a problem which arose with Rudolf—mutually agreeable housing.

> "Rudolf was unhappy when he first moved into my apartment and kept talking about a marvelous one he once had near the East River. He wanted to remodel mine, which he didn't like and didn't own, so we moved to the Pierre for a couple of months at his expense. He did it his way, then pulled his furniture out of storage and installed it. It was heavy, had belonged to his grandparents and was full of beetles, which got into my carpets.
>
> Sarah-Ann, who was still living at home, moved to a Village apartment, which I was not in favor of but Rudolf encouraged, and then he moved pretty much into the whole place, so I really just had my bedroom. In Danbury we also had separate bedrooms—he the master and I the second one—and there was a sort of closet with washbasin in each room, which is German. Since the time Dick Hall and I began leading separate lives, my husbands have always had separate bedrooms. It depends on your economic status, I suppose, but if I loved a man, I'd want to share his bed."

The question of whose territory was whose, among other housekeeping concerns, didn't occupy much of Dorothy's time or thought; her life with the *Post* didn't leave much of either left over. It was a busy one, covering publishing, politics and causes, and Rudolf played a part.

Rudolf had known Dr. Albert Einstein for some years in connection with his support of the Zionist cause. He arranged a meeting in Princeton during which the three discussed and deplored the retaliatory Israeli raid on Kibya (which resulted in the death of many Arabs and a strong censure by the UN Security

Council). Dorothy's subsequent "Dear Reader" column in March, 1955, had an unexpected and unpleasant repercussion.

Saintlike, simple, gentle Professor Einstein was sitting in a chair facing a large picture window. In front of him was a table laden with marked books and sheets of white paper covered with tiny, neat symbols He wore a faded blue sweater over his tieless blue shirt, gray trousers and brown mouton slippers on his bare feet. An old-fashioned steamer rug had slipped off one knee, and an electric blanket was beside him.

"How are you?" My husband broke the ice. As well as expected for his age was the depressing reply. I told him seventy-six wasn't old, thinking of my husband's mother, Churchill, Senator Green and Bernard Baruch, who are alert and energetic despite being in their eighties.

Einstein, who used to love to play the violin, told us he no longer fiddled because "you can't play it alone." However, he does improvise on the piano.

Did he think there were intelligent beings on other planets? "Of course," he said, "this is just an unimportant little planet. There are many of much greater magnitude." If they are more intelligent than we, why haven't they been able to communicate with us? I asked. After all, we have been unable to make contact with others in our own world, he parried.

We talked about the H-bomb. Through radiation it could wipe out life on this earth, he said. I got the feeling that this lovable man was so worried about the possible use of the weapon he had helped to create that he was in danger of becoming one of its first casualties.

There was an etching of Gandhi in the room. Yes, Nehru had been to see him. They had understood each other immediately. Nehru would like to be like Gandhi, but had found that he had to use force. Nonviolent Einstein seemed to sympathize. Does he read the newspapers? One only, and your first guess will be right. "It is my adrenalin." He chuckled.

No one in government spoke for the whole world, he said sadly. Even Roosevelt, whom he loved, had found it necessary to compromise several times because of pressures at home.

About Israel Einstein said large nations could control small nations, but who was to control the large nations? Standing on the stairs as we were leaving, the disillusioned idealist called to my husband, "We had great hopes for Israel at first. We thought it might be better than other nations, but it is no better."

Einstein publicly repudiated the final quoted sentence, claiming that he had been exploited and that portions of the column did not reflect his views. Rudolf wrote Einstein that when Dorothy drafted the column, "I could find nothing inaccurate to the best of my recollection, and encouraged its publication. Indeed, some of my good Zionist friends felt that your moral observation about Israel was both timely and well stated."

This exchange led to further correspondence and the story was reprinted in the Jewish press.

"Jimmy Wechsler had suggested I cut the last line of my column, because he foresaw that it would get me, and maybe the paper, in a lot of trouble. When Einstein said it, by the way, I said, 'Let's hope it's not worse,' and he laughed, standing on the front step of the house, looking like God. After it was news, he was put under pressure, became frightened and repudiated me. I had wanted to go live with him and take care of him, this old man with sort of a halo, who looked like my childhood idea of God. To be denied in writing by God was too much.

He had agreed to make a broadcast on the anniversary of the state's founding that year, but instead went to the hospital. After he died, some of the pages he had written for it were found on the night table. The same thing, pretty much, was said in other words: 'When you live among wolves, you must travel with the pack.' Rudolf thought I was making too much of Einstein's denial—Rudolf wasn't all that sensitive—and he encouraged me to print the line, but he could take it; he had a terrific position in the Zionist group. I think it needed to be said, too, so in doing the right thing it got me into trouble. I had killed my God, but my protector—tall and strong—turned out to be somebody who pushed me into a barrel of worms or worse. It was bad."

Dorothy's sense of hurt in being let down by what appeared a deliberate and dishonest retraction was severe, and in time this sense of loss was transformed into guilt.

"It seemed I had killed that God the Father; I had hurt him by revealing a secret that he didn't want made public. I knew he wouldn't want me to print it, but I did anyway. At least the anger was turned against me because he

said he hadn't said it, and he was believed. I had thought
he was God, you see, and he turned out not to be God. He
was a little, petty man who wouldn't stand behind his
statement, and while I understood the problem he faced,
I was very disappointed.

When I discussed this with an old friend, Dr. Lawrence Kubie, the analyst and cousin of my then lawyer,
General Greenbaum, he thought I needed to go back to a
psychiatrist. I told him I preferred a woman, and he recommended one. Larry and I may have talked about my
father . . . about his being such a mouse with my mother. Now I see I may have found somebody as replacement
for my father . . . the President, for instance.

In my first session with this new psychiatrist, sitting
opposite her at her desk, when she asked what was trou-
bling me, I told her that I thought I had killed Einstein.
She said that he was a very old and sick man, and after
all, I wasn't omnipotent. 'Oh,' I said.

She was a Freudian and, being badly crippled from
polio, did needlepoint all the time. I had given up mine,
and she asked me why I had stopped. I said I thought it
was a waste of time. She thought that was a great mistake—a hobby was very good for you—with which I went
out and bought a piece of needlepoint and have done it
pretty much ever since.

I told Dr. Rollo May at a Max Lerner party that I hadn't
completed my analysis with Sullivan, and he asked me a
million questions about him; he admired him very much.
And he said this is very interesting because it's exactly
what Sullivan did with his analyst, a woman. He broke
off his analysis, and Rollo said that Sullivan's interpreta-
tion was that when a patient broke off his analysis, it was
finished, but he didn't think that about mine.

For the next few sessions she and I just talked, as I
didn't want to go back on the couch. But I found myself
back on it for another two years."

Dorothy says her new doctor was "much warmer and more
gentle than Dr. Sullivan." The sessions were five days a week,
and she went before going to the office. There her activities continued as busily as before and without apparently being affected
by her psychotherapy, which in the clinical sense may have
been more supportive than analytic.

"Once I was on the couch again, it was as if I had found a—I was going to say friend—someone to talk to, and who wouldn't tell anyone. She was a nice person with a very white face and dark hair, which may have been dyed. I used to wonder how old she was and once speculated out loud. She asked me how old I thought, and I guess I took off some years. I still don't know, but she may have been older than I suspected. She was so terribly crippled by polio it was painful to watch her, and she told me I must tell her my feelings about it. I think I did quite a lot of editing, so as not to. . . . At some point I asked her where she lived and whether she was married; she may have said politely such things were not my affair. What I was wondering was whether a woman so badly crippled was married. I suspect she was not and lived alone. Or with a woman.

I told her my dreams, and we would analyze them; we did free associating, too. I don't think I was able to be any freer with her than with Dr. Sullivan, but I did get reassurance. There was a lot of talk about my marriages and guilt, particularly about the last one. At one point she told me I was promiscuous. I resented this because to me promiscuity means having more than one affair at a time—on the whole, I didn't.

I think she was interested in me partly because of the *Post*—having a finger in the pie. We talked about the paper a lot, and when the need arose to increase the price of the paper from five to ten cents—it had already gone up from three to five—I told her that Jimmy Wechsler was very opposed but that Rudolf was in favor of it. By her questions, I thought she sided with Rudolf, and this taking of a position bothered me; I didn't think an analyst was supposed to give business advice. She was right from a financial point of view but wrong from the professional one.

About two years after we started, something came up which changed our way of working. The arrangement was that my secretary had the telephone number of her office but was to ring it during my hour only in the greatest emergency. Well, a call came for me with a male voice, which she answered, and it turned out to be the business manager. He thought I should know that a press had caught fire—they always get frightened when this happens, as it cuts circulation—and they call me immedi-

ately. I made my answer as brief as possible, saying I
would be there in half an hour.

When I hung up, she said angrily, 'Who was that man?'
I told her and she said, 'But you know you're not supposed to receive calls.' I said it was an emergency, and
she calmed down, but I was very worried. I went back the
next day anyway, which she said was very mature of me,
and stayed with it the rest of the week. I remember her
saying about the call, 'I am only human,' but it was July—vacation time—and everyone was going away.

I wrote to her from Europe, saying I would not return
to sessions and explained I wanted to try going it alone.
She wrote me a nice letter, saying she was there if ever I
needed anything, and I thanked her. Had I felt such a
need, I would have gone to another therapist on account
of the phone call incident. Also, I think I had gone as far
as possible, though I do remember her suggestion once
that perhaps I should try another therapist. And I said,
'Oh, no.'

She may have felt defeated by me, which worried me
for her. By that time I felt terribly sorry for her, because I
realized I meant a great deal to her, I think she had become emotionally involved with me, but not I with her. I
don't think the transference thing took place in either of
my therapies, but there may have been a sort of counter
one here.

It is interesting that both my attempts at analysis were
broken off by me after two years, and I guess the fact I
lost Dr. Sullivan's letter and can't remember what we
were working on . . . but maybe there just was nothing
more. Anyway, for those who need it, I would recom-
mend therapy and have. As was said to me by the doctor
who had referred me to Dr. Sullivan, 'There is nothing
wrong with psychoanalysis, provided you have the right
analyst.'

I know I still lack self-confidence—esteem—which
may be due to too much tearing down as a child. My
cousin Carola Rothschild said that my mother was a scary
lady, even if she did add that I was good at managing my
father, implying that there was something between him
and me. But if he was overfond of me, I certainly wasn't
aware of it.

My mother used to say, 'Dolly always bounces back,'
and Sarah-Ann thinks I'm amazingly resilient. But I

think of myself as weak, dependent and supersensitive, though when I am hurt or disappointed, something always comes along to take my mind off it—people, usually. Everything is people in my life; I'm not an abstract type of person, so I always want a 'for instance.'

When I am hurt, of course, I'm too proud to show it, and like all self-centered people, I'm supersensitive. I'm forgiving with people—have been for many years—but I wasn't always, and I don't bear grudges. I never did any homework as a child, so I didn't think I was bright. I suppose I must be, though; people tell me so, but I'd rather be intelligent than bright; brightness implies superficiality.

Sometimes I think nothing troubles me except not having answers. There are times, even now, when I panic and think I will never get through the day. I want to cancel everything and hide in my room, but then trays will come and everybody will be terrified. It's easier to hide in my office and not have to explain; after all, the feeling of security of a lot of people is involved.

At the *Post*, I think they see me as professional in my relationship with them and know that I am not zonked by them. They may be shocked, too, by the fact that when they don't do things the way I think they should be done, they hear from me. I don't do these things tactfully; I'm not sensitive enough about their feelings to be diplomatic. I'm so involved with what I want the paper to be, I forget about their feelings. If you hit them hard, it gets done, but to creep up on them takes too long. I don't know if there is a way to correct them without their being a little hurt. Anyway, if I were less direct, I wouldn't be me.

It's been brought home to me that I sometimes scare people I meet on social occasions, but I never think of it until later. I forget that they may be a bit overawed and that I'm not just an extra woman at the party. If they are awed, it's only because I'm Dorothy Schiff of the New York *Post*; otherwise, I wouldn't be at the party. I expect to be treated like any other woman, and I wish I were more like them. Not being so gets in the way of a lot of things.

I've been told by a much younger man recently that I have sex appeal—eroticism, he called it—but I can't believe that at my age. . . . I'm told I have charm, too, but I have never been aware of it and certainly not of using it.

If I do have an effect, I would call it salesmanship. I admit I have a special way of selling a point of view or advertising by appearing interested in the person. That's easy, because I am."

Dorothy was interested enough in the idea of meeting Fidel Castro to leave a dinner at short notice when Rudolf managed to arrange through his Cuban oil products interests for *El Primo* to come to their apartment in the spring of 1959. He was escorted by aides, "all of whom had beards and liked to drink," Dorothy remembers. There was plenty of liquor in the apartment, but because it was 10 P.M., food had to be sent out for. The street was closed by the police for security reasons, which made it hard for Dorothy to get to her home from the dinner. She says that Rudolf had not wanted her to attend the dinner anyway, since it was a Jewish holiday, and gives him credit for an original way to get her home early.

> "It was Castro's first glimpse of a New York penthouse, and when he looked at the view from the terrace, he said, 'To think there was nothing here three hundred years ago; someday Havana will be like this.'
> He was absolutely fascinating, I thought—very male, charismatic and a little anxious, which may have been due to the lack of warmth in his Washington reception. When I asked what had been the hardest part of his struggle, he said, 'Not the fighting, the administration. And if it doesn't work in three years, I will resign.' Although Nancy Wechsler was skeptical, after he left, Jimmy said, 'Jesus Christ must have been like this when He walked over the land.'"

In May, 1959, Dorothy's world was to undergo another major change. It was one which would lead her to settle for a life peculiarly her own and a solitary one at that.

> "The night Rudolf returned from a business trip—they had a refinery in a place called Petrolia, Pennsylvania, but I never went on these trips—I was upstairs in the living room of my apartment talking to a CBS head, who was interested in becoming part of the *Post*. It was cocktail time, and we were having a good talk when I heard

Rudolf come in downstairs. He was making it known that he was back, moving around slamming doors, but he didn't dare come up. He was interfering with my business, and I was irritated. After my guest left, I went down to ask Rudolf how his trip went, but he was much more interested in the interview.

Dinner was announced shortly—we had a live-in German couple—and as usual, he sat at the foot of the table and I sat in the middle. He was the kind of man who wanted it known he was the head of the household, even though I owned the apartment. If anyone had to change his seat, it would be me and not him.

The second course had been served, we were talking, and then, as he had a forkful of food halfway to his mouth, everything stopped. He got a silly grin on his face, and I thought he had something stuck in his throat. I said something, but he just kept that sort of vacant smile, and the hand didn't move. I thought he was going to choke, but he just stayed that way, and there was no response when I spoke to him; he couldn't talk or anything. My heart began to beat very hard—something terrible, terrible had happened, and I panicked.

I think I must have called the butler—a very strange type, always completely calm—then I flew downstairs to call Rudolf's doctor. I found the telephone book, but I couldn't remember his name. I tried hard, but it didn't come, so I called mine. He lived nearby, and when I said, 'I think my husband has had a stroke,' he asked who his doctor was. I told him I couldn't remember his name, and he said, 'Try to,' and I said, 'I have, and I can't.' He said he would be right over, and he was. By that time, I think, Rudolf's hand was down.

The butler helped the doctor lay him out on the floor; then, after some tests, the doctor said, indeed, he had had a stroke but that he responded to command. 'You must remember the name of his doctor,' he said. 'You have to remember his name.' I said, 'Well, I can't.' I remembered the first letter of his name, but that was all except that he was charming and divine. He was a very gentlemanly person, but he would *ask* you; mine *tells* you.

My doctor had me get the classified directory—I didn't even know MDs were in the yellow pages—and he read out all the names beginning with that letter. When he came to it, I remembered, and he called him. He was on an emergency at the hospital and asked mine to take over, saying there was no room there anyway. My doctor called an ambulance and got Rudolf a room at his hospital, although there was a strike and no nurses were available.

By the time the ambulance arrived Rudolf was completely out. The doctor said I could ride in the ambulance with them, but I said, 'No. I have to do some telephoning.' I had never ridden in an ambulance, even when Morti was taken to a hospital with pneumonia as a little boy, and I couldn't. It wasn't really the ambulance, though. I just didn't. . . . I really wanted to run away, and I knew I couldn't.

It was all too much; I didn't want any part of him. I had a lot of duties—the *Post*, the children and all—and here was this man who had collapsed completely. He was supposed to look after me—that's what he said he was going to do—and he didn't. Well, he did for a while . . . the best he could.

When I got to the hospital, in a daze, I was asked endless questions about him I couldn't answer. They had put him in a thing like a crib at the hospital and given him what they give drunks—formaldehyde—no, paraldehyde. Then he was delirious—raving—and Rudolf's sisters sat in, there being no nurses. It was terrifying to see, and I couldn't go to the office for a couple of weeks or more.

Rudolf was a very handsome man, but the first few days they did nothing about him; there was a barber in the hospital, but I had to arrange for him to be paid. I remember thinking how marvelous he looked after he was shaved—he had the most beautiful profile—and I thought how awful I would look if I were that sick, with my hair all mixed up and everything. He looked like those bishops on their stone coffins up at the Cathedral of St. John the Divine.

He came out of it gradually and after six weeks was moved back to the apartment, together with nurses and therapists—the works. Getting him well was the center of all attention; everything was geared to that. It meant extra help in the apartment, air conditioners and different ways of doing things. Finally, Rudolf and I had a scene— between servants and nurses and their frictions, nothing worked—and I called Morti. As usual, he said, 'Well, what do you want me to do? Throw him out?' I said, 'No. Never mind.'

There had been a personality change or something. Oh, I suppose I had provoked him . . . it was awful."

For six years the apartment's life revolved around Rudolf's determination to recover fully and Dorothy's, when not with him, around the *Post*. She seems to have given the paper even more thought and effort than before, with the result that in these years its position was enhanced and her professional standing was confirmed.

In 1965 she decided that the part of her life dedicated to Rudolf's recovery must come to an end. She was secure in the certainty that she had done as much as she could, for as long as she could, and so told Rudolf. The constant conflict with the young nurses she hired at his insistence and the household help became unmanageable. And yes, as with the termination of life with all her husbands, it was a July.

"Rudolf had a lot of possessions," she says, very quietly. "He would have left them, but we decided they should go to storage. When I found him he was in a hotel, with his furniture in storage, and when he left, he went to another hotel."

X

_____

"I could say that it was money that killed them—they weren't as reckless as I have been."

From the early fifties on, as sole owner and publisher of the _Post_, Dorothy was more and more involved with politics and politicians on the national scene as her memos show. One of the men she knew particularly well was Adlai Stevenson, not only because he was the Democratic Party's standard-bearer for two campaigns but because he was so close to her friend Alicia Patterson, of _Newsday_.

This first memo concerns a meeting prior to the 1956 election.

Complaining of the Chicago heat, Adlai took off his jacket, exposing a huge paunch. I mentioned that Norman Thomas, the Socialist who kept running for President, as he said, to oblige his lecture bureau, once told me that if he had not been married to a woman with independent means, he couldn't have afforded it. Adlai's comment: "Marry a rich woman and become a Socialist."

Upon my saying that Joe Alsop had called him a man without a mission, Adlai said angrily that he had a mission to beat Republicans and that he didn't think much of crusaders anyway. On Senator Joe McCarthy, he said that Eisenhower didn't do anything about him when he was lambasting Democrats, only when he turned on Republicans. He made many extremely partisan remarks, and when I told him the type of campaign that De Sapio was conducting against him—"mentally, temperamentally and physically unfit for the Presidency"—Adlai, shocked, said that at least he had intellectual self-confidence.

I realized that he was, in fact, saying that he lacked another

250

Dorothy and her friend Alicia Patterson (behind Stevenson's hand) watch as Stevenson addresses the Democratic Convention in 1952.

kind of self-confidence. I remembered what Alicia said when they became lovers, "With Adlai, sex is not urgent."

As I was putting on my coat, he suddenly came close to me. He put his arm around my shoulder, squeezed it hard and said, "You're a goddamned provocative woman!" I blushed because in spite of the gossip, at last this was a real man and I felt quite overpowered.

Jokingly, he added, "I would like to disport myself with you at the Lido this summer." I told him I was going to a cold climate.

In the spring of 1957 after the election Dorothy had cocktails with a dispirited Adlai Stevenson at his Savoy Plaza suite. In her memo she described how she put out some rather cautious feelers about his becoming an associate publisher of the *Post,* a gesture she would make increasingly to others as time went on.

Left to right: Dorothy Schiff, Blanche Helson (Mrs. Henry Helson), Dorothy Norman and Adlai Stevenson.

When I asked him what he was going to do with the rest of his life, he said he didn't know, but did I? I said it was obvious that he had two sides to his nature, politics and newspapering. He mentioned that he was going on a long trip and then became quite pitiful, saying, "Dolly, I haven't had any fun in Europe for years and years. It's just work, work, work all the time."

Dorothy was fond of Stevenson and believed in him politically. However, she remembers that Alicia Patterson was not impressed by him at first, and she told Dorothy on their trip to Europe that he had once proposed to her, but he wasn't glamorous. He would arrive late for country weekends and would hurry in with his briefcase and scurry upstairs like "the rabbit" his friends called him. Alicia and he had their affair after he became governor of Illinois. A well-known columnist acted as cover during their governor's mansion rendezvous.

Commenting today on unsuccessful candidates in general, Dorothy talked first about Wendell Willkie and then about Adlai.

"Willkie died a little before Roosevelt of, I always thought, a broken heart. He had high hopes in 1940, and nothing went right after that. He wouldn't run for governor of New York State because Helen Reid of the *Herald Tribune* told him that would have been a comedown after having run for President, although Jim Farley told me he could have won. I think she was wrong, but he followed her advice and not mine.

I think it's possible that he did not disagree with Roosevelt as he had been a Democrat and a delegate to one of the conventions. He was picked because they felt that as a liberal Republican he might cut into the Roosevelt vote, which indeed he did. His girlfriend, Irita Van Doren, who was book editor of the *Herald Tribune*, was extremely liberal.

Anyway, he came up against what he called 'the champ,' and the people around Roosevelt were quite worried that he might make it. Wendell fell apart at the end; his voice gave way.

As for Adlai Stevenson, nothing turned out the way he had hoped. He really wanted to be a Senator from Illinois, but Paul Douglas got that. Adlai didn't want to be governor at all; he was interested chiefly in foreign policy. He spent most of his life on foreign policy in Chicago and lectured on it, was on all kinds of committees and really wanted to be Secretary of State. Then he was shoved into the Presidential nomination, which he didn't really want. It was obvious to him Ike was going to win, I'm sure. We thought Stevenson had a chance; he was sort of the liberals' god. He was much more sophisticated than Gene McCarthy; he belonged to my world, I suppose.

When he got the UN, which I think he loved, he couldn't get anywhere; he had to do what the President wanted, which wasn't what he wanted. He was very ineffective. I think the UN should have been a good spot for him, but I think he thought it was rather a bore, with all the entertaining that had to be done for all the delegates. He wasn't good at that sort of thing, although he appeared to be a marvelous host and all that. I don't think he ever knew what he wanted. He liked to write and was a really good speech writer. But he was not one who could communicate with unsophisticated people.

I don't think Adlai was ever happy; he was fundamentally a very discontented man—discontented with himself—and no matter how much adulation he got from the people he admired, he still lacked self-confidence. That was a neurotic thing, which made him fascinating to people like me. When he died, I was appalled. I thought, do I want to live in a world without Adlai Stevenson, his wit and brilliance and inefficiency and so forth? But the next day I had forgotten. Because the show must go on."

Dorothy's interest in and importance to the Democratic Party often brought her together with Eleanor Roosevelt, and her contacts were reinforced when Mrs. Roosevelt became a *Post* columnist in 1957 and she and Dorothy met often at dinners. As time went on, Dorothy admired her more as a person than as the

Dorothy with Eleanor Roosevelt.

writer whose syndicate she was paying $35 to for columns; she had been hurt by not being able to persuade Mrs. Roosevelt to switch her column to the *Post* until she was dropped by the competition.

One memo describing dinner at Mrs. Roosevelt's apartment in the mid-fifties gives a good view of her.

She and her constant escort, Dr. Gurewitsch, kissed each other warmly. He is recently divorced, had gone to school in Switzerland and remains silent most of the time. When prodded, he will talk of his own field, neurology, but has told me that he is lately more interested in psychiatric rehabilitation than the physical.

He is disdainful of psychiatrists who believe in deep therapy, saying they were interested only in eggheads and people with money. Mrs. Roosevelt told me that Dr. Kubie, who had been her constant guest at Hyde Park, had been teaching her about psychoanalysis. Apparently, she did not like what he told her, because she has dropped him cold. Probably she didn't want to recognize her relationship to her father.

This evening she had on a steel blue brocade dinner dress, obviously made by her dressmaker. Its neckline started out to be square, then had a terrific dip, going too low on one breast. After dinner, she told me she wanted to read the Brussels sprouts story. It was a privately printed book by Mrs. Kermit Roosevelt, the first copy of which was sent to Lady Churchill and the second to Mrs. Roosevelt. It described a White House dinner party at which FDR complained to the Churchills about English cooking. He went into Brussels sprouts, claiming they should never be boiled and that they were an American national dish. Mrs. Churchill later accosted Ambassador [John] Winant in London about Brussels sprouts, which Winant [another suicide] described as a near international incident.

The story wound up with FDR's standard line, "Don't you love it?" Mrs. Roosevelt turned to me and said, "You were with him so much; isn't this typical—just the way he always talked? And the 'Don't you love it?' at the end. . . . Do you remember that he always ended his stories that way?"

She is a very shy person and is afraid of showing any kind of emotional involvement with people, concentrating on their good works and their policies rather than on anything more personal. Yet she is a person of extremely strong feeling, and it must be hard for her to sublimate all this into her work, which

she tries to keep as impersonal as possible. Perhaps this is why
people think her column is dull.

She seems to have forgotten her irritation and unhappiness
with FDR. She speaks of him as a hero now, anxious to return
to the old days and even to me. Perhaps, after the pasha is dead,
the number one wife and the concubines enjoy reminiscing
about him.

One of the friends Dorothy saw a good deal of through this period was Alicia Patterson, editor of *Newsday* (her husband, Harry Guggenheim, was publisher). She and Dorothy had a long
shoptalk at the 1959 spring convention of the American Society
of Newspaper Editors. During it the editor of *Newsday* made
some interesting comments to the publisher of the *Post*. One that
amused Dorothy was Alicia's abhorrence of monopoly situations
in their field, in spite of the fact that *Newsday* had become the
next thing to it on Long Island. It was doing so well, in fact, that
overtures from the *Daily News* and the *Herald Tribune* had been
turned down.

"Her editorial writers emphasized local issues, seeing
themselves as the watchdogs of Long Island, and hated
the city, referring to us as 'slum bums.' Alicia mentioned
that the influence of newspapers is overrated, and when I
told her that we might start a drive to reclaim *Post* readers
who had moved to Long Island, she didn't seem too worried. But she suggested we think about Westchester,
where the local papers are weak.

Alicia wanted to work with me once and suggested
buying a Washington tabloid. I didn't want to, nor did
her husband and *Newsday*'s majority owner, Harry Guggenheim, who didn't approve of the *Post*. At that time the
antitrust laws were different, and we could have merged.
She had forty-nine percent of *Newsday*, which she had
founded to show her father she could do it and was
qualified to inherit his New York *News* (which I once
tried to buy). Harry told me he kept control because he
knew she would leave him if she had that additional two
percent. She was great at asking for help from people,
and I wish I were. I don't know why asking for help is
impossible for me."

With the paper taking so much of her time and politics absorbing even more, Dorothy found she had to give up her column. She abandoned it in 1958 after a gubernatorial election which still has some political leaders outraged and others bemused. Five days before the gubernatorial election in which incumbent Averell Harriman was being challenged by Nelson Rockefeller, the *Post* endorsed Governor Harriman for reelection, but the afternoon before election day Dorothy had the final edition front page pulled and remade to reflect her endorsement of Rockefeller. She repudiated Harriman because she felt his claim that Rockefeller was pro-Arab and anti-Israel was unjust.

On October 31 Harriman had charged on Barry Gray's WMCA show that Rockefeller was a White House adviser on foreign affairs in 1954, "when the first appeasement of President Nasser of Egypt took place," and that "big business oil interests" influenced the change of American Middle East policy from support of Israel to neutrality.

The switch brought joy to the Rockefeller forces, who collected available copies of the edition to put where they would do the most good. Rockefeller credits Dorothy with his substantial victory, and in the Harriman camp, feelings ran high.

The day after the election, the *Post* ran a story in which the Liberal Party's vice-chairman and Dorothy's friend of years, David Dubinsky, attacked her switch.

"This so-called liberal paper," Dubinsky said, "had no opinion five days before the election and yet, five minutes before its last edition (on Monday), a decision was made, not by the editor, but by the publisher because of her power and position."

Dorothy Schiff made this comment upon hearing of the Dubinsky statement:

"Election night was a tough night for a lot of people, including the leaders of the Liberal Party. On Friday, I shall discuss the *Post*'s position in the election."

This she did on November 7, but it was neither said lightly nor written easily.

Nelson Rockefeller had a wonderful bipartisan reputation as a man of honor, integrity and selfless devotion to helping the

Dorothy with Nelson Rockefeller.

advancement of the aspirations of mankind all over the world. The only thing wrong with him was his membership in the Republican Party. But, in various ways, Nelson had been making it clear, before and during the campaign, that he was not in sympathy with major policies of his party.

Averell Harriman also, for a long time, had had a fine record. His views had been typical of those of the liberal Northern wing of the Democratic Party. He had been a good governor of New York State. But, probably under Truman's tutelage, he had bowed to the city machine more often and more abjectly than any Democratic governor in our time.

The *Post* might well have endorsed Nelson Rockefeller instead of Averell Harriman had it not been for the disappointing breakfast-with-Nixon incident. To us, Nixonism has replaced McCarthyism as the greatest threat to the prestige of our nation today.

I spent a weekend of soul-searching. Overwhelmed, for inspiration I looked at the large portrait of my forceful, outspoken grandfather, Jacob H. Schiff, hanging opposite my desk. I was sure I knew what he would have done. No one had dared or cared to refute Harriman's unfair insinuation that Rockefeller was hostile to Israel. As the deadline arrived, I stopped the presses and tried to correct what seemed a shocking injustice done to a dedicated humanitarian.

Dorothy says that she still thinks her decision was right, but that her mistake was in waiting so long before making it. More than 400 letters came in, outrage being expressed on behalf of both candidates, but the one that threw her was from Rose Schneiderman, a fiery labor leader she had long known.

"She wrote that it wasn't worthy of me," Dorothy says. "And that hurt. Later I found out not only ideology but perhaps patronage was involved; a favorite nephew worked in the Harriman administration."

Dorothy says that her column "was the most satisfying thing I've ever done and I'd like to get back to it someday; in the meantime, I have my needlepoint." She continued to make appearances at political gatherings, however, and without the column, she was freer to take strong stands when she felt them justified, as this May, 1960, memo makes clear:

Yesterday afternoon I went to a reception for Senator John F. Kennedy at Gracie Mansion. I was introduced to Representative [Charles] Buckley [Democratic leader in the Bronx], who was standing with Dick Lee, the political reporter of the *Daily News*. I asked Representative Buckley what the Democratic Convention was going to do. He said he had no idea but would like to know what the *Post* was going to do.

I said I wished I knew, and Dick Lee said, "They'll support Khrushchev, of course."

I reported this to our business manager this morning, saying that I had no wish to remain in the Publishers' Association in partnership with the *Daily News*. He suggested that I call F. M. Flynn, publisher of the *Daily News*, and ask for an apology from Lee.

I had a brief telephone conversation with Flynn and asked him if this reflected the opinion of Lee's superiors. Flynn assured me that it did not, saying they didn't agree with us but would fight to the death our right to state our opinion. He tried to find out, tactfully, whether Lee had been drinking. I told him that I thought Lee was sober, although I had seen him many times when he was not.

I have decided to let the matter rest because I feel sure that
Lee will be reprimanded by his superiors.

Joseph P. Kennedy very much wanted the backing of the *Post*
for his son John's Presidential candidacy. The endorsement
shouldn't have been a problem for Joe Kennedy; to him its publisher was Dolly, a friend since the twenties in Palm Beach. And
she liked the Kennedy boys. But . . . she wanted to do it in her
own time. This she could afford to do, and it was exactly what
she did do. So Joe Kennedy had to remember that patience is a
virtue—and he could use some virtue in the eyes of many.

There were some hard choices here for Dorothy, among them
Adlai Stevenson, but once John Fitzgerald Kennedy had the
nomination (a victory which wasn't the pushover Joe Kennedy
felt he had a right to expect), Dorothy's problems were simpler.
Of JFK she says, "Unlike many liberals, I was never really
against him; I didn't know him well. When I saw him at a party,
I told Gore Vidal I had never seen such narrow hips. Ever since,
Gore calls it a sex line. But I didn't mean it that way."

Despite her vote for Rockefeller for governor in 1958, it was
almost inconceivable that she or the *Post* would endorse the
Richard Milhous Nixon Presidential candidacy in 1960. But
Dorothy can be more independent than her independent paper.
And so the Kennedys continued their soft sell, an example of
which was the candidate's visit to Dorothy's office in mid-Octo-
ber.

We talked for three-quarters of an hour, during which he said
that, as to Quemoy and Matsu, he guessed he had better make it
clear that he didn't intend to make a present of those rocks to
the Chinese and that, anyway, nobody knew where they were.

He did ask for the *Post*'s support, and I told him frankly that,
although we had planned to come out for him, after the second
Nixon debate I was concerned about the militaristic approach
and decided to wait for the third debate. When I asked him
whether he minded my being brutally frank, he said no, he was
used to it (he does not respond to personal remarks).

He talked about the newspaper industry, saying that our
strikes were not a matter for government intervention and that
he was opposed to compulsory arbitration. He said with some
passion that although he was officially supported by labor, they

hadn't contributed to his campaign, and he added that he
thought the government should pay for political campaigns. I
brought up his father's contributions, saying I supposed his father couldn't pay for the whole campaign. He agreed and said
that his father had been very helpful during the primaries, but
not now.

I mentioned to him that we had some Negro readers, and I
thought the more honest and least opportunistic among them
inclined toward Nixon. This led us into Lyndon Johnson, who,
I told JFK, I had heard had asked for the Veep nomination.
Kennedy said absolutely not; that there were two reasons why
he asked Johnson to be his running mate: One, he didn't think
he would accept, and two, he thought that, if he did accept, he
would be better as Vice President than as a disgruntled, frustrated Majority Leader. He said he was a very peculiar and
difficult guy, torn in five different directions. Obviously he
hates him.

On being asked who his Secretary of State would be, he hesitated. I said, "Adlai Stevenson?" He looked terribly pained,
and I realized that he was reluctant to lie. I said that most of my
friends and our readers were counting on Stevenson, but I
could understand if he did not appoint him Secretary of State
but sent him instead to the UN. He looked extremely relieved
and said that that was exactly what he would do.

On political debates, I asked whether they were not a great
strain, and he said yes, that he started off with a minute and a
half, and then Nixon had several minutes in which to tell five
lies. I told him that I knew Democrats who didn't like the Kennedy family and that I needn't repeat the things being said
about his father.

He became very defensive, saying that he (Joe) was not a politically minded man, he liked people. He liked Justice Bill
Douglas—they had been out together—and Joe McCarthy, because he was an Irishman. He doesn't like Adlai Stevenson, has
never liked him and thinks he is "an old lady." He said, "My
father would be for me if I were running as head of the Communist Party."

I told him I thought Jackie was very good on *Person to Person*. He said that she was much better than in personal interviews. He was utterly cold in his remarks about her, and I had a
feeling he had very little interest in her except as she affected
his campaign.

It is hard to figure what are Kennedy's convictions. He

seemed much more conservative than he has appeared to be during the campaign, at least on domestic issues. His tone toward labor leaders was far from friendly. I thought of the Wechsler phrase for him, "lone wolf." In his favor, I would say that besides being very good-looking, he is extraordinarily frank, even where it might hurt him. He never once used the phrase "off the record," which reminded me of Roosevelt, who trusted the people he talked to.

In December after Dorothy and the *Post* had endorsed JFK and the election was won, she was taken to dinner at La Caravelle by Joseph P. Kennedy.

Joe, quite changed, looked his age. He has retained his figure but seemed depressed and nervous. He ordered tomato juice and didn't drink a drop, which wasn't much fun for me.

He talked about how appalled Jack had been that topflight newspapermen had to stand in the pouring rain in the street all day outside his house. The tremendous Secret Service protection gave him absolutely no privacy, and he said he didn't think Jack had realized what it would be like to be President.

Joe did nothing in President Roosevelt's 1944 campaign because he didn't believe he should run—that FDR was sick and "didn't know what he was talking about" most of the time. The President told him to go on working to keep America out of the war when Joe returned from England, but at the same time was telling the British the opposite. Joe said he didn't like that.

On Bernie Baruch, he mentioned that FDR often said that he could have Baruch "any time he allowed him to put his feet under his dining-room table." Joe said that Herbert Hoover knew more about government than anyone else in the country, but nothing about people. He said FDR knew nothing about government, but a great deal about people.

Twice when Joe was present at dinner with Winston Churchill, he said, Randolph Churchill had been so rude and behaved so badly that Churchill left the table crying.

Joe doesn't seem to care anymore about money, women or anything else except his children and grandchildren. He said he could lose a million dollars in the stock market and not turn a hair, but if the slightest thing was wrong with one of his children, he went into a tailspin. All within eighteen months, Joe, Junior, was lost, his son-in-law Billy died and his daughter Kathy was killed in a plane accident, and he pretty much cracked up. When he said he has tried about twenty-five times to read a book Jack wrote about Joe, I thought he was going to cry at the table.

He kept referring to my father and how he must be turning over in his grave because I am a liberal publisher. He added that my father must have told me many times that most of the men who make a lot of money are stupid; no brains are required to make money, he said. I don't know whether or not he thought he was the exception.

Dorothy is ambivalent about Joe Kennedy; she respects his success and is loyal to the memory of their friendship, yet she questions the means of his rise and a certain ruthlessness she felt in him to the end. His and his wife's social ambitions she finds amusing—Rose's need for social acceptance by the in crowd, as well as Joe's way of bypassing the climbing process by getting himself appointed to the Court of St. James's.

"I don't think Joe cared about the ambassadorship; it was Rose," she says. "As to the social people, they were all Republicans and wouldn't have advanced his sons politically anyway. I don't know about his integrity, but he was a good friend—rather like Max in a way. They became great friends, and Joan and Teddy spent their honeymoon at Max's place in the Caribbean. She thought he was dreadful."

Dorothy's reservations about Joe Kennedy do not extend to his sons, whom she has known well. The President was the first she became close to, and as an admirer of his success, political and personal, she became increasingly curious about the man he vanquished, Richard Nixon. What was he up to, besides licking his wounds?

Her interest went back to Nixon's successful Senatorial campaign in California, in which he smeared Helen Gahagan Douglas. ("I would have found Hitler interesting, too.") An old friend of Dorothy's and a financial backer of Nixon, producer Sam Goldwyn, invited Nixon to his Hollywood studio for lunch with her. It was September, 1961, and the day was sunny.

Nixon's hair is blacker, curlier and oilier than I expected. He looked suntanned and happy, but began to sag after two hours of questioning. My attitude was deliberately friendly because I believe in the fly-catching-honey maxim.

I asked him what had made him suspicious of Hiss. He said that after Chambers had accused Hiss, Hiss had insisted on testifying and was so convincing and articulate the members of the committee believed him, but Nixon thought he was too glib. Hiss' denial of the charges against him could not be proved or disproved, but his avowal that he had never met Chambers was subject to proof. He said Hiss was like a lawyer who overstated his case and that he needn't have gone so far. Had he said that he had met Chambers once or twice and knew him slightly, no case would have followed.

DS: What do you think of Senator Goldwater?

RN: He has an attractive personality but lacks depth. He hasn't studied the issues and is superficial.

DS: What do you think of Rockefeller?

RN: He has an attractive personality, too, but he also lacks depth. He is a task-force man. He has to get down to studying the issues himself.

DS: You are in the middle between the two, aren't you?

RN: Yes.

He seemed obsessed with the idea of money, saying that there was no money in government and that he had come to the conclusion that men worked only for money, sometimes power. As a great anti-Marxist he seems to believe that a vast majority of men are governed by materialism. He favors cutting taxes for $100,000 men, saying they are the most valuable people in America. He added that there were only 1,000 topflight people in the country, then amended it to maybe 10,000.

He expressed contempt for university and foundation people, saying they should be made use of in government but only in an advisory capacity. He seemed to be referring especially to Rusk and called such people "marshmallow people." He pointed to Frederick the First, who said that the way to lose a province was to send a professor to administer it.

DS: What about FDR? He had the Brain Trust.

RN (almost nostalgically): He was a great leader.

DS: Why do you think you are hated by most intellectuals?

RN: There are certain enemies that it is good to have. Most intellectuals have socialist backgrounds.

DS Why is it that you want public life, while private life seems much more pleasant and lucrative?

RN: (emphatically): For a creative person, private practice is unsatisfactory. No matter how big the client, you are nothing but a messenger boy, representing his interests.

I am convinced that Nixon was once a New Dealer but sold

out for a higher salary when he was offered the original Republican Congressional nomination and that he has no regrets about this. He is hard, tough, austere, self-centered and is as ambitious as Hitler and Khrushchev, whom he obviously admires. For years he has grabbed at what he thinks is the main chance. A lonely man, he is tremendously impressed with the rich and powerful, but he has a contempt for socialites.

In the early sixties Dorothy made a major decision about the *Post*'s hierarchy which had the effect of involving her more directly in the news side and of separating the news operation further from the editorial. Paul Sann remembers the historic moment vividly.

"See, from '49 to '61, she had a guy who was editor in charge of the news section and also the editorial page. She decided there should be a total separation of the news and editorial operations and moved Wechsler upstairs. The story around was that I had done some plotting with her to boot Wechsler the hell out so I could be the editor. I wasn't thinking about this at all.

"Dolly asked me whether we could work together, if she moved Jimmy upstairs and made him a columnist. I was shocked by it, but, you know, I didn't fall off a chair. It was decided right then and there in two and a half minutes; there wasn't any discussion of money or anything else."

Jimmy Wechsler speaks with a certain amount of tension. "I remember Dolly saying—I guess this was a very gracious way of putting it—'I'm tired of hearing about James Reston and other columnists, and I think you ought to be a columnist and have the editorial page.' We never really argued the merits of whether I should or not, and I have very ambivalent feelings about it. I sort of enjoyed the fun and games of the city room.

"On the other hand, I have to say quite honestly in retrospect that, in terms of writing a column, she has total tolerance about what is sometimes known as Wechsler's follies. I don't mean it wasn't a difficult period of transition, but I never felt I was out of things. Paul and I have never really gotten along since. We barely see each other, but when we do, we always have sort of a strangely warm relationship. When the 'revolution' happened in '49, I think that Paul thought that I was going to be editorial writer and he was going to be editor. He very genuinely differed with my view of the news columns; I was keeping what he regarded as lively stuff out of the paper because of what he would call cause stories. In the end that view prevailed with her.

"I don't think Dolly's was a frivolous decision. What she really meant was, 'Look, you've had twelve years of this. I'd like to run this paper now.' She's obviously far more involved in the daily news operation, as well as business, than she was then. The distance between the editorial and the news side is, I think, one of the honest points of difference between Dolly and myself. I think it relates partly to her view that Roosevelt ran an effective government because he kept his executives away from each other.

"I used to urge her to allow the advertising manager and me to have discussions in front of her about the allocation of news and advertising space. Her rejection of that—and I'm mostly reading her mind—was based on two things; she really felt that she could deal better unilaterally with her executives than having bull sessions, and I don't think she likes to have to preside over confrontations.

"I think there was also a Rooseveltian sense that there are times when you tell one Cabinet officer what a great job he's doing, and at the same time you let the other one cut the news space."

A third view of this shake-up is Dorothy's own.

"People came to me saying I had to make a change. Circulation was slipping, which was blamed on too much editorializing in the news, and morale was low. When I came back from vacation, Jimmy went for his, and the editorial writer couldn't write editorials.

Jimmy is right about my not liking confrontation scenes; I didn't and don't, having seen quite enough of that with my parents. The advertising manager is not the one who sets the size of the paper, regardless of Jimmy's thinking so; the publisher and business manager are. Generally, there is a sixty-forty ratio of advertising to news linage, but we've never been up there, alas.

Of course, the idea that advertising isn't of value in itself is absurd. The consumer is overwhelmingly a woman—she buys for the family, except the car, the color of which she chooses, and we are here to serve the public, which includes the consumer. Even on welfare, she is the consumer; she loves most ads, and so do I. But I turn down or drop ads if I find out they're misleading. The other papers take practically everything these days."

Dorothy disagrees with Jimmy's comparison of her and FDR's way with executives ("to identify me with him is at least a compliment"). Not even FDR, great optimist as he was, would have predicted her success or her executive efficiency. And she needed all her strength when, shortly before Christmas, 1962, she realized she was about to face the most critical test of her career. It was one that many people were convinced would mean the end of the *Post*, and well it might have. The newspaper strike, which began December 7, lasted for 114 days, and shut down the New York *Times*, the *News*, the *Journal-American* and the *World Telegram and Sun*, all members of the Publishers' Association. Other members, the *Post*, the *Herald Tribune*, and the *Mirror* suspended publication to keep a united front. The issue was the usual—wages and hours.

The *Post* was not a giant among the papers involved, and Dorothy was looked down on by other members—particularly the *News*—because she represented too liberal a newspaper. She was tolerated, but it was clear early in the strike that major association decisions were going to be made with the *Post* excluded. It was also clear that her protests would receive polite hearings—too polite for this lady—and that that was all the effect they would have.

In an effort to simplify her life, the better to concentrate on the negotiations, Dorothy took a suite at the Hotel Pierre, which didn't stop her from going to a Chinese restaurant with a lower-echelon adviser of the *Herald Tribune*. Dorothy was gently reprimanded for doing so by Walter Thayer, the *Trib*'s main force and Whitney's man of business and companion, who explained that the boys just didn't operate that way. From then on she dined only with publishers.

Dorothy liked the *Times*' Orvil Dryfoos, saying that although he was just a son-in-law, "he was a very nice person and good at getting sandwiches." As the only woman in the association Dorothy held her end up bravely, however much she was seething underneath. Hanging over her was the threat that all she had worked for in the last twenty years might be about to disappear, and with it, those hundreds of jobs.

"She was hard as a rock in that time," Paul Sann remembers,

"maybe stronger than some of the rest of us. She was cool, and there was no real desperation that I was aware of. But there was some brooding about how awful it was not to be publishing.

"Her public image was something else. On TV and radio it had the sound of the paper folding tomorrow morning—not shrill, but menacing."

The projection of disaster as to what would happen was not insincere on Dorothy's part; for all her bravery before her staff, she was very, very scared. Bernard Baruch called her after the strike had been on for a while to tell her he had seen her on TV, as Dorothy has recorded in one of her briefer memos.

> BB: I saw you on television [this was at the beginning of the strike]. You are a brave girl and made a good fight. Don't give up the ship. You have had a tough life, Dolly, and I don't mean only in business.
> DS: How did I look on television?
> BB: You looked so sad you wrung my heart.
> DS: How are you?
> BB: At ninety-three I can only look and admire you on television.

Dorothy had cut her teeth on the seventeen-day strike in 1958 but she hadn't counted on anything like this. Increasingly, she felt excluded from the association's decision-making and, as a loner, suspected she might be better off out of it altogether. In the strike's third week, however, she was persuaded not to withdraw by those who convinced her it was to the interest of all to have her stay in the trade association.

So great was the city's loss caused by the strike that on the fiftieth day Mayor Wagner entered the negotiations. He had been persuaded to do so by Ted Kheel, who has been called the most powerful man in New York. For all that, this heavyset, reassuring man of quick mind and warm eye is careful not to make his influence obvious.

He recalls: "The strike had been on for about fifty days when Bob Wagner asked me to join a meeting of the publishers in City Hall on a Monday; he sent out this invitation on Friday, and there was great consternation.

"The publishers were very fearful that this was going to be a political effort on his part to appease labor. I did all the ground-

Dorothy, Ted Kheel and Bertram Powers.

work on the mediation until the strike ended; still, his presence was an important presence.

"Dorothy appeared before me and insisted that the other publishers be there; we were feeling each other out. They were fearful that this was a trap to get them to give more for Bert Powers' [president of Typographical Union 6] benefit, and I was trying to establish my credentials as a professional mediator. After one week I had a confrontation with Amory Bradford [vice-president] of the *Times.* I said, 'If that's your position, forget it. I'll step out,' and I left. Orvil Dryfoos came up to my home and pleaded with me not to step out and not to be offended by Bradford.

"Now, the thing that intrigued me is the word I got that Dorothy wanted to be close to the situation because I was going to be the next candidate for Senator."

Dorothy says her interest in Ted Kheel had nothing to do with his political ambitions, nor did she know he had any. "I had discovered the hard way, and almost too late, that Ted was Mr. Labor in New York City. I saw then that he was the only man who could settle the strike, which is what he did. He was a true professional, even if he did throw me at one meeting by admiring my Chanel suit."

"The other fellows," Ted continues, "were thinking, will they get a good settlement or a bad settlement? Dorothy was saying, 'Oh, this is going to make him the next Senator, so I better be involved in it!' Which is so typically Dorothy. It's one of the things that makes her very intriguing and actually helps her as a bargainer. I don't know at times whether it's a technique or just the way her mind operates normally.

"When there's a labor dispute, it is handled routinely by her staff, who are very devoted to her. They're pretty competent, professionally, and they always want to keep Dorothy out because they're fearful that she may say the wrong thing or do the wrong thing. Then, at the most inappropriate moment, she'll step in. The fear of a professional is that if your principal comes in, it will show anxiety and weakness.

"She will so completely mystify the other side by talking about things that are totally unrelated to the discussions, they think, 'Ah, we've got her on the run now. She's worried and that's why she's coming to the negotiations herself.' But she'll say, 'Well, do you think the Liberal Party is really going to do this, that or the other thing.' It turns out to be a good bargaining ploy, you know?

"The negotiations shook down to three people on the employers' side: Jack Flynn of the *News*, Walter Thayer of the *Trib* and, to a lesser degree, Orvil Dryfoos. Dorothy was completely shut out in those negotiations."

This was in the third month of the strike. Dorothy had moved that her labor lawyer be appointed to the small negotiating committee and, on being voted down, was furious.

"It was like a fit of pique, I see now. They had gone through the motions of including me at a publishers' meeting the previous night at Gracie Mansion which got nowhere, but this was too much. I stood up, took my handbag and announced that not only was I resigning from the association, but I was going to call Bert Powers at once. Actually, I didn't even have time; Orvil beseeched me to ask what Bert would settle for before telling him my decision, which, of course, had been the name of the game.

Bert and I met at the Pierre for lunch, but the kitchen was on strike, so we had to go elsewhere. When I told him I was resuming publication, he was horrified; he said he'd order the men not to come back. I argued and argued with him and finally won him over. I might not have, if his refusal to go along hadn't been due to his fear that we'd lose our advertisers. He was afraid that they would punish us and didn't want the responsibility for it; at least, I *think* that was it.

We were back on the street March 4 with a lot of Easter linage, but our major accounts—department store and national ones—didn't come back until the other papers resumed publication."

Powers persuaded Dorothy to hold a press conference to get the most mileage out of her break with the association but had to tell her how to go about it. Shy as she is, it wasn't easy for her, but the photograph of her, sitting at ease surrounded by reporters, doesn't give a hint of what she calls her mild panic. As for the reaction of her former fellow association members, Ted Kheel says that her agreeing to "a sort of most-favored-nation pact" with Powers, in which she agreed to pay whatever the others would, was a factor of some tension.

"Of course," Ted continued, "it wasn't the same as giving him what he wanted. The publishers were annoyed and sneered at her, Bert got some value out of it in public relations, but no real value in negotiations, and she got back to work sooner. For a little while there, her circulation was zooming.

"When Walter Thayer [*Herald Tribune*] broke with the association in 1965, it was under very questionable circumstances and a lot more divisive than Dorothy's. She had the argument she couldn't take it anymore; when you break that way, it's like being on the employees' side as a strikebreaker. With Thayer it was different; Jock Whitney had to be in a better position than Dorothy."

It wasn't easy for Dorothy to make such a major break with allies—as an original and a loner she takes loyalty very seriously—but her sense of injustice at being shut out of the negotiations, energized by her pique, made it possible. She anticipated cen-

The Post *resumes publication on March 4, 1963.*

sure; there were a lot of critics and few defenders, partly because
it looked as if she had broken ranks out of financial greed. The
feeling was that as a Schiff she could take her losses pretty much
as could Jock Whitney. The fact is that she simply wasn't, and
isn't, in that economic class. She faced the possible loss not of a
mere item in her investment portfolio, but a property of major
interest, personal and financial, to say nothing of all those jobs
that would have been lost.

Two years later there was more labor unrest to plague Dorothy and the other New York papers, and there were times when it looked as if the settlements finally reached with the unions in 1963 were not going to stick. There were slowdowns, "chapel meetings," work stoppages and mysterious mechanical break-downs with implications of sabotage. For Dorothy, while there were some advantages to being no longer in the Publishers' As-sociation, it was a little lonely. The fact that the *Herald Tribune* had now pulled out of the association after a twenty-six-day strike didn't make her feel any less so; they didn't have much in common editorially or by readership.

The *Post* was in the black, if not as much as she would have liked, but the uncertainties of the labor situation were a worry. She had been negotiating with Bert Powers over automation of the composing room, and finally permission was granted to the *Post* and *Times* to set stock market tables by computer, but pay-ment to a joint fund of an amount equal to the straight time sav-ing had to be made. This was a form of compensation for jobs lost and was a breakthrough.

In June, 1965, Dorothy rented a computer and typesetter which, as Ted Kheel explains, "is a very serious business; you have to train old people with new skills and so on. They invited me to come in as mediator, the story went all over the nation, and she became the symbol of the publisher fighting for automation against the union."

Ted says that Dorothy and he met with Bert at her apartment for days trying to work out agreements on such things as further automation, retirement and manning. (The latter comes down to the question of job protection, or how many men will watch another man work.) "Dorothy would say, 'Bert, we're both liber-als, and we have to stick together.' And he'd say, 'That's right, Dorothy, we have to stick together.' 'Now,' she'd say, 'on this computer. . . .' And he'd say, 'Dorothy—no.' We tried all sorts of things and nothing worked. Finally, she gave up on it."

Dorothy says that to the extent that there is anything enjoyable about negotiating sessions, she liked those with Powers. After she appeared with him on TV, he told her, "Never again! My mother-in-law said, 'How could you do that to that lovely little lady?' "

That winter the *Post*'s competition continued to worry Doro-thy, particularly the *World-Telegram*. It had become more readable, and she envied them their columnists and being backed by the strength of the Scripps-Howard chain. The *Journal-American,* of course, had a conservative readership the *Post* had no hope of attracting. Adding to her concern were the rumors she had been hearing for a couple of weeks of a merger of these giants, including the *Herald Tribune.* It was a threat she dreaded and knew she could do nothing about. And on March 22, 1966, it happened; the *World Journal Tribune* was announced.

As Dorothy describes her reaction to the birth of this three-headed monster, soon known as the Widget, her mask is reinforced so that she looks even more remote than usual.

"I was petrified. Here we had Jock Whitney, William Randolph Hearst, Jr., and Jack Howard teaming up in our evening field and competing with the New York *Post.* I thought, 'This is the end; this we will not survive.' I asked Walter Thayer why I had not been asked to join the combine, and he said, 'Oh, you wouldn't want any part of that; it's an impossible three-headed thing,' or words to that effect.

Well, with hindsight, I think he probably expected that it would not work. He was trying to get Jock off the hook, I suppose, so that they could all go down together. But since this was supposed to be a new paper, it seemed to me that we should have a chance to bid on the columns from the former three papers. It was the *Herald Tribune* columns that I really wanted; I knew I couldn't get the *Journal* and the *World-Telegram.* A funny thing happened; we had lost Murray Kempton to the *World-Telegram,* but they dropped him in the merger, and he came back. They had had too much reader complaint.

When I saw the first edition . . . I was overwhelmed. There were lots of features; for the women's pages it had not only Eugenia Sheppard from the *Herald Tribune,* but Suzy from the *Journal-American,* and it looked great—in fact, terrific. It had a lot of circulation, but—I wasn't sure at first—it didn't have enough advertising. I mean, the mass advertising; they had the class, of course. But it's better to have the mass than the class; it means more volume."

The typographers' president Bert Powers was also taken aback by the Widget; a lot of jobs went with that merger. He would be called the "paper killer," blame he does not take lying down. But he has praise for Dorothy. This large man with steel-rimmed glasses and watchful eyes speaks of her with a hint of Boston Irish in his voice.

"She's the only publisher with balls. As negotiator she was decisive and fair, but never meek. When she walked out of the association, I thought it was in my interest for her to resume publication. There was pressure on her to stay in, but she doesn't seduce easy. It was a real break for us, and I remember she called a meeting of her staff and said, 'I have decided we are going to publish.' Very imperial."

In order to have a crack at getting some of the better columnists from the three papers, Dorothy tried to prevent *WJT* from capturing them. She went to Washington in August, 1966, with counsel, hoping to persuade the Attorney General that the three-headed monster was a new entity and thus couldn't claim the columnists of the former individual papers, but the Justice Department took no action.

For about a year Dorothy worried about the Widget and then came to realize the *Post* could live with it after all. Her staying power didn't surprise Bert Powers, who says the paper had "a large Jewish base which she never abandoned and they didn't abandon her.

"If she had tried to duplicate the *World-Telegram,* she would have lost her readers; already they were turning to TV and the suburbs."

The *World Journal Tribune* was pulling almost 700,000 readers daily, so Dorothy was astonished to be told by a former *Trib* executive at an Associated Press luncheon in late April, 1967, "They're going to fold very soon."

Dorothy says she couldn't believe it, and she still couldn't when this *Post* story appeared May 5:

> The announcement, signed by WJT president Matt Meyer, said: "It is with a real sense of personal regret that I must tell you that the *World Journal Tribune* is permanently ceasing publication with today's issue. Your employment must terminate at that time."
>
> Later Meyer amplified the statement and attributed the decision to shut down largely to the recent wage settlement reached by the printers union with the *Daily News.*

Meyer said the WTJ publishers "have contributed over $10,000,000 to keep the paper alive," in addition to paying $7,000,000 in severance to former employees.

"The settlement with the *Daily News*, if applied to all unions, would add $10,500,000 to present payroll costs over the contract," he said. "Mr. Bertram Powers, head of Typographical Union No. 6, has stated that this will be the pattern for all papers.

"His specific language referring to the WJT was 'all they can do is pay or shut down.' Under the circumstances, it is totally impractical for the WJT to assume this increased burden."

Powers, arriving at the WJT plant to confer with the publishers, was asked to comment on Meyer's statement.

"That's to be expected," he said.

The closing, which put more than 2,500 people out of work, was a dark day for the city, always newspaper-responsive. In addition, it meant further expansion of other media, and some saw this as almost as serious a disaster.

The first act on Dorothy's part was an editorial reassuring the *Post*'s readers, as well as the columnists she hoped to get, that the management was aware of its responsibilities and (perhaps a little tactlessly) its opportunities. She, herself, was not that sanguine.

"The night it folded I went to a dinner with people involved in papers and politics, and they were all terribly excited. Someone said I was the only person there who wasn't, and it didn't seem to me I had reason to be. What I did have reason to be I was—and very much so—scared.

I was sure a paper would start up right away in the terrific vacuum in the evening field which had been created, just as I knew we had to increase production and couldn't out of our plant. Soon the *Daily News* and *Times,* even *Time* magazine, were doing surveys, making up dummies and planning. When I went to the *News* to see if we could print out of there, which we could have without interfering with their production, I was told that they'd like to think about it. Then I tried the Widget plant, which was idle, of course, and was told that it was not available. Then I tried our present building; Hearst had old presses here but the foldover was the same size as a tabloid, so it seemed a natural to rent. They were smart, though, and wouldn't. It was a chance to unload a white elephant, and I bought it, as is, for a million and a half, out of long-term accumulated profits we'd been saving for new equipment and other purposes. You see, no stock dividends have ever been paid.

Nothing had been done to the building since the twenties, so we had to get engineers—I didn't use an architect—and went to the bank for millions. I ordered new presses and a major remodeling and notified our West Street landlord; he was so glad to get rid of such a dirty tenant—ink and grease—he paid us to get out (he was stuck with a lease from the time I had sold the building).

I became increasingly nervous with all this—the huge debt I was taking on, papers threatening to start up, wondering how I would ever pull it off with our tiny staff . . . I mean there were all these big, successful men who had collapsed! And here was little me, and how was I going to cope with being the only evening paper in the largest city in the United States?

I probably wouldn't have been able to if I'd had time to really think about my problems, but I was too scared of somebody filling that void to take the time. After all, our circulation almost doubled—there were some people who just wouldn't buy the *Post,* of course—and we got more advertising, class and mass. People kept saying it was only temporary, we'd find out! Only we didn't.

My anxiety attacks became so severe I had to do something, and I knew going back to a psychiatrist wasn't it this time. Instead, I called my doctor and described my symptoms—anxiety, shaking all over, fearing I was inadequate and unable to cope with this huge situation—and he prescribed a tranquilizer, Librium. I took it for a day or so, I guess, but I was so busy I kept forgetting to. Anyway, those anxiety attacks were the scariest things that ever happened to me.

Bert Powers has always said he didn't kill that paper, and after all, it wasn't struck. They were in a precarious position, but I know what I would have done; I would have raised my price. I learned from a friend that the triumvirate weren't getting on and didn't want to stay; they faced millions of dollars in severance pay, which they could divide, and they would go down together—no single proprietor had to close down—and everybody's face was saved.

It certainly solved the problem of our getting columnists, and others, too. Clay Felker, who had been running
the Sunday New York section, was out of a job, and Jeannie Campbell arranged a meeting at her house. He came
an hour late, was in a bad mood, and I think was prepared
to hate me. For us, he had awfully big ideas, and a mutual
friend told me he's very difficult, that Clay and I
wouldn't last five minutes together. I'm not sure that's
true, but in any case, we've become good friends. Still,
it's funny to think if he had come to the *Post*, there probably wouldn't be *New York* magazine. He's done a good
job with that."

The rest of 1967 was as much concerned with construction,
engineering and financing the new *Post* building and technical
improvements as it was with publishing and editing. Dorothy
was so busy she didn't have time for politics for a while or even
wondering how soon she was going to have competition again.
It was the end of the year before she began to relax on this score.
She says about the rise and fall of the Widget:

"It's hard to account for it. I could say it was money
that killed them—they weren't as reckless as I have been.
Of course, they had huge expenses because they had to
sell all their papers late in the afternoon; the kind of readers they had wanted the stock tables. We sell our papers
throughout the day, beginning in the morning, but they
had to have an enormous number of trucks and presses
and everything.

I don't know. . . . Maybe they were just more businesslike than I—more concerned about profit. It was a
bad business deal, they thought, and they didn't know
how to make it pay. Certainly, the *Post* was a terrible
business deal and had to be made to pay. It almost didn't,
you know; but I survived.

Sometimes, this Dorothy reminds me of that Dorothy
in *The Wizard of Oz*, to whom earthquakes and terrible
things were always happening. She underwent strange
adventures, yet always seemed to come back right side
up. And I guess, maybe, that's what those big men on the
World Journal Tribune did for me; they saved me. But I
don't think they saved me on purpose, do you?"

XI

"Please don't do anything about New York State without asking me."

The sixties brought Dorothy, along with anxiety for her husband's health and concern about the continued existence of the *Post*, increasing attention from the nation's political leaders. Her memos from this time reflect the need of Presidents and Presidential aspirants to court her goodwill. For example, her visit to the White House in May, 1963. She found JFK well settled in, and the decor had been changed for the better since FDR's days, thanks to Jackie. Otherwise the house felt familiar, even if the time was not the 1930s.

He sat in his wooden rocking chair covered in white crash, with a little pillow for the small of the back, and asked me to sit at his right in one of the armchairs. I told him he was doing a good job in the South, and he said that they weren't getting any help from the press and the ministers, but were from the business community. The pressure on these men seemed to be paying off.

I said, "Economics does count then, doesn't it?"

"Yes. Marx was right to this extent."

I asked him what he was going to do after his second term and if he'd like to be a newspaper publisher. On his saying that he would, I said that I would keep the *Post* warm for him until he was ready. He said, "What would you do then?" I said, "I'll be too old." He laughed and said that if he became a newspaper publisher, "I'll be saying these 'Goddamned unions.'"

He suggested a walk in the Rose Garden, and I wondered if perhaps his back was bothering him. Indicating a small flower

Lyndon Johnson visited the Post *on October 15, 1963.*

bed, he said, "When I showed this to Ike, he said, 'We took all
that stuff out when I was here. It was too expensive.'"

I had the feeling that he regarded me as a family friend from
the old days. He was very straightforward, seeming unhurried
and not too worried about anything—it was very quiet where
we were, and the whole thing was informal. He said he liked
his job very much.

Dorothy found time for the Vice President, too, but not until
fall, when Lyndon B. Johnson came to her office.

Our contact man said he had taken LBJ to the Washington
Post, where he had been very nervous with newspapermen and
intellectuals; that, on being questioned about some trip he had
taken to the Far East, he brought out a lot of photographs and
passed them around and discussed them all through lunch,
thus evading any really serious conversation. The contact said
that Johnson, under the influence of President Kennedy, whom
he had grown to admire, was beginning to read for the first time
in his life.

Before he arrived, security agents had been through the plant and instructed our representatives as to what he drank, which is Cutty Sark with soda. We were told that he liked to have the soda bottle beside him with a tall glass so that he could keep sipping it and refilling the glass with soda. We were instructed to provide Sanka and not regular coffee.

He asked for the bathroom when he arrived and disappeared for quite a long time, a guard at the door. When he was ushered into my office, he looked extremely pale, sat on the sofa and spoke inaudibly with his hand in front of his mouth. Some thought he might have had a drink or two, which would have been possible for him with a flask. He drank scarcely any of the drink offered.

As questions were asked at the lunch table, a recording machine was set up next to it by one of his people. I was shocked and assumed that permission had been granted but that I had not been told through oversight. It had not been.

He said he had been to Vietnam and, when asked what he thought of the Diem brothers, compared them to the Kennedy brothers, with Bobby as Mr. Nhu. He said twice that JFK was a man of enormous self-discipline, had a terribly difficult job and that at Cabinet meetings, he (Johnson) always hoped he wouldn't be the first one asked his opinion.

He seemed really to admire JFK—almost in awe of him. He mentioned a rich custard dessert that had been served at some dinner and that JFK took a good-sized portion. Seeing this, LBJ, who is supposed to be careful of his weight, took a large portion, too. JFK did not eat his but only toyed with it, but LBJ couldn't resist cleaning his plate.

When Lyndon Johnson was Vice President-elect, he told Dorothy that as a young Congressman he had been introduced to her by Helen Gahagan Douglas on FDR's 1940 campaign train. When he tried to engage her in conversation, he said, she had paid absolutely no attention to him. Dorothy was amused but apologized, explaining that she "had other fish to fry." She does vaguely remember "a tall, lanky guy and that someone said he was Congressman Johnson."

The day he came for the *Post* sandwich, she liked the way he shook hands with everyone, saying, "I'm Lyndon B. Johnson," when she took him through the plant. It had made him happy, Dorothy thought, and in his new self-confidence he told her that

Lady Bird was overworked, seeing "people no one else would have anything to do with" when they came to Washington.

Five weeks later Johnson was flying east on Air Force One as escort to JFK's body and widow. The thought of Lyndon Johnson occupying the Oval Office took some getting used to for Dorothy, and she was surprised by a call from him the week after the assassination. Her memo recalls:

> The President (in a Texas accent) said: "I've been thinking of you all evening, honey. I have been reading that wonderful newspaper of yours with the stories about Lyndon Johnson, his life, his family, his ways, and I think it's just wonderful."
>
> He said he had had a very busy day, but he guessed that all my days are busy. I said, "Not as busy as yours, Mr. President." I don't think he is used to being called that. I said I had been thinking of him, too, and of his wife.
>
> He said, "She is right here and she wants to talk to you, too." Lady Bird came on and said she was trying and she would do the best she could. I said I was sure she would do extremely well, as she has always done.
>
> When I was about to say good-night she said, "Wait a minute. Lyndon wants to talk to you again." He said, "I would like you to come down and see me next week."
>
> I said that I didn't have my calendar beside me and I certainly would try to. He said, "I will call you next week, and I want to thank you for that wonderful sandwich at lunch."
>
> I muttered something about little did we know, then said, "Please don't do anything about New York State without asking me." LBJ said he would not.

Less than three weeks later Dorothy's intercom buzzed just before lunch and she was told there was a woman on the phone with a message from the President. Dorothy says she thought it was probably "a nut," but it turned out to be Liz Carpenter, Lady Bird's press secretary, asking Dorothy to meet the President in Adlai Stevenson's suite at the Waldorf at two thirty.

> There were a dozen or so people standing around a large hall. Liz Carpenter came up to me and asked if she could take my coat; then Adlai Stevenson came over and shook hands, and Marietta Tree was standing there but didn't speak to me. All looked awfully serious and were not talking to each other.

A woman emerged from the group and said, "I am Lady Bird Johnson," and we shook hands. I had met her a number of times before; she always says this. She is small and slender, with dark hair and very white skin.

I was immediately ushered into a reception room and the President came right in, kissed me and called me Dorothy. We sat down, and he hitched his chair up to me so that we were knee to knee, and I could smell his breath, which was odorless; he obviously hadn't had a drink before lunch.

He started out by saying that he reads our paper every day and appreciates so much what I and Jimmy Wechsler had done for him. He said he can't say this publicly, but he has no hope that the civil rights bill will come out of Congress through petition. He said he wanted to wipe out pockets of poverty that still existed in parts of the country.

I asked him about the Vice Presidential candidate. He said he wasn't even thinking about it during the thirty-day mourning period but that he noticed various candidates had been on the air over the weekend. I remembered only Sargent Shriver, and he pointed to the hall: "Adlai wants it, too."

I said how would McNamara be for Vice President? He said he couldn't imagine being President without McNamara as Secretary of Defense; he is simply wonderful. He said, "We call him the 'Staycomb boy.'" When I looked blank, he explained that his hair was so slick because he used Staycomb on it. He said he was sending him out to Vietnam because things are in a mess out there.

Lady Bird joined us, and we moved to the other side of the room. She looked at a Peale portrait of Thomas Jefferson hanging on the opposite wall and said she thought there was another one like it in the Yellow Room at the White House. I wondered whether she was trying to be like Jackie.

The President told her about having lunch at the *Post*. I spoke of the sandwich and that I had been worried that he hadn't had enough to eat, since he had gobbled it up very fast. She said he always gobbled and was on a diet; a sandwich was plenty.

The President asked me if I had seen anything of what I understood to be "Ellen Douglas." I looked blank and said, "Mrs. Lewis Douglas?"

He said, "No. Helen Gahagan Douglas."

I said I hadn't seen her recently. He said that he wanted to find a place for Helen in the administration and got quite violent about Nixon, saying that he had been so vile to Helen when she ran for the Senate in California. He said that Sam Rayburn had urged him to run for the Vice Presidency because Nixon had called Rayburn and Truman traitors and "Sam didn't want *that man* to win." That was why he was finally persuaded to run.

I told him that everybody was for LBJ, even my Republican friends. He said, "They won't be in a few weeks." I think he is worried about Rockefeller, although his name wasn't mentioned; LBJ said he had no idea who the Republican nominee would be. (It was Goldwater.)

LBJ was telling about all the things he was doing, had been getting about five hours' sleep, and needed more than that. He gets in a swim every day. He was up until 1:30 every night and got up at 6 or 6:30 A.M. I asked him if he rested during the day. (People who have had heart attacks usually are ordered to do so.) He said no, that he feels a bit let-down about this time of day, after lunch.

DS: Can you sleep on the plane?

LBJ: No.

A little earlier a small man, introduced as someone [Jack] Valenti, came in. The President said, "Get the name straight. It's Valenti, not Valachi."

When I went out into the hall, Adlai and the others were still standing around. Adlai asked me if I knew where to get my coat and took me into his bedroom. I went down in the elevator with Marietta Tree and two men, one of whom was a Congressman whose name I don't remember and the other was Senator Fulbright. When he heard my name, he said, "Are you the New York *Post*?" I said I guessed I was. I found him delightful.

In talking to Lady Bird, she seemed quite different from what she is in public. The Southern accent isn't nearly as strong. She seems quiet and laughs rather ruefully—very, very modest, but sophisticated and I liked her very much.

LBJ seems unsophisticated and tried harder than he needed to, never stops selling.

Dorothy wasn't surprised by an LBJ ranch call on January 1, since she assumed he was following what she calls "Jim Farley's policy of calling people to wish them a Happy New Year." The President did just that, even though Dorothy got ahead of him. Her memo explains he hoped for "a New Year's gift."

He wanted me to go to Liberia "as a person of Presidential caliber to represent him." He was sorry he couldn't go himself, but he had to work on our "archaic budget to find some more money to help people."

Appalled at the thought of taking off for Liberia suddenly without clothes, hairdresser or someone to accompany me, I said, "Well, thank you very much, Mr. President. I am afraid I can't do this."

He then pressed me very hard.

Squirming, I said, "I am going to be very frank with you. I don't like to fly."

He softened immediately and said in that case, he understood.

DS: Of course, I do fly occasionally, but I don't like it at all. What would I have to do?

LBJ: Well, you just speak for me. You would sit in the Presidential box and you would report back to me how the people are getting along and what the conditions are there. You would be my personal representative.

DS: What is the occasion?

He didn't seem terribly clear himself and said something about a 100th anniversary. Then he said, "Why don't you think it over and call me if you decide to go?"

DS: Well, I think I had better be definite. Thanks so much for considering me. It's a great honor and I certainly don't like to say no to you.

LBJ: Thanks for that meager little sandwich you gave me.

DS: I'm getting an inferiority complex about that sandwich.

LBJ: I will be glad to give you something better than that when you come to see me.

DS: I bet you will.

In just a month, Dorothy chatted with him at a dinner of Mary Lasker's in New York, during which he said jokingly that he hadn't brought Lady Bird because he knew he was going to see Dorothy and that they had been mentioned in a gossip column. When Dorothy looked blank, LBJ said, "Don't you read the papers?"

"Only the advertising," she said as she walked away. Then she remembered that this was the President.

In mid-August Dorothy interrupted her stay at an East Hampton inn to attend a White House dinner for U Thant. Her memo shows she wasn't happy about it or about "the tremendous effort of all the necessary preparations."

I came to New York a day early to look for a summer-type dress and found a white chiffon with white cotton lace over-blouse, spangled with rhinestones and white tear-shaped beads, bateau neckline in front and U-shaped décolletage in back. Fortunately, I had white sandal-type slippers, a white beaded bag that I bought years ago in Paris and long white kid gloves, left over from a dinner for the Queen of England. I decided that they wouldn't go with the outfit and wore white stretch satin inexpensive gloves that I had. The day turned out to be unseasonably cool, so I took my out-of-date mink stole because I didn't want to buy an evening coat, thinking I would only wear it once.

At the Carlton Hotel the limousines were all taken because of the dinner. Bobby Sarnoff [chairman of the board of RCA] said he would be happy to share his with me, but when I got downstairs a few minutes late, there was no one in the lobby. I looked in the bar where there was a party of men and one of them looked up and said, "Hello, beautiful." I quickly walked away, but he called loudly, "Come here, beautiful." To my horror, he followed me into the lobby continuing to say, "Come here, I want you."

The hotel employees pretended they didn't notice, but at that point, Anna Rosenberg Hoffman, her husband and the "Mike" Cowles came out of the elevator and the man disappeared. They were dressed to the teeth—white stoles made out of material—and I tried to hide the mink under my arm, knowing it was out of date and tacky. My friend accosted me again, so I went to the bell captain. At that moment Bobby Sarnoff arrived, apologizing because he was late.

When we entered the White House grounds, we had to show our invitations. Mine was not asked for because it was assumed that I belonged to Bobby, I suppose. I produced it, anyway, and again when we entered the House. In the East Room line-up, which was alphabetical, I was between Bobby and the Howard K. Smiths. It reminded me of school and always being at the wrong end of the roll call. Lynda Bird came along; she is a large girl who looks exactly like her father. In a strong Texas accent, she said, "I want to meet everyone who is here. My name is Lynda Bird Johnson," and introduced herself. Standing a few people away in the lineup was a very tall, dark and handsome man. I asked Bobby if he knew who he was. Bobby looked at me quizzically, said it was Gregory Peck, and would I like to meet him? I would and did.

The President seemed delighted to see me and gave me a resounding kiss on the cheek. He started introducing me to U Thant, who said, "Of course I know Mrs. Schiff." This time Lady Bird did not say anything to me except "How do you do?" (The last time she had complimented me on my dress.)

The Washington *Post* report mentioned that the wines were American. According to the menu, they were not. "Puree Favorite" turned out to be puree of broccoli; the last time we had puree of string beans. The dessert, "Coppelia U Thant," was a bombe of what I thought was chocolate mousse but, according to the Washington *Post,* was coffee. The food is light, small portions, not rich, and excellent. While dessert was being served, the Air Force string band, in white uniforms, came in. Fifteen to twenty boys played schmaltzy music on violins and spread themselves throughout the room, so each table had a violinist, as at Monseigneur in Paris.

At the end of dinner, the President made an excellent speech before the toast to the guest of honor. U Thant then responded with, I thought, a not-too-subtle criticism of the Bay of Tonkin affair. I walked out of the dining room between Lady Bird and Anna Rosenberg.

Lady Bird seemed uncomfortable and ill at ease but looked lovely in a yellow chiffon dress with a beaded top. That morning I had been to a needlework shop, and they told me that she had been in to buy some needlepoint, because Mrs. Angier Duke (later killed in a plane crash) and a group of Washington wives were making chairs "for the White house." I asked Lady Bird how she was coming along with it. She seemed annoyed, said she wasn't doing any, and her needlepoint was for a friend.

In the East Room a stage had been installed and Peter, Paul and Mary entertained us. Apparently they are very famous, but I had not heard of them. The two bearded men looked like beatniks, and so did the girl, with her long yellow straight hair. A place was cleared for dancing by the front door, and one of the ushers asked me to dance.

The President came along, grabbed me, and the next thing I knew we were fox-trotting around the room. I felt it incumbent on me to say something, so I told him that Jim Farley had said he would carry most states. The President said, "If I carry twenty-five, I will be satisfied," and held me closer, placing his right cheek against my right cheek and holding me firmly, with his hand across the upper part of my back. This was not a good position in which to have a conversation. The President is extremely portly around the middle, which his excellent tailoring conceals, but while you are dancing, it is very noticeable, since you can't get close to him. The only way to dance with him cheek to cheek is to stick your fanny way out.

We danced in silence for a while and then the President said, "You are a lovely dancer, Dorothy." I looked up at him and said, "You are a wonderful President, Mr. President!"

I wondered if I was going to get stuck with him, since no one cuts in, and whether I should break it up. After quite a long time the music stopped. I quickly said, "Thank you, Mr. President," and started to walk away. He held his arm around my waist and walked with me to the edge of the dance floor, at which point I fled, running smack into Adlai, who kissed me.

I introduced myself to Everett Dirksen, saying that I was afraid that our editorial writers had not been very friendly. He said, in not the funereal, sepulchral tones that I expected but much more normal, "Oh, well, it's all in the day's work."

I thought I had made the most of the dinner and had better look for Bobby. He was ready to leave.

The waiters at the White House are tall, young, beautifully trained Negroes. The service is excellent. The White House was so clean that even the bottom of my white dress wasn't soiled and didn't have to go to the cleaners.

The President was in a white dinner jacket. About half the people were in dark dinner jackets and half in white. I understand there is a controversy about which is correct. In the top social circles in which I have traveled, white dinner jackets are not considered *comme il faut*.

Later that summer LBJ's nemesis, Robert F. Kennedy, came to her office and her memo describes their discussion of his campaign to unseat Senator Kenneth Keating.

I asked him why he thought the Jewish vote was against him. He said, "Oh, my father in the 1930s, and my membership on the McCarthy Committee." He was careful, when he met Everette, my chauffeur, to call him "mister," but he seemed most confident with Irish-sounding names.

With Bobby Kennedy at the Democratic Convention in 1964.

He wears a black tie, on which reporters often comment without realizing that this is a sign of mourning. There is a great similarity in appearance with JFK, although I don't think he is nearly as good-looking. The accent is pretty much the same, but RFK's voice is harsher. JFK was more relaxed, had more polish and was more aristocratic. Bobby seems upper-middle-class; probably this is due to Jack being older when their father was ambassador to the Court of St. James's, and the British upper classes having rubbed off on him.

Bobby has tremendous drive, is very intense and serious, but has the same sophisticated sense of humor as his brother. His accent is definitely on youth, and he seems to have contempt for older people. In discussing Senator Keating, he thought rather than calling him names, as I suggested he should stop doing, he could just refer to him "as a nice old man."

I don't hold any of these things against him, but he is definitely a young man in a hurry and has a bit of "What Makes Sammy Run" in him. Untactfully I said at one point, when we

were discussing slogans, that it wasn't what New York could
do for him, but what he could do for New York that must be
emphasized. There was a painful silence.

Another slogan that he repeated earlier had been Ethel's,
whom he now *does* call his wife or Ethel, and not Mrs. Kennedy, as I suggested Arthur Schlesinger pass on to him. That
was: "There is only so much you can do for Massachusetts."
When she came up with that, they told her to go and sit in the
back of the bus.

Dorothy had met Jacqueline Kennedy only at a large White
House reception and had mentioned this to RFK. Her memo recalls:

A little after seven last Friday night [October 9, 1964], the
Post operator called me to relay a message to call Mrs. Jacqueline Kennedy at the Carlyle Hotel, Apartment 19C. I had told
Bobby Kennedy how much I wanted to meet Jackie. He said he
would arrange it for the following week, but I had not heard
any more about it by Friday morning. I was sure that Bobby
had a lot more important things to do and had forgotten his
promise. Really all I wanted was to befriend her.

I felt self-conscious about calling Jackie after I got the message and had to steel myself by taking a couple of drinks. After
the drinks, my courage returned, and I put in the call nervous-
ly. Jackie answered the phone herself, and I told her that I had
a message from the *Post* to call her. She said rather plaintively,
"I called there because I didn't know where else to call," and
that she would be in town over the weekend. "Will you come
and see me for a drink or something at the Carlyle?"

I said I would love to tomorrow and what time? "Whatever
time you say."

We went into a Gaston-and-Alphonse routine, and finally I
said, "Five or six o'clock?" "It's up to you; whatever you like."
I said, "Five would be fine."

After the call, I made notes so I would have something to talk
to her about: (1) the Kennedy Foundation; I had been meaning
to make a donation but had not done so; (2) I had known both
her father and father-in-law; (3) suggest a woman's page column in the New York *Post*; (4) Bobby's campaign. (I put the
notes in my purse and forgot to refer to them.)

As I drove up I saw Jackie going in and a group of kids stop-
ping her. Since it was just five o'clock, I sat for a few minutes in
the little lobby outside the bar.

I debated with myself whether to go to the desk and be announced. However, there was no one available behind the desk at that moment, so I got into the elevator and asked for the nineteenth floor. I got out at the nineteenth floor and rang the bell at Apartment C. Nobody answered. I was sure she had gone upstairs, and I had given her time to fix herself before opening the door. There was a chair in the vestibule outside the apartment, but not the Secret Service men I had expected.

After a while, I rang again. No answer. So I went downstairs. By this time I was in a dither. There was a man behind the desk, so I said I had an appointment to see Mrs. Kennedy and gave him my name. He looked at me suspiciously and said, "Wait a minute." He put in a phone call and then said, "Go right up to Apartment 18E."

I went up to the eighteenth floor, where there was a Secret Service man in the hall, and a very plain-looking maid answered the door. It was a cold day, and I had put my otter coat over my new gray suit. With a gesture, she showed me into the living room where Jackie was sitting on a sofa with her back to the door, with little John, playing records. (The record was *Peter and the Wolf.*)

She made no move and didn't seem to hear me when I came in. I said, "Hello." She didn't seem startled, got up and said, "How do you do." She was wearing a beige skirt and a white silk blouse and had on very little makeup. She was beautiful.

She turned to John and said, "Make your bow to Mrs. Schiff."

Little John has a long face like his father, light brown hair and, on that day, a sad expression. Caroline was not there. He shook hands, saying, "How do you do," and making a little bow.

Jackie immediately took me through a smaller room into another, a little dining room. I felt warm and opened my jacket, which has three black buttons on it. Two of them immediately snapped off and fell to the floor. I said, "Oh, dear, the buttons are all coming off my suit." I bent down to pick them up. She seemed not to notice and made no comment.

There was a bar table set up in the dining room. She asked me whether I would care for tea or a drink. For the first time in my life I said what people are always saying to me, "What are you going to have?" I didn't want to drink alone if she wasn't going to have a drink.

She said she thought she would have a dubonnet. I said I would have a scotch on the rocks, with a little water. She fixed the drinks herself. When she handed me the glass, I saw it was straight scotch. I said, "This will be too strong for me. May I save half of it and have water?" She went out to the kitchen and changed it.

I said, "How is the decorating getting on at your new apartment?"

She said, "Decorating!" in a scornful way. "There is no decorating. Just packing boxes."

She said she had been to the apartment that afternoon. She had taken it in summer, when it was warm and lovely. When she visited there today, it had been cold. The wind was whistling all around, and it seemed very drafty. She was sort of scared about moving in.

She started to go back into the smaller room between the large living room and the little dining room. When we got to the door, I hesitated, to allow her to go first, as one does in the White House for the First Lady. She walked through ahead of me. We went into the small sitting room and sat together on a sofa before a coffee table. She closed the door, leaving John (whom she does not call "John-John") in the large living room by himself, telling him to play the records.

I started out talking about her father-in-law, saying that I had had dinner with him just before he got sick and that he had said such wonderful things about her, but surely she knew what he thought of her. Jackie said, with some vehemence, "And I was supposed to be afraid of him. It's so unfair what people say about him." She discussed his illness and referred to him as "Mr. Kennedy."

I told her my husband had had a stroke, so I knew something about the aftereffects, but that my husband was able to speak and walk and I knew that Joe could not. She said she thought that when the brain had been damaged, it would be better if nature would allow the person to become a complete vegetable so that he would not know what was happening to him. To have only partial functions was a terrible thing. I went on to her father, Jack Bouvier, with whom I had danced at parties when I was a debutante.

I told her that I, too, had been brought up as a Republican. She said that when she was a child, there were two things she was threatened with when she was bad: One was Hauptmann of the Lindbergh case, and the other was FDR. (The Duke of Windsor was told "Boney" [Napoleon Bonaparte] would get him.) She said that the trouble with resorts like Newport was that everyone was Republican. I said I had found that, too, and that is why I had left Long Island so many years ago.

I brought up Bobby's campaign. She was definitely interested in this. She said, "He must win. He will win. He must win. Or maybe it is just because one wants it so much that one thinks that." (She talks in the third person a great deal.)

Several times the little boy, John, came in, looking depressed, saying that the record was scratchy. She would firmly tell him to go back and play it. He left the door open one of the times, and she got up and quietly closed it. The third time he came in she took him out to the kitchen, where the maid was cooking supper, and asked the maid if she needed someone to help her. From then on there were no interruptions by John.

About Bobby she said, "People say he is ruthless and cold. He isn't like the others. I think it was his place in the family, with four girls and being younger than two brothers and so much smaller. He hasn't got the graciousness that they had. He is really very shy, but he has the kindest heart in the world. One time he went to a hospital to see a little boy who had his head bashed in by one of his parents." Jackie started to describe the condition of the child, said he came from a broken home. She said Bobby wanted to adopt him, but Ethel was having her eighth child, and they had only four rooms (I assume four bedrooms), and he had to be talked out of taking the child home with him. (Max Lerner says sentimentality is the other side of ruthlessness.)

She wanted to talk about columnists. She said she read the *Post* and that those six [*sic*] center pages were wonderful. On Jimmy Wechsler, she said that she had met him and that he didn't look at all like his picture. She said, "All the columnists have pictures that must have been taken twenty-five years ago." She said she supposed Max Lerner's picture didn't look like him either. I don't think she knows Lerner but think she wanted to show me how carefully she reads the paper or was trying to show me she had intellectual interests.

I said I thought the boys were all quite vain, as probably we all are, and often men more so than women. She said she thought so, too, and she had heard a lot of men were dyeing their hair. She thought men over sixty were often more attractive than younger men; for instance, General Maxwell Taylor was marvelous and lean, while classmates of Jack's (she always referred to him as Jack, unlike RFK, who speaks of "the President") had let themselves go and looked awful. She said, "General Taylor is over sixty and plays tennis and is lean." I said I thought many men were fearful of aging and losing their virility. They worried about this more than women because of what was expected of them. She said she thought that was very true.

In discussing newspapers, I said everybody wants to write about international affairs—even Elsa Maxwell did when she was with us and we had let her go. She went to the *Journal-American,* where she was much better because they gave her a lot of help.

She said the *Journal* was an awful paper. I said they have good gossip writers I wished we had, like Suzy, for instance, forgetting that Suzy had cracked at her many times (including items implying that Jackie and Bobby were lovers). She made no comment, and I said columnists were much better when they went out and did legwork, instead of just sitting behind a desk and reading newspapers. She said Jack felt that way so strongly. He said so often that Washington columnists should go out on campaign trains with him.

I went into my own former column, leading up to asking her to write a column for us, "You could just write about things you go to and anything you like."

She said, "Oh, I can't write," and that there had been a lot of requests from magazines, which she had barely looked at. They all wanted her to write about "gracious living or fashion." She cried out, "I am interested in the same things Jack was interested in."

She said that she had left Washington not because of the tourists but because of the "old haunts," that she just couldn't bear to be reminded all the time, that she had wanted to move into the house they had lived in when he was a Senator but had not been able to get it because someone else had it.

I said, "What happens when you go out of New York City—are you mobbed?"

"No. People will pass me and turn their heads sometimes."

I had a feeling that that is not something she objects to. She said she was a private person, and perhaps she had been chosen for that reason to complement Jack, although he really was a private person, too. When he was Senator, they hardly went out to dinner, only to Joe Alsop's "because the food was so good."

I said without thinking, "Oh, I didn't think Jack was interested in food."

With a faraway look and smiling, she said, "No, he wasn't, really."

When talking about Jack, tears came to her eyes. "People tell me that time will heal. How much time? Last week I forgot to cancel the newspapers [this was a reference to the publication of the Warren Report], and I picked them up and there it was, so I canceled them for the rest of the week. But I went to the hairdresser and picked up *Life* magazine, and it was terrible. There is November to be gotten through . . . maybe by the first of the year. . . ." (She obviously couldn't bear to mention Christmas.)

I quickly said, "There is only one thing to do, and that is to find a substitute in work that is all-absorbing. It will never be the same thing, but you can lose yourself that way."

She said she knew that was true and she would like to do that. She said, "I don't want to be ambassador to France or Mexico. President Johnson said I could have anything I wanted. I would like to work *for* somebody, but the list is. . . . One is expecting someone to come home every weekend, but no one. . . ."

I said I thought most women were that way and that anything else was just a substitute. "You know, you are the most famous and admired woman in the world. It is quite a responsibility."

She half smiled and didn't answer; then she talked about the White House and "all that furniture. One would be on the telephone all day and in the evening one's voice would be tired. Oh, well. . . . One tries to keep fit during the day, but the evenings. . . ."

At one point she said that the children loved being in New York. I tactlessly said, "Usually they hate New York." She said they didn't like the muddy park in Washington.

I said I used to hate Central Park as a child and one day was walked French and one day was walked German. She said that is exactly what had happened to her—Russian ballet and music lessons, etc.

The phone rang. I had the feeling it might be Bobby—and the maid answered outside. It was six o'clock, and I thought I ought to leave. She found me my coat, walking through doors ahead of me without urging me to go first, and took me to the elevator.

I said, "Will you lunch with me?"

"I would love to."

"Are you always in town weekends? Saturday is my best day."

She said, "Oh, no. It is better to go away weekends."

A short time later it was announced that she had rented a country place for weekends in Glen Cove, Long Island.

A month or so later, on the weekend before the anniversary of JFK's death, Dorothy had lunch with Jackie at the latter's Fifth Avenue apartment. Dorothy's memo notes that Jackie seemed so anxious to please she wondered if Bobby had asked her to do it for him.

Jackie answered the doorbell and had on a very simple white silk shirt, open at the neck, and a brown, heavy cotton skirt with a loose belt around the waist. She seemed to be wearing a dark slip which showed through the blouse, and she had on black silk stockings and the new kind of loafers with chains across the instep.

She had lost a great deal of weight since I last saw her, and her skin was tanned and a little leathery. I have seen her looking radiant, but she had white circles under her brown eyes, which were dull. Her hair looked dusty, with no gleam to it, and she seemed depressed.

A not very large table was in the angle of the dining-room windows, where one could sit and contemplate the view. White wine was served in long-stemmed water goblets with a small bowl of ice, broken into little pieces. When I tried to put mine in the wine, little pieces slid off the teaspoon onto the tablecloth. Having tried to retrieve them with the spoon, I decided the only thing to do was pick them up with my fingers and drop them in my glass. Jackie made no comment, deftly serving herself with the spoon.

She had seen her father-in-law in Palm Beach and said his mind still works, but he can't speak. He can only point to things and is locked in. Recollecting Jim Forrestal, she remembered that when he was staying with them in Washington, her stepfather had called upstairs and asked her to lend Jim her sneakers. She had been embarrassed because her feet were so big.

The story of her cook's memoirs had come out in the *Post* this day, and she said that it was very hard with staff to know what to do in terms of that. She now was using younger girls from Europe to take care of the children, and one of them was attending Marshall McLuhan's lectures. I asked if she understood what it was all about. Jackie said, "Yes, of course." I don't.

Because of the anniversary of the assassination, various New Frontiersmen, all men, had been dropping in to see her during that week. Over that particular weekend, she said, she didn't know what to do. I told her about my last meeting with Jack. She said, "What did he say?" and I was careful to be tactful.

She had never told him anything or shown him anything unpleasant, she said, and when he got home, she always had his favorite drink, a daiquiri, ready for him and his favorite record playing, with perhaps a few friends. She said he never kissed in public or anything like that and really hated public demonstrations of affection. Campaigning, she said, was exhausting; you go to your hotel room at night completely drained, but the next morning "the adrenaline starts to work again." Jack, of course, had an adrenaline deficiency.

She mentioned that he'd had to make a speech about Southeast Asia and had asked her to translate ten books in French for him. She stayed up all night working on the books, saying, "He has got to ask me to marry him after all I have done for him. . . . And he did," she said triumphantly.

In terms of writing, she said that all she'd really like to write about would be Yucatan, where she had just been, and to use the money to help the poor people in that area. She said that she liked running her fingers through the earth there and finding what we would call artifacts but she called bones. When I said I thought she had been very brave to go to all those places in Southeast Asia, she bridled and said, "It's safer there than here." She added she felt very, very disorganized.

I said that she was an eighteenth-century woman: "You should be the mistress of a king or a prime minister." She said she doesn't like the five o'clock thing; she would rather be married.

On account of the children's not having a father, she likes to be home at their bedtime and have other people there so they won't be alone and could have people to say good-night to. As we walked down the hall toward the children's rooms, she pointed out the photographs of Jack with the children. She said that she had found old frames for these and that there were no photographs of Jack in any part of the apartment except the children's rooms.

She said that she had offered him peace, tranquillity and
serenity, but that now "the board has moved, and all the little
pieces change places."

It was hard talking to her. She let silences go on. She is odd
and different, very much less the queen than she was. I think
she was scared of me, in a funny sort of way.

The last meeting with a Kennedy that year of 1964 was with
Bobby just before Christmas. Dorothy had been of significant
help in his victorious Senatorial campaign and it was something
of a thank-you visit that he made to Dorothy's office.

When he says "the President," he means his brother, and
thus, when we got on the subject of the FBI and I said "the
President," he looked confused at first. Then he said, "Oh, you
mean Johnson."

I asked what J. Edgar Hoover had on the President (LBJ had
not fired Hoover, despite his attack on the Supreme Court and
Dr. King), and Bobby looked very pained. He said that for two
reasons Hoover had to be kept; he has a vast fund of information about everybody, and it would be very difficult to replace
him. When I asked whether some of the Walter Winchell items
about Communists came from the FBI, he looked nervous. Finally, under pressure, he said he thought some of them did.

He was cautious about Martin Luther King until I said we
had the story of his frailties from several sources, and I told
him what we had. He then said, "We kept away from him for
two years." When I asked why one felt so much more shocked
by this than when one's friends are involved, he said, "Well, he
is a clergyman." I added, "Yes, and we are used to Adam Clayton Powell."

Bobby said, "We never expected anything of him. We never
put him on a pedestal." But, he said, without Martin Luther
King there would have been violence, but there had not been
violence. This was a wonderful thing.

As to the future, Bobby said he wasn't sure he was going to
like the Senate. He really thought he was more suited to the executive branch. He liked to get things done and didn't like to
wait.

I said, "Now you have it, you aren't sure you want it. I can
understand that; it has happened to me in life." He laughed.

I asked if he would resign if he didn't like it, and he said no,
he would stay. I said that six years is a long time. He seemed

very sad and said Washington wasn't the same anymore. [He was assassinated three and a half years later.]

Just as she had ended the year with a Kennedy, she was close enough to the family to begin the next, 1965, in their company for an evening on the town. For it, the Kennedy charm was cranked up and the Schiff eyes and ears were functioning.

> When I came down to the front hall, Bobby was waiting rather pathetically in front of the elevator. I asked why he hadn't come up and he said the elevator man said not to.
>
> At the Caravelle, Mrs. Peter Lawford and the Stephen Smiths were at the Kennedy table, always in the center in front of a semicircular banquette, but we moved to a larger one. Steve was on my right, Bobby on my left, Jean Smith sat next to her husband, and Bobby's sister, Pat, whom he calls Patty Cake, next to him. There seems to be a tremendous affection between them, but she looked badly. Her hair needed doing, she had on a nondescript black dress, is quite tall and on the gawky side. (She and Peter are not getting along, I am told.) Jean Smith, who had on a white outfit, was extremely quiet.
>
> In a few minutes the Radziwills arrived. She looked very chic, and he—with a black mustache, gray hair and overweight—looked old enough to be her father. In fact, I remarked on how much he resembled Jackie's father, "Black Jack" Bouvier.
>
> While Bobby was talking to Pat, I told Steve Smith that when I was sitting next to Adlai one night, he was complaining of the inability to communicate with the nonwhites at the UN. I mentioned Bobby's ability in this respect, whereupon Adlai got up and ran from the table. When I refused to repeat the story, Steve did it for me. Bobby, pleased, said, "Did he really?"
>
> In the car, after leaving the restaurant, Bobby cried out bitterly, "Why do people hate me so? Don't you think I was a good Attorney General?" I was quite shocked and said soothingly that perhaps he was upsetting the status quo and that people who do are not always the most popular.
>
> At the Plaza, where we went to hear Diahann Carroll, we were at a table to the right of the dance floor. I was wedged between Bobby and Radziwill, who said that when Bobby had invited them for dinner, he told them he was having "the woman who is responsible for getting me elected in New York." He asked me if I enjoyed having all that power, and I said I never

thought of it that way. I was saved from having to make further comment by the show's starting.

The Kennedys seemed rather pathetic—lost and shabby— and obviously still reeling under the blow of the assassination. They are not polished, but I find them appealing, and I felt as though I had been at a children's party. The seating arrangement was not very sophisticated—husband and wife not being separated—which doesn't make for good conversation. They are a very closed group, and I don't think they do anything without a purpose. Many people speak of Steve's rudeness, but I have never seen this. He knocks himself out when I am with him, I suppose because he considers the *Post* essential to RFK. I have a feeling that they are worried about keeping me in line.

Her next encounter with LBJ was at the President's Club dinner at the Waldorf-Astoria in May, 1965. The President had Mrs. Lasker on his right.

I went to LBJ's table, and Mary Lasker moved over on her little gilt chair to make room for me. The President kissed me, then said how great Max Lerner had been at a dinner recently; that he was the only newspaperman there who had asked important questions. (Max came away dazzled by his talk with LBJ and ready to be a propagandist until I unbrainwashed him.)

I became miserably uncomfortable on about a quarter of the little chair and asked one of the Secret Service men to pull up a whole chair for me. The man made no move, and LBJ turned to him and said, "Bring Mrs. Schiff a chair." He did.

LBJ discussed at great length the Dominican Republic problem, stating that we were trying to form a moderate government but that terrible things happened every time we thought we were on our way, such as the killing of a young colonel recently. He went on and on, and finally I said, "Mr. President, this isn't a terribly good place to talk. And I wish you would send for *me*, as well as my staff." (I think he got the message that I thought he was trying to subvert my staff over my head, as all politicians try to do.)

LBJ said he hadn't invited them and seemed stunned by my remark. He made no move to kiss me when I arose. I leaned over and kissed him, but he remained unresponsive. Dancing with Morris Abram, my lawyer, I said I thought maybe I had gone too far.

He said, "Dolly, you were absolutely right."
"But he is the President of the United States, and I can get
very rough."

Another confrontation for Dorothy was just a month away, an
appointment with Cardinal Spellman at the "Power House"
(archdiocesan residence).

> When I asked him how he thought Bobby Kennedy was do-
> ing, the Cardinal answered that although he had married three
> Kennedy children, he had not been on very good terms with the
> family since his difference with the President on the constitu-
> tionality of aid to parochial schools. He said strongly that JFK
> had been wrong and damaging to the Church, and that it had
> shown in his face.
> On Vietnam, he recalled that he had seen Diem several times,
> that he was a good man and should have been given a chance.
> He said he knew that President Kennedy had been asked to de-
> cide whether Diem should be removed by assassination and
> that, on the recommendation of American officials in Vietnam,
> had decided that it was all right. JFK had thought about it over-
> night and changed his mind. It was too late; Diem was already
> dead.

Near the end of 1965 Dorothy spent an intimate evening at the
Nelson Rockefellers'.

> Happy, in a sleeveless late-afternoon dress and black suede
> shoes with low, squarish heels, apologized for Nelson, saying
> he seemed to be detained and she was always waiting for him.
> She took me on a tour of the Fifth Avenue apartment, which
> had been broken through to the one next door, doubling the
> space or more. In the bathroom were "His" and "Hers" marble
> basins side by side, with gold fixtures and a raised marble tub.
> She said, "This is my favorite room in the house. I often come
> in here to get away from it all."
> Nelson said the newspapers are always taking cracks at him
> and telling public officials what to do, but they can't solve their
> own problems. He said that he had suggested to the publishers
> after the *Post* left the association that legislation be enacted for
> compulsory arbitration.
> I could feel antagonism when the name of Bobby Kennedy
> was mentioned, although nothing was said. I asked him why

he wanted to run for governor again. He looked a bit startled, then said that there was some unfinished business—low-cost housing and drug addiction—which he would be able to solve in his third term. With him, it always comes down to money, and he mentioned figures in the millions and billions with great assurance. He talked about loyalty as the most important thing to look for in an assistant, saying that then you worked through an individual you trusted. He is very positive, very optimistic, but not quite as enthusiastic as he used to be.

He seemed terribly anxious to be friendly with Lindsay and said, "You and I are the only two old New Dealers left." He added that we thought big. At one point, he said, "Happy and I sit here so often talking about things." I had the feeling that these two were pretty lonely but very much in love. I wouldn't be surprised if she cried herself to sleep occasionally, missing her children.

The next morning, while shopping at Bergdorf's, I ran into the first Mrs. Nelson Rockefeller. She looked extremely happy and insisted upon telling me about a furrier downtown who, unlike the uptown ones, would give you an allowance for your old fur coat.

Dorothy had been asked to run as delegate-at-large to the State Constitutional Convention that fall of 1965, and although she had reason to think she could have the endorsement of all three parties, she had declined the honor. Her feeling then, as now, was the newspaper publishers should not hold political positions and that their contribution to the public well-being is best served from behind their desks. Such service, however, includes occasional politicking, and that can mean lunch with RFK at the Côte Basque in February, 1966.

Bobby had ordered filet of sole with a cream sauce, grapes and puree of mushrooms. Most of the men I know eat only plain broiled things, but I have noticed that the Kennedy family is apt to go for rich, exotic dishes.

Looking at the murals on the walls of the Côte Basque, Bobby said his father had liked them so much he had the painter come to the White House to do scenes of Hyannis Port and the Kennedy boats on the walls of the swimming pool there. Bobby was highly entertained by the thought of LBJ swimming around and having to look at them.

On being asked how things were with him, he said he had done enough for one week—abortion (he was for it) and the CIA (he had defended it).

I said, "You are always taking positions," and he said, "Yes, I don't seem to know how to get out of it the way other people do."

He said they had a wonderful cook, "who has come back to us. She is a Negro and about three hundred meals a week are served in our house, starting at six A.M. I don't get home until nine P.M." He added that there was also a Puerto Rican girl, and both these women were doing this as a Witness to God. He said several times, "They are dedicated and are both saints."

About Jackie, he said she was distressed about the Manchester biography and that it was unfair to her. When I said that I didn't think a political history of the New York *Post* would be very interesting, he said, "But your relationship with my father would be interesting." I told him, "That's what Frank Roosevelt always says to me."

About halfway through lunch Leonard Lyons joined us and told Bobby that he had been seeing a lot of New Frontiersmen out at night. Bobby asked for their names and Leonard said Bill vanden Heuvel, Arthur Schlesinger, Ted Sorensen and Rowland Evans. Leonard did not stay at the table long; I think Bobby makes him nervous.

After he left, Bobby explained to me that he didn't mind his people going to nightclubs and that "You have to remember if you've lived in Washington, especially a man like Arthur, there is absolutely nothing to do at night except go to people's houses."

Bobby took me to my car but did not speak to Everette. That evening at Gracie Mansion, when John Lindsay took me to the car, he shook hands with Everette, saying, "How are you?"

When Dorothy had gone to Washington on *Post* legal business in connection with the Widget in August, 1966, she also paid a visit to the White House. This time, the memo reveals, though the day was warm, the atmosphere was cool.

A stony-faced man ushered me into a large room. I waited about fifteen minutes and had a strange, shut-in feeling—perhaps paranoiac—that I was being watched or listened to. The stony-faced man opened the door after a while, looked at me, closed it again; then I was taken through a secretary's office into the room where I last saw JFK. The rocking chair was still there, and it gave me a turn.

The President was way over on the right, where the desk is. I stood at the door for a minute; then he turned around and said, "How do you do?" There was no kissing. He was holding some papers in his hand and gave Bill Moyers, press secretary, instructions about millions of dollars. He was brusque and looked the way men do when they have just come from the barbershop and have had a shave, with hair slicked down, etc. So did Moyers.

I had assumed that we would sit where I had with JFK—the place where the two sofas and rocking chair are—but LBJ said, "Let's go into the other room." He took me into a tiny little room next to the Oval Office with heavy curtains drawn. He seated himself in a large swivel chair, put his feet up on a hassock, then told Bill Moyers to join us. I sat on a cushioned sofa on his left and Bill in a low chair at the President's right. It was cocktail time, but I was not offered even a glass of water. The President looked extremely stern; in the morning papers the Gallup Polls showing Bobby Kennedy more popular than LBJ had been printed. I think I was quite frightened, and I did not feel any sympathy radiating from him. When I said I had seen Frank Roosevelt recently, he froze.

He talked about "Jewish power" and raved about David Dubinsky, saying that Dave had been for him for Vice President, while George Meany had wired Kennedy not to take him. He added that Dave always said of him, "He doesn't give me all I ask for, but more than I expect to get."

In speaking of the Liberal Party in New York, I asked if its members would not be better off in joining the Democratic Party to develop some good candidates. He answered that the Liberal Party was making both parties watch themselves, and anyway had always been 100 percent for him.

He spoke highly of Nelson Rockefeller; he had told someone, "Twenty years from now Nelson Rockefeller will be looked upon as a great governor of New York State." Nelson had asked, "Will you say that to use in my campaign?"

The President said that recently he had spent three hours with Arthur Goldberg, whom he had sent to Iron Curtain countries and to Moscow. Neither he nor Averell Harriman, the best possible men, could get to see anyone in any of these places. He added that Arthur had emphasized the importance of U Thant's remaining with the UN and that it would be a disaster if U Thant resigned; some African would take over, and the UN would fall apart.

I said, "I have found late in life something you probably have known for years: that everything is a negotiation." He was thoughtful, then said, "That's all very well, but Ho won't negotiate. He is worse than Hitler. If only they will negotiate, we will give up bases, do everything."

He said we had stopped the bombing for a while and it hadn't done any good and added with great relish that we are killing lots more of them now than they are of our men. He went on, saying, "Why don't Lippmann and Fulbright, Clark and other dove Senators hit *him* instead of me? When *he* was hit on the prisoners of war, *he* gave in." He was very angry and defensive, saying, "I told Bobby Kennedy, sitting right on that sofa, that they won't negotiate."

After an attempt by Moyers to terminate the meeting, the President began talking about Negroes. He said that [Stokely] Carmichael was a dangerous but attractive and articulate young man. He was extremely annoyed and added, "I will tell you what we are going to do with them. We are going to draft them. We are going to put them in the Army, and we are going to teach them discipline. We are going to get them up at six A.M., and they are going to learn to polish their shoes. When they come out, they will be on our side, and the leaders will come from among them."

I answered that usually the Young Turks win in the long run, then twitted him, perhaps foolishly, about a recent dinner at the White House for the nation's publishers. All New York publishers were there except me, who had not been invited. Again, he became angry and said that I had been invited to the White House a number of times. He had just told Lady Bird that they must have Fulbright and some other Senators for dinner and said if I wanted to come, he would put me on the list. He was terribly defensive.

While a taxi was being sent for, Bill Moyers took me into his office and said that Morris Abram had spoken to him about the antitrust aspect of the New York newspaper merger and the harm it might do the *Post*. He was surprised that I had not brought up the matter with LBJ.

As a newspaperwoman I have a hesitancy about going to the President as a supplicant. Also, he mentioned Lippmann as one of his great hates and Lippmann is at the top of the list of columnists we want. So are Evans & Novak, who are supposed to be terribly pro-Bobby Kennedy. This time when I reminded the President of the sandwich he'd had at my office, he didn't smile.

After the Widget collapsed in May, 1967, one of those who was worried about another paper starting and cutting into the *Post*'s circulation was Bobby Kennedy. He dropped in at Dorothy's apartment in August of that same year on what seems to have been a mission to get the feel of the *Post*'s future. Probably, he wanted to be sure that if it should leave her control, it would go to friendly hands; to the Kennedys it was as important as it had been to FDR.

> Several times I told Bobby that the independence of the newspaper was the most important thing in the world to me. He asked me if I thought that another paper would start in the fall. I didn't. Nor did he.
>
> On Vietnam, he said that Arthur Schlesinger had called him, asking him to make a Senate floor speech against the bombing of North Vietnam, and Bobby said he had answered, "Okay, and after that what do we do?" I asked, "Why don't you go to see Ho Chi Minh and make peace?" He said that could be treacherous, and he wasn't sure they would let him in anyway.
>
> About the race riots, he agreed that money was only part of the problem—it was jobs, equality, etc. I told him I was sorry I had not seen Stokely Carmichael. He said that I wouldn't have gotten anywhere with Carmichael; the person to see was [Floyd] McKissick, who was reasonable.
>
> Bobby wanted to know if I had a lot of offers to buy the *Post*, and I said that those who always keep turning up are usually involved with one political party or another. On leaving he said, "Stay with it."

Her next memo reveals her unique way of shuttling between the opposing camps of LBJ and RFK, as she attended a White House press luncheon a few weeks later.

> Whitney Young had just returned with a group of observers for the Vietnamese elections, and he said that Negro noncoms there were a good type for employment here, having been taught all kinds of skills, including computers. They want to reenlist, and he didn't want them to.

I asked him if he thought they would be like the Peace Corps, who were dissatisfied with life in the United States after having been overseas with power and prestige. He was worried about it, too, and told me about Negro women earning more money than when they were confined to domestic service; they don't know how to shop and buy things they cannot use, such as in the South electrical appliances when they have no electricity. In the North they buy the most expensive things in the supermarkets.

The President was standing between the dining room and the reception room in a receiving line consisting of the Vice President, Hubert Humphrey, and Secretary of State Rusk. He thanked me for coming to lunch, and I found myself sitting at his right. Dick Berlin, president of the Hearst Corporation, was at his left, and at my right was Catholic Archbishop Lucey of San Antonio, who also had just returned from Vietnam.

Red wine was served; the President said he didn't want any, but his glass was filled anyway. During lunch he, a table pounder, knocked Berlin's glass of water onto him and a few minutes later knocked a glass of red wine all over him. Berlin, mopping himself, said, "Now I've had two baths." Later LBJ knocked over his own glass of red wine, and I pulled my chair back quickly to avoid the spill. He didn't seem to notice these little accidents; he looked very well, but had a noticeable girth and smelled of cologne.

Archbishop Lucey wanted to know whether the *Post* was liberal; he turned out to be to the right of Cardinal Spellman—stupid and a violent hawk. I tried to have a civilized conversation with him, but he was viciously critical of Bishop Sheen, who has suddenly turned doveish, referring to him often with heavy sarcasm.

I turned back to LBJ, who talked about the new government in Vietnam. He told me what he wanted, making no pretense that this was an independent government—civilians in government, the bad generals out, and no more corruption. When I said, "How are you going to do that in Asia when we can't do it in New York?" he seemed stunned. He said, "But you have to keep on trying, don't you?"

He also wanted to build a two-party system, saying with enthusiasm that it was inspiring to see the birth of a new democracy. He compared it to when George Washington was elected here and said with a sneer that teachers, ministers and intellectuals were always against war. Then he asked an aide to bring him some typewritten sheets and read me speeches starting with the War of 1812 down through Lincoln, Wilson and, I think, Truman, criticizing the military efforts. Later a lot of these people changed their minds, he pointed out. He turned suddenly from me to Dick Berlin and talked to him for the rest of the lunch.

The President seemed very nervous, on the defensive, and hostile to the press. He implied we didn't know what was going on, that he has tried everything, but Hanoi won't negotiate. He said Ky and Thieu have said during their campaign that they would meet with the Vietcong and would stop the bombing for one week. The bishop interrupted and said what he had said to me, that we have tried it and it doesn't work.

LBJ brushed him off impatiently and said, "But the times are different now."

Otto Fuerbringer of *Newsweek* asked a question I had in mind, "Why won't Ho negotiate?"

LBJ said, "Simply because he wants South Vietnam and always has wanted it. But he isn't so sure now that he is going to get it." He said the bombing was hurting badly. That's why they wanted it stopped. "People in this country," he went on, "should stop eating each other up. Why don't we hit Ho instead of each other? Don't let him think that in 1968 it is going to be easier for him. The man who succeeds me will be harder to deal with than I am."

As I was planning to ask another question, he said that he had answered all the questions that he was going to. He then read the pages he had read to me, and I got restless. He said, "The American people would not support a President who withdrew from Vietnam," and when he finished what appeared a campaign speech, he sat down, looking depressed. The guests rose and applauded.

I didn't know what to do since I did not want to applaud. So I jumped up, shook his hand, and said, "Good-bye, thanks and good luck." Then I fled.

Dorothy was pleased on being sought out by one of her favorites, RFK, at her apartment in January, 1968.

He said that he, Bobby, had a lot of enemies. Labor didn't feel it had anything in common with him; or business, the newspapers or even most of the pros, and probably for selfish reasons.

I said, "Who is for you?"

He said, "The young, the minorities, the Negroes and the Puerto Ricans."

I said that the war in Vietnam was not being debated and that no one was paying any attention to Gene McCarthy. He said, quite angrily, that McCarthy had not come to him to ask for help or advice; that he has said that he won't get out, and he has raised all that money. I told him that when McCarthy came to see us in December, he said that Bobby had told him how to campaign in New Hampshire. He added that it would be the way Bobby would campaign, walking up and down the streets.

Bobby said, "I told him how *I* would campaign. I did not urge *him* to campaign."

After a discussion, Bobby asked me point-blank if I thought he should run. I said, "I think you want to run, and I think you will be true to yourself, whatever that self is." He said that was very perceptive of me, "as usual."

I realize now that I did try to push Bobby into running. Of course, he expected LBJ to run against him in the primaries.

He made public his decision to run after New Hampshire, which was a fatal error in timing. Had he announced before, he might have forced McCarthy out, and he might not have been assassinated in California. I have always thought Bobby was too controversial to make it to the Presidency.

After President Johnson announced that he would not accept the Presidential nomination, Dorothy received a touch-base call from Bobby Kennedy, in which he explained why he was now a candidate. He mentioned that the New Hampshire primary had shown there was a division in the party, and on Dorothy's reminder that he had told her on his last visit that power groups, as well as individuals, were against him, he assured her he was aware of the problems he faced.

They had lunch in April, at the Côte Basque as usual, and it was their last meeting.

In mentioning that he had sent his oldest daughter, Kathleen, to Putney, he said that she had gone to a Catholic school before and that at Hyannis Port, now the Boston Catholics had made money and had summer places, she was totally surrounded by Catholics; the world wasn't that way, he said. At Putney she would meet other kinds of people. He said that she loved it and that it was very good for her to have to defend her position.

I said, "About politics?"

"Not so much politics as about God—religion and why she believes what she does."

I asked him if he wasn't afraid that he would be hurt by all the wild crowds that he attracted, and he smiled and said no; the crowds were very friendly, and he was only afraid the children would be crushed.

In terms of the Vice Presidency, I asked if Jesse Unruh [the political boss of California] had been offered it. He said he hadn't offered it to anyone, hadn't even thought of it. Then he said, "What about you? It's about time we had a girl."

He still didn't think much of Senator McCarthy. "The people who are for him are the old Stevenson crowd."

As always, when I asked about Ethel, he said that she was fine and "loves those children so much." This said with a faraway, fond smile.

The night of his death, June 6, 1968, Dorothy was on the phone to Jimmy Wechsler as they watched his election victory reception. They had been discussing a suitable editorial, Dorothy remembers, when Jimmy said, "Wait a minute, something's happening." As the tragedy became clear out of the confusion of that night, she was reminded of that conversation she and Bobby had had about the possibility of his assassination.

"Bobby had taken a very strong position to get the Jewish vote, and I thought he had done everything. He shouldn't have expected Gene McCarthy to withdraw; he was in competition with the Kennedys. Bobby couldn't allow an Irish Catholic to get ahead; Kennedys were always in a hurry, and if Gene made it, it might mean an eight-year wait. He didn't think him very good and didn't trust him, although he did send emissaries to sound him out about withdrawal.

I have no personal feeling about Bobby's death; I thought he was asking for it. He'd made new enemies and maybe, he'd had it. After Jack, whom he adored and was a follower of even unto his death, was shot, he might have thought it a glamorous end; the Presidency was tough, and it may have seemed a good way out. Anyway, Bobby was not going to let McCarthy have it, even if it killed him.

I suppose I wasn't emotionally involved because it's

not my business to be emotionally involved with politicians, even if they're personal friends."

But Dorothy was surprised to find she was moved by President Johnson when she went alone to a dinner for him at the Plaza Hotel in January, 1969, a week before he left office.

> In the receiving line, LBJ put his arms around me and asked, "Will you still let me visit with you even after?"
> I started to cry and said, "Yes, of course."
> I sat between John D. Rockefeller III and Justice Arthur Goldberg at a table on the dance floor, with both Mayor Lindsay and former Mayor Wagner, as well as Muriel Humphrey and Aline Saarinen. I danced with both my dinner partners and had a hard time following Rockefeller; he was quite fancy in his steps.
> When I asked him what phase of the Rockefeller interests belonged to him, he seemed surprised that I didn't know, saying he was a philanthropist and the foundation was his interest. He asked how old Teddy Kennedy is (thirty-six); he thought that his son [John D. III's] Jay could be President after Teddy. He hadn't known Teddy was so young and said that Jay (thirty-one) hadn't found himself until he was thirty.

In May, 1969, Dorothy was with other Rockefellers on another evening.

> Happy and Nelson came for dinner before the theater. He really doesn't like Nixon; I guess he thinks he's cheap. He said that if you look at his investment portfolio, you see the kind of man he is; for a Wall Street lawyer to show a half-million-dollar net worth in a resort stock told the tale. Talking of others, he said he really didn't hate anyone, and I said I didn't either, anymore.
> After the theater, Happy and I waited in the car while he signed autographs on the sidewalk. I asked how she signed hers. "Happy," she said. "I don't know how to spell Rockefeller."

Dorothy was inquisitive on another night that May, this time in Sol Hurok's opera box. The draw of the evening was not the production or even Hurok; it was another impresario, Henry Kissinger.

He was with a young giraffe, introduced as Miss Maginnes. She seemed very possessive and, when he went to call Washington, became almost frantic because he was so long.

I have never seen as many millions represented as there were in the bar—Rockefeller, Whitney and Paley. McGeorge Bundy did not seem too pleased to see me; I wondered if we had attacked him recently.

Three people introduced me to Kissinger, and presently I found myself alone with him. I told him I had become very interested in Bismarck and asked which was the best biography. He said, "The trouble is there is no good biography in English. I was going to write one when I went to Washington."

Kissinger said Bismarck was a man with great power, who understood the limits of power, and was a liberal. This is strange for a German, he added (he does not consider himself a German, in spite of a very German impression). He said Bismarck was a genius and that a country can produce only one genius in a generation. I jumped in and said, "We hope you are going to be the genius of this generation." Kissinger: "If I were, I couldn't say so."

He warmed up and said, "Now Vietnam; the trouble is you can't say what is really happening. This present stage may be the final one; if not, there will be a long pause and the next one will be the final one. Nothing that is said in public is what they really want. The Vietnamese are the most elliptical people there are" (an elliptical remark, itself). He said he didn't know much about other Asian countries; then again, "The Vietnamese are subtle, and they survive occupations."

DS: Like the Jews?

"Yes, but infinitely more subtle."

I said, "We have mutual friends—Clare Boothe Luce and Nelson Rockefeller." Kissinger did not seem to care much for Clare but thought Nelson was great. When I told him Clare had told me she had gone to see him at the White House, he said, "She told me to get married."

"Are you going to?"

"No, but *she* wants to."

K. is very serious, speaks with a German accent and is definitely European. I felt he is someone who would listen to another if he respected him; otherwise, he would be quite rigid.

The year 1969 seems to have been one of relentless questioning for Dorothy, and a dinner party given early that summer by a

Kennedy consultant, Ted Sorensen, was no exception. There Dorothy concentrated on André Meyer, chairman of the banking firm of Lazard Frères and financial adviser to Jacqueline Kennedy, who had recently married Onassis.

Meyer said he had spent two weeks trying to persuade Jackie not to marry Onassis. He had tried to get a settlement for her but had failed because she flew over and married him suddenly. He said she wanted to marry Onassis, for whom he seemed to have contempt, more than Onassis wanted to marry Jackie.

I think she did it in reaction to Bobby's death. She was shocked and in despair; the kind of support she was looking for was not what some say—money.

André Meyer is seventy-one years old, has a very big stomach, a strong accent, and sits like a huge toad, listening. This was the first time I have ever seen him out with his wife; she must have been pretty when she was young.

The Kennedys continue to attract Dorothy; Teddy has star quality, and she predicts, barring further scandal, he could go a long way—in fact, all the way. But in June, 1972, she was visited by another star who, she decided, wasn't going all the way.

Senator McGovern looks very healthy. I told him to sit down, as I went to the pantry. He still was standing on my return and asked, "Where shall I sit?"

Conversation did not flow easily. He said he had been to a church in Harlem that morning, and very few people were there. I mentioned that perhaps it hadn't been highly publicized; McGovern said ruefully that had it been, there might have been still fewer people.

I asked about inflation, and he said the way to stop inflation was to stop the war. That ended that. As to labor unions, he said he thought collective bargaining should take its course. He, of course, is very anti-Meany and said so later.

On the subject of newspapers, I told him I had read in the Stewart Alsop column about family-owned businesses which would be exempted by McGovern from estate taxes and asked if it would apply to newspapers that had gone public where the family still had control.

He didn't know what to say and turned to a staff member, who said no, it would not include papers that had gone public.

McGovern said he guessed that they should pay some tax, but the time should be extended.

I said, "Then you believe in dynasties?"

He said, "What does that mean?"

"Kings and princes."

Next, he went into a diatribe against the Alsops and Evans & Novak, saying that they had been wrong on everything.

I asked him whether he was planning to broaden his base and move to the center more. He was quite testy about this, saying absolutely not; he was a radical, had campaigned as a radical and had won "all those states" as a radical. He said he didn't like the words "right" and "left."

Asked if he was frightened about being assassinated, McGovern said he was a little and had thought of running for President after Bobby's assassination. He seemed to think Teddy Kennedy on the ticket would be fine, but when I said, "What would Teddy add to the ticket?" he couldn't think of an answer. He said that one might as well give up on the South; no Democrat could win there, and he wasn't planning to try.

As to George Wallace, whom the Senator had visited after the attempt on his life, he said he thought he was very sick and had been surprised by his deafness.

I told him that Gene McCarthy had said that New Yorkers are the most provincial people in the world, which brought up John Lindsay. McGovern seemed disappointed that he had not supported him and asked if his support would have been useful. At the moment it would be the kiss of death here.

He said he had been surprised at the strength of ethnic feeling in New York and, with much hesitancy, that "the Jewish people are opposed to the encroachment of the blacks in their communities, and the blacks and Puerto Ricans are against each other." He added that he had been surprised that the tensions were not due to class differences—as the middle class against the poor and vice versa—but along racial and ethnic lines.

McGovern seemed worried and not happy during the questioning, and I was disappointed in him. Obviously, he is a nice guy, but I didn't think he had many well-thought-through positions. I was surprised at his referring to himself as a radical rather than a liberal, but maybe he was given the wrong briefing about us. I was not impressed with his intellect, and he is a one-issue man—anti Vietnam War. He certainly isn't a star of the first magnitude.

Dorothy's political interests are not limited to the national scene, and in New York she often meets with rough-hewn types, political bosses not excepted. She enjoyed the company of the Brooklyn Democratic boss, Meade Esposito, brought for the office sandwich by Pete Hamill in September, 1972. Pete had yet to desert his *Post* column for the fourth time.

Esposito is a Godfather type, drinks scotch, has rheumy eyes, very little education, is short, stoutish and quite funny. He told some jokes in his crude way, and I liked him very much (then I remembered that Lincoln Steffens warned against falling for the bosses).

Anxious to be loved, he said at one point he felt I didn't like him. He's interested in housing in Brooklyn, for which he wants our support, and offered us political advertising from his borough, if we didn't already have it.

Asked if he had seen *The Godfather*, he said he had left very depressed because of what it did to Italians. Twice he mentioned the bad way we select judges; he was pleased that Manny Celler had lost, leading me to suspect the organization had been behind Elizabeth Holtzman. He said she was too rigid.

We discussed the other county leaders; he said he was the biggest leader of them all. He liked Cunningham, hated Mattie Troy, whom he called all kinds of names and said was a liar, and Rossetti was a liar, too. On the mayoralty, he said he didn't have a candidate. He thinks Brooklyn should be a city by itself.

I asked him how he felt about Biaggi. He said he pleaded the Fifth Amendment.

Badillo? He called him every kind of name and said he was a ninny or words to that effect.

When I brought up the possibility of a woman, he spoke highly of Bess Myerson.

He said he had offered the Rooney Congressional job to Pete Hamill, but Pete said he didn't want it.

Another Democratic power in New York who can charm Dorothy is Joe Crangle, former state chairman, of whom it has been said that if he could get the black votes he controls to the polls, he would even be a national political force. He also received the accolade of an office sandwich that fall of 1972.

Joe, who is an awfully nice guy, talked about the upcoming national Democratic meeting in Washington and the election of committeemen. I suggested a black woman for vice-chair-man, Pat Harris, who makes an excellent impression on television. Crangle said the black male leadership resented having a black woman chosen to represent blacks. (I didn't think until just now that the person chosen would have to be cleared with Shirley Chisholm.)

I told Crangle that I feel strongly that two Catholics should not head the national committee and possibly nominate a fellow Catholic. He thinks Congressman Carey would be a great candidate for mayor, possibly followed by the governorship, but said Abe Beame might be the candidate. I said he should stay as comptroller, nothing more.

Crangle is worried about Rockefeller's running for President in 1976, thinks he is formidable. He will be sixty-seven.

Dorothy's political, as well as calendar, year of 1972 wound up with another tête-à-tête office lunch with Nelson Rockefeller in what she calls "his sexy dining room." Her host was a little late, permitting her to inspect "a photograph of President Nixon with an enthusiastic inscription."

We settled for dubonnet and got on to the subject of his vast holdings in Venezuela. He said that he had had a bad time on his last visit and sadly admitted that he hadn't been back for four years; it was dangerous to go there with two little children.

He said that people thought that because he had supported Nixon, he was expecting a Cabinet position, but of course he would not work in the Nixon administration. My information is that he expected to be made Secretary of State but didn't get it because Kissinger wouldn't allow it and that Nelson is not aware of this.

I asked him whether he had gotten Kissinger his job in the Nixon administration, and he said he had not, but when it had been offered to Kissinger, the latter had called him to ask him whether to accept. NR told him that he must. He was constantly in touch with Kissinger and sees him a great deal.

On the subject of John Lindsay, he complained that he couldn't understand why John had turned on him since he had urged him to run for mayor the first time. In fact, John had said he wouldn't run unless the Rockefellers put up a lot of money, which he said they had for his campaign.

On Attica, he said that he had made a terrible mistake, and while I thought he was going to say by not going there, he said in backing his new commissioner. He said they should have broken the rebellion right away, and he asked me if I had seen in the papers that one of the prisoners had just got a fifteen-year term. We talked about Tom Wicker's acting as a negotiator, and I said that had an editor or columnist in our organization been asked to act in that capacity, it would have been cleared with me, and probably I would have said no, I'd go myself. He insisted that he should never have gone himself, that it would have been unsafe to go into the prison.

On Rogers as Secretary of State, NR said he was merely a representative of the State Department at the White House, not the White House representative at the State Department. He added that Nixon was his own Secretary of State through Kissinger, saying that Kissinger was a "tough Israeli politician here."

Nelson has aged a bit, has a potbelly and looked as though he had nothing of interest going on in his life. While essentially a liberal, like so many of the rich kids—Averell Harriman, for instance—in his effort to become President he compromised with the right wing even more than he needed to.

Dorothy's final editorial chore for the year of 1972 was a confrontation with Mayor John V. Lindsay at her office. He came with aides to complain about the *Post*'s views of the city, editorially and in the news columns.

DS: Do you think we're in an adversary position? Probably.

JVL: I think that your paper is missing the boat. You could have a wider readership and make more money if you had a greater understanding of the people of the city and what they really want. They are sick to death of reading about negatives—death and destruction—that is supposed to be eye-catching when it hits the newsstand. If they are going to read about bad things, they'd like it to be in context, and your stuff has not been in context. We are trying to grapple with street crime, vandalism in the parks, muggings—

DS: If I may interrupt for a minute, despite your insulting remarks—

JVL: Not insulting.

DS: And tactlessness.

JVL: They're not intended to be insulting, Dorothy, and I don't regard them as insulting. This is an opportunity to talk about the *Post*'s general approach and its awareness of the need of balance and support for the city in a fair way—

John Lindsay and Dorothy. © 1975 Helene Galliet

DS: Excuse me a minute. We had a circulation manager when I first came here who said, "There's no good news today, meaning bad news, so we won't sell many papers." Of course, we need to sell papers, and we do sell more and more, but that's not why I'm in this business.

JVL: All I'm asking for is fair and accurate reporting.

DS: We try to do that, and I am sure we often fail, as we all fail at our jobs. Our paper is run for the people of New York City.

An acrimonious discussion followed in which Dorothy complained that the Lindsay administration was ineffectual in solving the traffic problem, ending with a charge that the Madison Avenue Mall plan was a plot against *Post* delivery trucks. She was just light enough to produce laughter which broke the tension.

DS: John, if you weren't so handsome, I would have thrown you out of the office when you made that terrible remark about my paper. [Laughter.] Will you have a drink, John—now that we're friends again?

JVL: Okay.

DS: John, you were a Republican until a short time ago with

a Republican governor and a Republican President. Why didn't that help New York's problems?

JVL: Damn few people understand what cities are all about and what their needs are. Most politicians are careful to avoid them—they're too hot, much too hot, and there's nothing but political loss in tackling urban problems. Frankly, I think in the '72 elections most of America voted their prejudices.

DS: What do you think of Teddy Kennedy's chances in '76?

JVL: Good, I should think.

DS: You think Nelson Rockefeller will run?

Voice: He'll be sixty-eight in '76.

DS: Sixty-seven, Crangle said.

JVL: Well, maybe he had the records changed. Dorothy, I've got to run—a correction officers' Christmas party.

DS: And in your meanness, you wouldn't let me call off this meeting until after Christmas! But Merry Christmas and Happy New Year.

JVL: Thank you, Dorothy. And the same to you.

DS: I'll try to be a better girl.

JVL: And I'll try to be a better boy. . . .

In speculating about John's political future, Dorothy said, "It's gotten him down, that job, and it need not have. If only he wouldn't keep picking fights with Nelson." After a thoughtful silence, she said that she always has regrets at the end of a year for not having offered help to those who needed it.

"But the New Year is always exciting and full of marvelous possibilities, even if by the third of January it's just like the old year. . . . So, you have to keep on trying to be a 'better girl.' "

The New Year, however, brought with it sad news—that of former President Johnson's death, the afternoon of January 22, 1973.

"My first thought was, gee, Lyndon is dead; I can't believe it. He seemed indestructible, in spite of the heart attacks, and was so strong, so large and so positive. He was a man, as Eric Sevareid said—no pussycat or weakling, with all his frailties. In spite of all his vulgarities and coarseness, he was not that way with women. I suppose Texans must have a Southern view of ladies, so they don't use that bad language.

I don't see Lyndon in history as very large; he was a very astute politician and a man of very strong feeling, but the Great Society will be forgotten along with the good legislation—civil rights—and if it isn't, it will be attributed to Franklin Roosevelt. I think he's a very sad case, who did a lot and then couldn't get himself out of Vietnam. He may have been misinformed or kidding himself, but I think he really believed that we were doing something great for dear friends. A lot of liberals who went to Vietnam and met the Vietnamese leaders were crazy about them; they thought they were patriots and came back completely sold on the cause of South Vietnam.

It would be interesting, by way of comparison with other political fathers, if there were a son to follow after him. For instance, I think Frank Roosevelt and Teddy Kennedy—and I'm fond of both boys—have suffered from being the sons of great fathers. They're not single-purposed, they get sidetracked by side issues, and they play around. Both are susceptible to girls, but in their lack of discretion they always get caught.

As to integrity, I think both these boys make deals quite easily, but I think Frank has made all his mistakes and learned that they don't pay off. He'll still compromise more than necessary, maybe, but he's bright. Teddy has more heart; Frank is less interested in individuals but loves children and is more hard-boiled. I don't think Teddy is all that ambitious, but he's running—being pushed by advisers.

No, I don't feel threatened by Lyndon's going—not the slightest. Too many people have died over the years for me to feel that way."

XII

"Fairy tales don't happen."

For some time Dorothy has recognized that much of her work is done. The *Post* is secure, her children's lives are far enough along so that those of *their* children—all fifteen of them—are largely predictable, and she herself is an institution ("horrible word").

The personal challenges she faces seem to be of continuation rather than creation, governed by the routines she has set up for her days which have become rigid enough to be almost fail-safe. No matter what ideas, events or people she may encounter, the unvarying pattern of her days insulates her. When a breach occurs, she can become a little lost.

For example summer vacations and even long holiday weekends continue to be a problem for Dorothy. They mean not only a break in the pattern, but a reminder of her dependence on others.

"My resentment of dependence is in being a burden to others. It's got to do with pride, of course, and I'm glad I don't show it. I can amuse myself and all that, but I'm a one-man dog—I become dependent on a single person, not people. I try to control it because I know what it does to the other person. I've always been this way—in need of hanging onto someone. It's pathetic that I am so thrilled when a man gets me across the street safely or into a movie, but other women take it for granted. I can't go downstairs in the office by myself.

One doesn't mind being alone when one knows there are alternatives—people will call and there are things to do. It's terrible to think no one will, or has, called. I can't believe that can happen to a man—he can always go to a bar. Yet more men commit suicide than women. When I was in Paris alone, I could hardly go out without an escort, so I'd sit in my hotel room alone. Maybe women's lib is a good thing, even if it's not for me.

The main thing about these four-day weekends is not to go into a depression. I couldn't sleep one night, and during it I took three tranquilizers, then a glass of wine, and finally a couple of vodkas. Then I overslept. I thought I was worried about a Newspaper Guild meeting, but it was really the weekend.

Such days are made up of sad thoughts—a misspent life, inability to make it work with another person. . . . I tell myself to get out of brooding and into the marvelous stuff I want to read and will have ideas about. I have so many things—a marvelous family I could see, who want to see me—but I don't; I'm alone and glad to be so. I enjoy my loneliness, which may be a form of self-centeredness. I may find it more interesting—this delving—than the problems of another.

None of the things one goes to, or does, is completely satisfactory. There is a sense of guilt in not being part of the dancing, drinking, sleeping thing of others. It makes me feel peculiar, missing these things, but I'm ambivalent. Half of me wants to be part of these things; the other half wants to be uninvolved.

Anticipation is usually better, or worse, than the reality. The weekend wasn't really that bad, and I got through it. My full briefcase made me feel better; I knew it would take me all three days to get through it, so I wouldn't be lonely. The suicide rate is up on these long weekends, you know. I am pleased that I survive them, with everybody off somewhere having fun.

If people have felt sorry for me, I never knew about it. Actually, I have been told that I am envied—the other side of jealousy. I would not want pity, because then I would be afraid that when people are nice, they would be doing it because they are sorry for me. It's so demeaning; I like others to feel equal, and I don't want to feel inferior. Maybe it's hubris—false pride.

I do know that I always hated being a child because of being in an inferior position; the grown-ups were such giants, and the child was humiliated, put in an untenable position, defenseless. I must have fallen down a million times, because my knees were always scabby, and I had childhood illnesses, but I don't remember people being sorry for me; they were only afraid John would catch something from me. At least, that's what I thought.

I don't know where my ambition came from out of all that. It did, though; I wanted to be of use, and now I want to be wise. Even if I don't get there, I hope I've tried."

Entertaining doesn't often seem the answer to lonesome hours, despite the suitability of her apartment for parties. The upper floor of her duplex consists of what used to be called public rooms—dining room, living room and a kitchen with butler's pantry. The lower floor's use is limited for the most part to her bedroom (sizable and with bath-dressing room) and the TV room (small, crowded with required reading and a color cable set). A former bedroom is now a yellow library-sitting room, and there is a guest room. The servants' quarters, also TV-equipped, have a faint and not unpleasant odor of O'Cedar mops and laundry.

The decor was executed by Dick Hall's sister, Marian. She was governed less by Dorothy's taste, which runs to the conventional, than by inherited items, such as the Lely and Lawrence portraits, a sizable number of porcelains and Meissen birds and English antiques. The high-ceilinged living room, almost as notable as the office, is long and of proportionate width. Arched french windows are at the far end, flanking a fireplace, and casement windows open on terraces. The feeling is of a country seat; emphasis on chintzes confirms this, as does a pair of Grandma Moses snowscapes.

The dining room, with three french windows opening on terraces, accommodates twenty guests, who are served efficiently by two party helpers, in addition to her couple, all well schooled in Dorothy's routines. The simple menu may consist of a soup or appetizer, a casserole, salad and cheesecake. The wine is a Pouilly Fumé (Dorothy doesn't go for red), and with dessert champagne appears, domestic label concealed by napkin ("one has to cut corners somewhere").

Cocktails precede dinner in the living room or on the west terrace, with canapés (smoked salmon and sliced hard-boiled egg with anchovies). The guest list will include one VIP and wife, often political, perhaps a lighter weight of opposing view, a few money types, certainly some liberal thinkers, and some "young" (the bottom thirties except for a grandchild or two in the twenties). The seniority range has no limit as long as he (which it's more apt to be than she) is interesting, presentable, influential or of note.

"I guess people have a good time," Dorothy has commented, "or they wouldn't write such nice letters. What I don't understand is why I am so seldom asked back."

Though always nervous as a hostess, Dorothy managed one of her rare dinners in March, 1973, for the Nelson Rockefellers. She didn't enjoy herself until the sexes rejoined each other in the living room over liqueurs, as her memo shows.

> Nelson sat down next to Joe Kraft and praised a column he had written about the Supreme Court coming out in favor of abortion. Joe, of course, was very flattered that he had read and remembered this column; I thought what a good politician Nelson is. Nelson, at one point, said he didn't always vote for Republican candidates and gave an example.
>
> Somehow or other we started talking about death; he said he wasn't afraid of death. I said I wasn't either, but I was afraid of the possible pain of a slow death. Nelson said that could be taken care of, and I said, "But you once told me that you believed in God. Isn't this against all religions, to hasten death?" Nelson said God did not intend us to suffer pain; he was quite positive about it.
>
> Later we talked about his ability to negotiate; he did not remember that he had once told me that he had learned negotiating from his father because that is how he had to deal with him. He said when he, Nelson, took over as manager of Rockefeller Center, the first thing he did was to fire four $80,000-a-year men because he said they were dishonest. He said the sons had bought the center from their father because of Nelson's having persuaded him to give them money, gift taxes being lower than inheritance taxes.
>
> He was worried about his weight; says he now weighs 205 pounds, which is "awful." I said no, I think it's very exciting. Everybody laughed.

One result of that dinner was that Happy Rockefeller came for the sandwich and to chat "about men and women." The tape records:

"Happy had asked for a chicken sandwich, thinking that was the easiest thing to order. What she doesn't know is that in the eateries downtown they call them chicken salad sandwiches; God knows what they're made of. Fortunately, I had a roast chicken cooked over the weekend, and there was some left. I left a note to make two chicken sandwiches on white bread without mayonnaise because I thought the mayonnaise might get bad if they hung around all morning.

At the office, I supervised the opening of the sandwiches because the very first lady of the state was coming for lunch and I thought we would have as few errors as possible. There was a debate about whether to give her one sandwich or both—I had ordered my usual BLT— and I said, 'Well, I think two sandwiches on the plate might put her off.' She was given one and a half.

She arrived in a gray wool; she dresses well—very simply—she doesn't wear jewelry, and I liked her shoes. I thought she was a little on the plump side; she doesn't look as well as she did when she married him. But she's a nice, warm, earth mother type.

First she said, 'What are you having?' and I said a Clamato. She said she didn't want a drink, then she said, 'If there is any dubonnet. . . .' It wasn't put out, so I squatted down, opened that ghastly little cupboard thing and couldn't see it. She spotted it; it just had some dregs. After we had talked for a while, she said, 'Gee, that makes me feel like having another dubonnet.' I had poured the three drops left and knew there wasn't any more. I didn't dare buzz because I would have gotten the answer there isn't another bottle.

We started talking about politics, which really was not the purpose of lunch. She and Nelson had watched Kissinger's broadcast together; she said he, K., was worried he had not mentioned Nixon often enough. I told her how anxious I was to see Kissinger again and that Nixon is hard to see. She said, 'He sure is,' indicating that Rockefeller didn't get to see him too often in the past. She said

within the family, the Nixon family—the entourage—
there were people who did not want K. to remain, and I
said there was always infighting around power. Happy
agreed that any man who has had a taste of power, such
as Kissinger's, would not want to relinquish it. She said,
'Let's just the four of us have dinner.' On Nancy Maginnes, who does research for Nelson, I said, 'I hear she's
Kissinger's real girl.' Happy thought it was an intellectual friendship but that one never knew about Kissinger unless one saw it with one's own eyes.

On drugs, she said they are now selling them in ele-
mentary schools; she's worried about her little boys. She
wants the pushers off the streets—I bet she gave Nelson
that idea—and in jail for life.

I think she was slightly overawed because she kept saying she hoped she wasn't interrupting anything and taking too much of my time. I expect people who come here
for lunch, especially a woman who doesn't go to an office
habitually, might feel that she is intruding. Even the governor's wife might feel that she isn't that important. Happy ate all three parts of her sandwich; other people do
not.

I'm glad that I saw her, even if I kind of lost control of
it. She got me to talk more politics than I intended to. She
kept telling me what a marvelous time Nelson had at my
party, that he always leaves parties at ten thirty and she
had to drag him out at twelve thirty. I think he had a better time than she had. I wouldn't want to be Happy
Rockefeller. It is too bad, because really she is much better for him than he is for her."

Not long after, in that same spring of 1973, the Nelson Rockefellers asked her to dine with Henry Kissinger. According to the
tape:

"I was told it would be just the four of us, meaning Kissinger, Happy, Nelson and myself, but when I arrived,
Nancy Maginnes was there in a red pants suit. She is very
tall, very serious, knows facts and figures and never
smiles.

Nelson, whom she calls Governor, got on local politics,
but Kissinger looked more and more bored, so I asked
how a recent speech of his went. He cheered up consider-

ably and talked about other nations, much as our labor negotiator at the *Post* speaks of those he deals with. He adores the Chinese and said that everything is highly organized, but you don't know it, and the police aren't visible. The schedule for visitors is made up of eight-minute segments, he said, so if it's running late, they just cut one.

As to the President's mental condition, he said Nixon rises to crises and doesn't panic. K. prefers talking about nations, and when we got on to foreign trade, Nelson said money doesn't matter anymore; it's become meaningless. I said, 'You still have to have it,' but he thinks in terms of barter systems. K. looks up to him and agrees with me that leadership is the most important thing to have.

Nelson joked with K., who said, 'Well, you chose me from Harvard,' and Nelson laughed. 'I didn't choose you; I don't know where you came from.' K. was on a committee for the Rockefeller Brothers Fund, which was composed of professors and was to make recommendations. Nelson said that what they'd come up with were tactics, but he wanted a long-term plan. K. said, 'Indeed, that is just what it was—short-term thinking,' and he was impressed by Nelson. Nelson and K. are at the same time employer and employee along with professor and pupil. I think K. wishes to God Nelson were President and has affection for him—as much as he can for anyone.

On trust, K. agrees that it is important in international relations, but I had the feeling he likes to see it backed up by power. I think he's delighted that Nixon recognized his ability and followed his recommendations. I did not get the feeling that killing, such as bombing Cambodia, bothers him one bit. He can be ruthless in his personal feelings, too, I think. And with women, for instance, I am sure he has been.

I think I fear him somewhat . . . this man is extremely . . . I was going to say cold, but it's more than that—calculating. He is without the usual kind of male charm, but his intellect is so terrific; at least, many people have told me that, and his wit is acid. I don't think he'd ever back out; he's too Prussian."

A year later, after Henry Kissinger and Nancy Maginnes were married, Dorothy's habitual curiosity led her to accept an invitation to a dinner dance in their honor, although she usually doesn't enjoy that kind of party. It was given in late spring, 1974, by the Nelson Rockefellers at the family's Pocantico Hills estate, a domain which is one of the few that could make her father's Northwood duchy seem a modest holding. Although Nancy Kissinger was absent owing to illness, Henry was very much there.

Dorothy, seated at a dance floor table in the gaily decorated tent, was anxious to have a word alone with Kissinger. As soon as the chair on his left was empty, she slid into it. Her tape says:

> "K. said he liked the recent *Post* series on him, in spite of there being a few minor errors, which he couldn't remember. Clayton Fritchey had reported that Mrs. K. hadn't been pleased by the mention of some of K.'s old girl friends.
>
> When I asked him how he liked being married, he said, 'Any woman married to me has to realize she can have only ten percent of me.' He added that Nancy was very bright and strong, that I should get to know her.
>
> I told him that Lewis Strauss had said that he and I wouldn't have worked out, because we both were strong people and when that kind married, there was always a clash. K.: 'I don't know; I've only been married three months.'
>
> K. said he keeps going back to the Middle East to say the same thing over and over. 'Are you a patient man?' I asked.
>
> 'No. Extremely impatient.'
>
> 'How can you keep going?'
>
> 'It is so important, I have to hold my temper.'
>
> He is trying, but it may be like the Vietnam peace—no peace at all. As to his ten percent thinking, I should have told him he needs a woman who can give only ten percent of herself. He sees himself as a combination of Metternich, Talleyrand, Castlereagh and Bismarck. He's very impressed with people who have established reputations and always refers to himself as a "statesman." I see his success as due to the impression he made on Nelson, who, like my grandfather and Franklin Roosevelt, learned not from reading books but from endless people around them. Beaverbrook, too, always milking brains.
>
> K. concentrates on you a hundred percent and makes more personal remarks than one expects a professor to, but I get a sense of his wondering how you can be useful.

Henry Kissinger and Dorothy at the party given by the Rockefellers in honor of the Kissinger wedding.

He's a powerful man, and I'm interested in power, but I prefer Dean Rusk, who was charming and was hit unfairly by the liberals; he was only following White House instructions. I could never work with a man said to be as mistrustful as K. and given to such outbursts of temper.

I don't think he forgets his Jewishness for a second; how can he? There is a lot of hostility there, or he wouldn't be overweight, but it's controlled. Someday I'd

like to talk to him about what Bernie Baruch told me—
that he'd turned down a Treasury Secretaryship because
he didn't think a Jew should stick his neck out. But people say times have changed. I wonder?

Had there been martial law during the armed forces
alert and K. one of those in charge, along with [James]
Schlesinger and [Alexander] Haig, I think he would have
given the order to shoot the rioters. I don't think he's interested in civil rights anyway; I think he'll make money,
write books, get a foundation job—a big one—and be set
for life, *if* he survives. I'd like to see more of him, in spite
of my criticisms; he's the second most important man in
the world.

Something was dead about the Pocantico evening—no
gaiety. The lovely grounds made the trip worthwhile, but
the atmosphere was better a few years ago. I think the
trouble is the gloom of the country and the feeling of impending disaster. There's a leadership problem, too; all
the leaders seem so old and shaken."

In July, 1974, Dorothy came to a decision about President
Nixon which she would have reached earlier had she not feared
that her enmity and distrust influenced her reasoning. Those
scruples overcome, the *Post* came out for his resignation, and
Dorothy awaited the departure of our first President to resign
from office.

"It's great we've won, but I do not want to dance on the
grave of Richard Nixon. I take no joy in this moment; I
have never trusted him, long knew what he was and always opposed him. But this is so sad for America, and
these are not crocodile tears.

I think it's our fault he was elected. This goes back to
'68 when we had the Bobby-McCarthy disaster, which
never should have happened; it should have been one or
the other. I think Lyndon Johnson could have defeated
Richard Nixon, or Gene McCarthy or Bobby, but since
they all got into it. . . . I blame Bobby a lot, frankly.

Why did he assume McCarthy would get out? Why was
he so arrogant? Poor Bobby, whom I loved, knew
McCarthy and knew he wanted to be President very badly or even be Vice President with Lyndon. We were divided, which showed lack of leadership. Any one of these

candidates could have been elected, but instead they knocked each other off—a case of divide and be vanquished.

Hubert Humphrey I knew couldn't make it. He may be the brightest man in the Senate, but he just didn't have the public personality. I have enough flair to know that, and so did lots of us, yet we allowed Nixon to win. In the long run it may be for the best in the best of all possible worlds; everyone has learned a lesson for a while.

Nixon's farewell to his staff showed him at his lowest ebb, looking for love and understanding. His reference to his sainted mother was significant, as was that to the "little man," his father. His 1960 farewell speech about the press not having him to kick around anymore didn't work, but he has learned not to show so much of his hate to those who hate him.

I'm not clever enough to do a psychological rundown on him, but I've never seen a man as cool under pressure. He couldn't admit his guilt for reasons of liability but went as far as he could in admitting poor judgment. His most serious flaw is lack of ethics; he has worked for the worst elements in the United States.

The assassination of the Kennedys should be reexamined; we know that Howard Hunt recommended assassination for Castro, but CIA Director Richard Helms, a liberal, wouldn't go along with it. Then there's Bebe Rebozo, a Cuban mixed up with Meyer Lansky and the Mafia, etc. The question is, who had the most to gain from these killings?

Ford has opened up a lot; he's a decent man, and having Nelson in, it could be a terrific combination; they don't have a neurotic bone in their bodies. How nice that Nelson is Vice President; he made Kissinger, and now Kissinger has returned the compliment by making him!"

As so often when she ponders national perils, Dorothy mentions the need for leadership. She is discouraged that so few leaders are available at this significant moment in our history, and in trying to define leadership quality, she comes back to the press lord, Max Beaverbrook. She remembers he once called her an old soul ("probably, he told all the girls that"). Reminiscing one evening, she spoke of a speech Max had given to farm labor voters in Norwich, England. As he finished, they rushed to him and carried him on their shoulders to the London train. Once aboard, Dorothy said, "How they loved your speech!"

"*Loved* it?" Max said. "I thought they were rushing at me to kill me!"

Dorothy says she doesn't dream much—more accurately, seldom has recall—but that night had a dream in which Max came through strongly.

"I had gone to see him in a London hotel with people around. He asked me to come into the bedroom to speak to me; I had with me two women—maybe employees— two children and perhaps a dog.

He said he had sent me a note and hoped I was going to do what it asked. I hadn't received it and asked where it had been sent. He said to my present apartment and wouldn't tell me what was in it. I couldn't understand why the two women wouldn't leave the room and asked them to. The children stayed; then Everette was waiting outside, and finally Max disappeared. It was daylight. I couldn't find Everette and didn't know where to go or what to do.

Max looked exactly as he did in '31 and I couldn't understand his hold over me—so alive—not having seen him since '51. I have no association with it at all and only know that with Max, I was too young. I'm still not very sophisticated, or maybe I mean cynical.

Max was extremely neurotic, with I think a subconsciously low opinion of himself, and when I suggested psychiatry to him at lunch at the Chambord, he screamed with laughter. Had he tried it, he might have thought twice about me, but it wouldn't have changed my view of him. It put me off when he made such fun of it, and I didn't tell him I had tried it.

My picture of Max in New York over the years is sitting in good restaurants at a good table, having personal conversations, being pooh-poohed and getting nowhere, as was the case at Claridge's in London. I thought the whole thing was dead until this dream. He caught me at a formative age, and got me into everything, and his influence was hypnotic. He made fun of sacred things such as motherhood, even though he liked children. Max was a very sad man, and I see now that I was right to leave when I did."

Returning to the need for national leadership, Dorothy points out that it is almost eerie how often the name of Franklin Roosevelt comes up in connection with current talk about a depression. She wonders if that combination of aristocracy, authority and humanity would work this time.

Her awareness of FDR and her sense of inadequacy in the relationship prompted a visit to Hyde Park, the first in thirty years. Her dread of the changes time might have wrought was offset by her anticipation at having as her guide Franklin D. Roosevelt, Jr. She has been both friend and political adviser to Franklin, Jr., who of all the sons looks and feels most like his father.

Today Franklin is better known for his name and for his success as a Fiat importer than for political accomplishment, in spite of his having served a term in Congress. His manner with Dorothy is a combination of the gallant and respectful, and he relates to her as peer and contemporary. Her manner with him is simpler; she is very glad to see him.

As Franklin drives Dorothy up the hill on which the Red House stands, she mentions that then the abutting fields had been open, instead of being a sizable housing development. "And the Christmas trees your father had planted were little shoots."

"You know, Dolly, I was responsible for getting him into growing trees. I studied the thing, while still at Harvard, and asked him to rent me some land. He took one look at my figures and said, 'If it's good enough for you, it's good enough for me.' The next thing I knew I wasn't in the Christmas tree business, but he was."

The frame house is of simple design, blends well into the site, and the color is very red indeed, setting off the white trim. The owner remembers the price he paid for it in 1947, together with the forty-five acres, as $25,000. Franklin calls it quite a buy, as he admires the superb view with its choice of seven mountain ranges.

"It always seemed so teeny whenever I came from Oyster Bay," Dorothy muses. "I'm glad nothing has changed; so much else just isn't anymore—the houses I grew up in, Max's Stornaway House in London. . . ."

Dorothy had only a brief look at FDR's Dream House; a Great Dane growled on the bank next to the driveway, his jaws on a level with the car window. Apprehensively, she suggested mov-

Dorothy and FDR, Jr.

ing on, saying the house would look prettier in the spring.
Franklin obliged and mentioned that the place had been left to
his brother, Elliott, who had sold it without telling their
mother.

"She was horrified," Franklin said. "And that ends the story of
the Dream House."

"Except for the fact that the pair of Delft cows I gave your father for his new mantel went to Elliott. I wish they hadn't."

Dorothy lost her look of bitterness as they drove to see the Val-
Kill cottage and the furniture factory Eleanor had converted into
a house for herself. She recalled how proud of Val-Kill the President had been, adding that at heart he was a frustrated contractor. "He didn't trust experts and was always saying they didn't
know anything."

Franklin laughed. "That's true, you know."

"And here's that swamp which had to be drained every year.
He never would quite admit it was a swamp."

"And this is the dam he put in," Franklin said, steering over it
with care.

"Is the bridge safe? It looks like Chappaquiddick."

They were convulsed for a moment. "I ought to slap your wrist for that, Dolly."

"Why—has it happened to you, too?"

The mood of the place stilled their laughter as they got out of the car. Both cottages seemed very closed up and in a way that spoke of more than winter. There was less a feeling of great names having been about, or large ideas having been exchanged, than one of abandonment. Whatever past there was had fled.

"Johnny lived here in the cottage until a few years ago," Franklin observed, his voice low. "Isn't it a lovely house? Mother's bedroom was up there in the old furniture factory by the corner of the porch."

Dorothy, her eyes on the pool, nodded. "At picnics *he* used to sit there in his chair."

After a bit they returned to the car, and Franklin broke the stillness by saying how different it looks in winter. "At Christmas we would come here for the big presents, as we called them. Mother used to give a marvelous Christmas for us kids—six Brooks shirts, a dozen handkerchiefs. . . . Everything had to have our initials on them."

"It doesn't sound a bit like her. I would have thought she'd go to Sears, Roebuck."

"No. I insisted that Brooks button-down shirts were the right thing to wear, so she got them for all the boys. I still wear them, although people think I'm square. I don't think my brother-in-law liked them, but he had to put up with it."

On the wood road down to the Hudson, Franklin mentioned that the drive to the Dream House was one of his father's favorites for scaring people. Judge Rosenman, he added, used to cross himself, and even the King and Queen of England had to be tried out on it.

"Edsel Ford saw him driving a Model T with hand controls and said, 'Oh, Mr. President, I've got to bring you up to date.' He replaced it with a Model A, and when the V-8 model came out, he gave him one of those, and the Model A was retired to Warm Springs. They were both blue, which was Father's favorite color, because he liked the sea."

Dorothy looked at him closely. "Are your eyes blue?"

"When they're not red."

She gave one of her best laughs and, relaxed in spite of the precipitous downgrade, tucked a leg under her.

Among the indications of Dorothy's emotional maturity is her having made a kind of peace with loneliness.

"I am convinced Mr. Right will not come along after all, and I'm glad; I really don't need any*one* now, but I do need people. If not freedom, this is independence. I can live with myself and recognize some of my qualities, which I suppose are unusual. I still need intense relationships, but it's on a different level; it's no longer a possessive, frantic kind of need, and I know that the other person must be free. I don't think I ever thought of that other person until lately, but involvement still hurts. I always see failure in an affair as my fault—I didn't try hard enough—and now I may have learned that it takes two to make it work. Both must give.

Fairy tales don't happen. I have learned, finally, that when one has a friend, one must love that friend and accept whatever happens—even be grateful for demands. The word 'sacrifice' comes to mind—self-sacrifice—putting the other person first. Adlai Stevenson used to talk a lot about sacrifice, but joking mostly; he would have said the one you love does the sacrificing. In a two-way relationship, one gives more than the other; I've never had any other kind. I probably didn't deserve it.

I did my best within the framework in which I lived, but not in terms of my potential. Even with the paper I don't think I've done as well as I could. My relations with my children have been fairly successful, even if I don't see them much, and they seem fond of me. I've failed desperately in my peer relationships, though—I've had at least a dozen close ones, and they failed. I haven't educated myself as much as I might have in terms of book learning, but in life learning, maybe I have done better than I know. As Abe Beame says, 'I get along.' I've become tolerant and understanding, but I'm indifferent about people too much of the time.

If I had to go back, I suppose I'd do it exactly the same way. I might be more calculating in my choice of friends; I like doers and eclectics—a spectrum. Too many people in the arts have only one topic—their world. As to physical types, they could be black, white, or in between, and short or tall. I'm thinking of men, which is funny; I'm not thinking of women.

Sometimes I wonder what those I have known would think of me now. Grandpa Schiff would be very pleased, but he would have gone through some agonizing moments. People have said to me, 'Your grandfather must be turning over in his grave,' but I think he'd say I've done all right. My father would think the same thing, but he would not have predicted that it would turn out all right. They were always worried about me, that I'd get into dreadful trouble that I could not get myself out of. Which I may be doing.

My mother wouldn't have understood any of this, having wished me to make 'a brilliant marriage.'

My brother, John, is the rock of ages for me, even though I don't see much of him. He is the most stable man I know; always does his duty and the right thing. In trouble, he's the man to call on, although I never have. I might ask for emotional support but never help for the *Post.*

People say we're so different, but maybe we're two halves of a whole, each a side of the medal—he's the good person, and I'm the bad—but he thinks I'm so terrific. At his birthday party he said, 'Come sit with me,' and I was stunned; it's the nicest thing that ever happened to me. He's a little afraid of me because of his fantastic idea of what I am, even when we were at school. Probably I was the darer as a child and he was the follower.

He looks rather awesome, so tall and so serious. I always feel he's going to disapprove—that's the conscience thing—but he never does. He always says 'fine,' and backs me up in whatever I do. I see him as Mr. Common Sense, but he is very withdrawn, restless, and has no sense of how good he is or of his achievement. He told me a few years ago that he always looked for the best in everyone; now maybe he's beginning to wonder whether life is that good and people are that good. He keeps in touch with all sorts of relatives. My father was rather like that, too, though a completely different type of person.

I suppose really I'm more like my father than John is; probably he's more like my mother, except that she was very naughty and advanced. It was called 'fast' when she was a girl; on her honeymoon she was asked to leave the Ritz Hotel in Boston for smoking in the lobby. And years later, in San Francisco, she was arrested for jaywalking; at first she thought it meant streetwalking.

John is very money-conscious, but also very generous. Leonard Lyons used to say that usually John's son David goes to work in his Rolls, but that John takes the subway. Often between board meetings, Leonard said, John would have a ham sandwich in the subway, which he buys at Grand Central. When asked what he would do if he saw a friend on the subway, John said, 'Well, I'd offer him half.'

It's useful in many ways to have a banker as a brother. For instance, to be John Schiff's sister is advantageous with certain advertisers. It means I cannot be as wildly left-wing as they had been led to believe, and they're right. All my life there has been someone that I have been careful not to offend, but I've gone ahead and done things anyway.

At the same time, he never discusses his racing stable with me or his annual Boy Scout things that take place in foreign countries; perhaps those pictures of him in shorts and Boy Scout uniform made him feel silly, and he didn't think it was serious enough. But being chairman of the board of NYU, that's okay. I see him as a very stiff, serious Puritan, and I never think of his power, really. Because he is my conscience, I would want to conceal things from him, as I did with my mother."

Dorothy takes pleasure in the company of her son, Morti Hall, and is amused by his tales of society types she no longer sees. "But he threw me when he said he was more scared of me than Uncle John," Dorothy almost whispers. "Awful; it made me think of my father, who was so terrified of his father."

She also enjoys her daughter Adele Sweet, who says of her mother: "She is, I think, the most current human being I know. She is also contradictory—wafts back and forth—and can be terrifically affectionate, extraordinarily generous and uncomfortable when she's praised. She can be vulnerable and open, but patience is not her long suit. If she's in an impatient mood, it comes out looking abrupt and quite unintentional.

"It beats me her inordinate physical fears—escalators, eleva-tors, flying and so forth. It's a monument to her self-discipline, her efforts to overcome her fears. I watched her speak at the *Her-ald Tribune* Forum—that's the only time I've seen her address a public gathering—and I died for her; I had vicarious stage fright because she was shaking. I noticed recently that just proposing a toast made her terribly uncomfortable; her voice was shaking, and it was like watching a child perform, completely centered on its discomfort.

"Her vulnerability is hard to define; she is a sensitive person and protests too much, I think, that she's not sentimental and emotional. She's quite insecure, too, but I certainly don't think that's the image that's projected. As to the woman, the word 'feminine' doesn't cover it all; she is very, very much a woman, but that gets lost in the shuffle.

"One of the most remarkable things about her is the intensity with which she views absolutely anything that touches her. She gave a dinner one night and asked me to be there at nine o'clock in the morning to make preparation; there had been any number of phone calls to make prior to that. She asked how many bottles of wine should she order, and I said, 'Now, let's see; how many people are you having?' But she wanted to know how many glasses of wine each person would drink, and I said, 'That's sub-ject to change without notice; you can't figure out that closely. Make a deal with the liquor store dealer, so he'll take back what you don't use.' She expects absolutely precise answers, and then there's the frugality—that penny-wise and pound-foolish thing that must go back to Jacob Schiff.

"One afternoon Uncle John and Aunt TeeTee were coming for a drink, and TeeTee arrived first. Mother said, 'What would you like to drink?' and Aunt TeeTee said, 'I'll have a scotch and soda.' Then Mother said, 'What do you think John is going to drink?' 'Probably a scotch and soda.' So Mother opened a quart size bottle of soda, and Uncle John arrived.

"'Scotch and soda?' Mother asked. 'No, I'd like a martini.' Well, she looked devastated and said, 'But TeeTee said you'd have a scotch and soda.' I knew what she was thinking—that she could have done with the little bottle. Waste is anathema to her; she loathes it."

Adele's half sister, Sarah-Ann Kramarsky—the only child of

Adele Sweet, Dorothy and Adele's daughter, Wendy Lynn Gray.

Dorothy and George Backer—enjoys a close rapport with Dorothy, perhaps because of being the youngest.

"I can't imagine anyone better as a mother, mother-in-law or grandmother," Sarah-Ann says, "but my father thought the men she married didn't give her enough to do. He thought she would have been happier as the wife of a President or a Prime Minister. Maybe her husbands felt inadequate because they couldn't live up to her expectations, and while I don't see her as essentially sensuous, men are attracted to her for a lot of reasons.

"The way she has changed with the times is extraordinary. I can't imagine her allowing herself to be just an old lady, any more than I can see her not having the *Post*. She's always let me have my own point of view, and it would take a lot of courage for me to tell her a lie."

Sarah-Ann's husband says Dorothy disproves all the mother-in-law stories. "I am very much in awe of her and, as a relatively aggressive male, I create tensions, but I don't experience them with her as a threat.

"Being known as her son-in-law is not a problem, and I can join those who criticize the running of the *Post*. She is an elitist, not an anti-Semite—one of those who demand the best of everybody, an attribute of the elite to which she belongs. In a sense her generational caste had very strict concepts of right and wrong; one did *for* those who were less fortunate, and she has translated this in contemporary terms.

"She is bright, intuitive and intelligent without being intellectual, in terms of pursuing an abstraction. I see her as a serious person, but given to flights of fancy. She has a mission, but I don't know if she has a sense of it. I find her open to ideas but less so to suggestions, and I see her involvement with the present as connected with her resistance to aging. She doesn't have to repair the past; she can concentrate on influencing the future.

"As to her being liked—revered—by those who don't know her well, she is pretty remote. There are few people I know of with whom she is on cozy terms; no one sees her as a joke, but some see her as a threat. There are those who think she does things arbitrarily and as a caprice, but they don't know her."

It is surprising how few of Dorothy's friends are aware of what goes on under the charm and behind the mask. Joe Kraft explains that before his column was in the *Post*, it was difficult for him to have an easy relationship with her. "Maybe I overdid the *Post*'s importance—probably it was something that I tended to imagine—but it was very hard for me. She tries to be informal, and since she is mainly a woman and a helluva dame, she is highly sensitive to boy-girl stuff.

"There is a difference in her relationship with Nelson Rockefeller and John Lindsay. She's really at ease with Nelson, and he with her; they can schmaltz it up between the two of them. It seems ironic that she and Kay Graham are both connected with liberal crusading newspapers, because they are themselves so far removed from the juiceless militant crusaders. They're pretty juicy people.

"Dorothy's Jewish background, in common with Kay, is a focus of a certain unease. I mean, there are problems for those old Jewish families who grew up cheek by jowl with Gentile society. In the thirties there really was a sea change that built up a self-consciousness about relationships that hadn't existed in the past."

Clay Felker, editor of *New York* magazine and the *Village Voice*, thinks Dorothy finds it useful to keep people off-balance. "I have always been struck by her asking direct questions, which are to the point and are ones no one dares ask. Once she called to ask if I wanted to join her and Ted Sorensen, who had asked her for dinner, right after he wrote Ted Kennedy's Chappaquiddick speech. She said, 'Let's find out what really went on.' So she was enlisting me as a co-questioner, although she was far better at that than I.

"This kind of questioning comes from her position; no one is going to take umbrage, or at least show it. Also, her intelligence is part of it; David Frost has it, too. I remember when she showed me her office and we went into a big room. I asked if it was a boardroom, and she said, 'I don't believe in boards of directors.' She's obviously sole owner; she is a one-person runner of things. If she should ever ask me if she should sell the *Post,* I'd tell her not to; publications have a way of taking hold of you body and soul."

The publisher of the New York *Times* Arthur Ochs Sulzberger, has said, "Dorothy is a very determined, gutsy lady; she tends not to run with the pack, but she's maybe not quite as fearful, now, that the *Times* and *News* are going to slaughter her. Dorothy is quite a woman, I wouldn't lie to you."

"Dolly is one of the brightest women I've ever known," Max Lerner says. "She is a very concrete thinker and is impatient when ideas are put in terms of abstractions. She has a remarkable capacity for getting away from the intellectual elite, and from their thinking, to the people on the street.

"In Dolly's case strength tends to become almost legendary; it's what I call authority. I don't think she would have had it if she hadn't come from the family she came from; it's a carryover of the sense of command she felt around her in that great family. It became a part of her, and she can no more help exuding it than she can help breathe.

"I think she has many angers in her. That mask she habitually assumes—a sort of deadpan calm—actually conceals an inner seething. A good deal of her vitality and drive come out of some of the clashes and frustrations that are involved there.

"I think she is very proud of the role that her grandfather, Jacob, had in the American Jewish community. She displays many of the characteristics of the wealthy, aristocratic branch of the German Jewish community. One of those characteristics is that along with the pride in what her family has done, there is a great reluctance to think of herself as primarily Jewish.

"It has shown itself in an unwillingness to make herself vulnerable, editorially or in news treatment, to accusations that what she is doing in the paper is because she is Jewish. The *Post* has taken a more open stand than the *Times* ever has on questions like Israel, and I find Dolly's liberalism more like mine; she is tough-minded rather than tender-minded."

Dorothy has still not found a successor for herself at the *Post.*

"The men I brought in were bright and looked as though they might be ideal. It was unfair to them because I should have told them what Herbert Lehman once said to me: drudgery is ninety percent of any job, but the remaining ten percent makes it worthwhile. I'm not sure all of them learned this: that really hard, grinding work has to go into a job. It was fun having these fun people with me, even if each was for only nine months, but I couldn't justify their salaries to the others. (Now I think about it, especially to myself.)

All these men cared a lot about the paper, but they didn't gain, or they lost, the confidence of the others. Somebody once said that I may not be able to work with anybody in such a position or that I don't really wish to. There may be some truth in both these charges, but I guess I'm sort of relieved these people are gone."

One problem in these relationships for Dorothy seems to have been that the amount of trust required was beyond her. These men were directed to speak and act for her, but never as if they were in her shoes. Some were given access to the books, a bit tentatively, but none to the book called Dorothy Schiff.

"I'd miss the *Post* more than it would miss me. It would go on and be even better, maybe, justifying my many years with it. I don't see my contribution to my time personally, but I guess it's through the *Post*. I've been striving all my life to reach the goal of complete wisdom and understanding, but I know that's impossible. I would like to understand the motivations of others

344   MEN, MONEY AND MAGIC

and be able to get people together for a durable peace, and while I know that I won't see it, you have to keep on trying.

When I took on the *Post,* I didn't have much faith in myself or the paper, and I didn't really think I could pull it out. Now, it's part of me—we are part of each other."

Index

Figures in italics refer to pages on which illustrations occur.

Abram, Morris, 300–1, 305
Adams, F. P., 109, 132
Aitken, Janet, 88
Alsop, Joseph, 250, 294
Alsop, Stewart, 313
American Labor Party, 203
Americans for Democratic Action, 230
American Society of Newspaper Editors, 256
Amherst College, 23
Annenberg, Walter, 172
Argyll, Lady Jean, 88
Arlen, Michael, 88
Ascoli, Max, 127
Associated Press (AP), 275
Astor, Alice, 34, 71
Astor, Lady, 44
Astor, Vincent, 51, 54
Atlantic Pact, 212
Atomic Energy Commission, 53
Attica prison rebellion, 316–17

Backer, George, (DS's second husband), 11, 27, 101–8, 113, 115–24, 126, 129, 132, 134, 146–48, *150*, 155, 169, 173, 185, 191, 216, 223, 238, 340; on New York City Council, 148–49; and New York *Post* acquisition, 161–64, 168, 175, 177–80, 182
Backer Kramarsky, Sarah-Ann (DS's daughter), 121, 122, 124, 173–74, 180, 186, 190, 195, 206, 219, *231*, 239, 244, 339; on her mother, 340
Badillo, Herman, 315
Baker, Edith (Mrs. John Schiff). *See* Tee Tee Schiff
Balsan, Colonel, 172
Balsan, Madame. *See* Vanderbilt, Consuelo
Barry, Philip, 132
Barry, Mrs. Philip, 132

Baruch, Bernard, 165–66, 194, 234, 240, 262, 268, 330
Beach Club, 64, 66
Beame, Abraham, 17, 220, 316, 336
Beattie, Bessie, 137
Beaverbrook, William Maxwell Aitken, Lord, 11, 80–92, 94–98, 102, 103, 105–6, 116, 117, 118, 119, 132, 139, 148, 161, 170, 183, 184, 193, 210, 225–26, 263, 328, 331–32, 333
Beaverbrook (Taylor), 83
Begin, Menachem, 201
Behrman, S. N., 108, 148
Ben-Gurion, David, 201, 227, 231
Bennett, Joan, 101
Berlin, Dick, 307–8
Berlin, Ellin Mackay, 36, 55–56, 60, 108, 116, 133, 219
Berlin, Irving, 55, *56*, 108, 116, 133, 147
Best People, The (Berlin), 36
Biaggi, Mario, 315
Bie, Mr. 172–73
Bie, Mrs., 172–73, 188–89
Bismarck, Otto von, 312, 328
Blumenthal, George, 147
Boettiger, Anna, 130, 133, 135
Bookman, The, 62
Bouvier, Jack, 290, 292, 299
Bowles, Chester, 207
Boy Scouts of America, 76, 78
Bradford, Amory, 269
Bradley, Colonel, 64
Brandt, Foulke E., 37–39
Brandt case, 37–39, 50, 60
Brearley School, 29, 32, 34–35, 47, 54
Bronx *Home News,* 197, 200
Bryant, William Cullen, 13, 161
Bryn Mawr College, 19, 47–49
Buckley, Charles, 259
Bullitt, William C., 157
Bundy, McGeorge, 312

Cartier, Pierre, 53
Cartier's, 85
Cambodia, 327
Campbell, Ian, Duke of Argyll, 88
Campbell, Janet, 95
Campbell, Jeannie, 180, 225, 278
Carey, Hugh, 316
Carmichael, Stokely, 305, 306
Carpenter, Liz, 282
Carroll, Diahann, 299
Casa Eleda, 65—Adele Schiff's house in Palm Beach
Cassel, Sir Ernest, 23
Castlereagh, Viscount, 328
Castelrosse, Valentine, 81, 83, 98
Castro, Fidel, 246, 331
Central Intelligence Agency (CIA), 303, 331
Celler, Manny, 315
Cermak, Anton, 143
Chesterton, G. K., 107
Chicago *Daily News*, 200
Chotzinoff, Samuel, 148
Chambers, Whittaker, 264
Chisholm, Shirley, 316
Churchill, Jack, Duke of Marlborough, 91
Churchill, Lady, 255
Churchill, Randolph, 183, 207, 210, *211*, 262
Churchill, Winston, 91, 183, 193, 231, 240, 255, 262
Civil Rights Bill (1963), 283
Clark, Ramsey, 218, 305
Clemens, Miss, 27
Cleveland *Press*, 175
Cohn, Roy, 229–30
Cold Spring Harbor Memorial Cemetery, 76, 112
Colefax, Lady, 13
Coleman, William, 13
Compass, 212, 228
Condé Nast house, 204
Cook, Nancy, 129, 130, *131*, 133, 135, 136, 140, 141, 143, 144, 146, 159, 168, 192
Costello, Frank, 231–33
Costello, Mrs. Frank, 232–33
Cotton Club, 55
Cowles, Mike, 286
Crangle, Joe, 315–16, 319
Cravath, Paul D., 39
Crouse, Russell, 132
Crouse, Mrs. Russell, 132
Cunningham, Patrick, 315
Curtis family, 161, 163

Daly, John Charles, 157
Dead End (Backer), 117, 163
Democratic National Convention: (1936), 134; (1948), 207

Democratic Party, 254 ff., 304
De Sapio, Carmine, 236, 250
Dewey, Thomas, 207
Dickerman, Marion, 135, 192, 200
Diem, Nho Dinh, 281, 301
Dirksen, Everett, 288
Dr. Sachs' school, 23
Dominican Republic, 300
Douglas, Gordon, 80, 81
Douglas, Helen Gahagan, 263, 281, 283–84
Douglas, May, 81
Douglas, Paul, 253
Douglas, William O., 261
Dryfoos, Orvil, 267, 269, 270
Dubinsky, David, 130, 201, 257, 304
Duke, Mrs. Angier, 287
Duke, Doris, 90
Duke, James B., 20
Dulles, John Foster, 235

Early, Steve, 194
Eckerman, Fern, 201
Eddy, Mary Baker, 44
Eden, Anthony, 98
Editor & Publisher, 204
Edmiston, Susan, 188
Einstein, Albert, 239–42
Eisenhower, Dwight D., 250, 253, 280
Emerson, Faye, 190
Esposito, Meade, 315
Evans, Roland, 303
Evans and Novak (column), 305, 314

Farley, James A., 133, *203*, 253, 284, 287
Federal Bureau of Investigation, (FBI), 298
Felker, Clay, 278, 342
Field, Marshall, 197, 206–7
Fish, Hamilton, 179
Fleeson, Doris, 156, 157
Flynn, F. M., 259
Flynn, Jack, 270
Ford, Edsel, 335
Ford, Gerald, 331
Forrestal, James, 73, 81, 173, 296
Fox, Charles James, 104
Foy, Sebastien, 11, 73, 85–87, 88, 104–5, 219
Frankfurter, Felix, 157, 158
Frankfurter, Mrs. Felix, 158
Franklin, Benjamin, 145
Franklin School, 23
Freud, Sigmund, 124
Fritchey, Clayton, 328
Frost, David, 342
Fuerbringer, Otto, 308
Fulbright, J. William, 284, 305

Gallup Poll, 304
Gandhi, Mohandus, 145, 240
Gardiner, Dorothy, 53
Gerhardi, William, 88
Gershwin, George, 104
Gibson, Charles Dana, 46
Gibson, Irene (Mrs. Charles Dana), 44
Gillette, Jean, 15
Godkin, Edwin, 161
Godwin, Parke, 161
Gogarty, St. John, 105
Goldberg, Arthur, 304, 311
Goldwater, Barry, 264, 284
Goldwyn, Samuel, 263
Grafton, Samuel, 194
Graham, Kay, 229, 341
Gray, Barry, 257
Gray, Michael, *231*
Gray, Wendy Lynn, *340*
Great Game of Politics, The (Kent), 127
Great Northern Railroad, 23, 72
Green, Theodore, 240
Greenbaum, General, 242
Greenberg, Byron, 16
Guggenheim, Harry, 256
Guinzberg, Harold, 127, 132
Gurewitsch, Dr., 255

Haakon, King of Norway, 173
Hadassah, 202
Haddad, Bill, 222
Haganah, 201
Haig, Alexander, 330
Hall, Marian, 54, *69*, 119–20, 126, 323
Hall, Penelope Wilson, 94
Hall, Mortimer (DS's son), 61, 63, 67–68, 70, 93, 94, 115–16, 123, 124, 180, 186, 200, 206, 225, *231*, 236–37, 248, 338
Hall, Richard B. W., (DS's first husband) 11, 51–53, 54–55, 56–62, 63 ff., 71, 74, 79, 96, 102, 112, 115–16, 147, 206, 239, 323
Hall, Sweet, Adele Therese (DS's daughter), 63, 67–*68*, 70, 93, 115, 131, 170–71, 180, 186, 206, *231*, 236, *340*; on her mother, 93–94, 338–39
Hallgarten & Company, 23, 58
Hamill, Pete, 315
Hamilton, Alexander, 12, 13, 161
Harriman, Averell, 67, 72–73, 80, 167, 212, 234, 235–36, 257–59, 304, 317
Harriman, E. H., 72
Harriman, Marie, 236
Harris, Pat, 316
Hearst Corporation, 307
Hearst Press, 37–38, 39
Hearst, William Randolph, 166
Hearst, William Randolph, Jr., 274, 276

Hellman, Geoffrey, 95
Helms, Richard, 331
Helson, Blanche, *252*
Henry Street Settlement, 78
Hill, James J., 23, 72
Hiss, Alger, 221, 264
Hitler, Adolf, 41, 80, 265, 305
Ho Chi Minh, 305, 306, 308
Hoffman, Anna Rosenberg, 168, 286, 287
Holmes, Oliver Wendell, 143
Holtzman, Elizabeth, 315
Hooker, Harry, 140
Hoover, Herbert, 53, 262
Hoover, J. Edgar, 214, 222, 230, 298
Hopkins, Harry, 152, 157–58, 165
Horder, Lord. *See* Simon, John
Hore, Lady, 99
Hore-Belisha, Leslie, 11, 89, 91, 97–99, 117, 170, 225–26
Horney, Karen, 132
Howard, Jack, 274
Howard, Ray, 175–76
Humphrey, Hubert, 307, 331
Humphrey, Muriel, 311
Hunt, Howard, 331
Hurok, Sol, 311
Hurst, Fannie, 146
Hutton, Barbara, 98
Hylan, John, 19

Ingersoll, Ralph, 207
Irgunists, 201
Israel, 201, 243

Jefferson, Thomas, 145, 233, 283
Jennings, Sarah, 91
Johnson, Lady Bird, 282, 283, 285, 287, 305
Johnson, Lynda Bird, 286
Johnson, Lyndon B., 261, 280–88, 295, 298, 300–1, 302, 304–8, 309, 311, 319–20, 330
Joyce, James, 63
Juliana, Princess, of the Netherlands, 192
Junior Assembly, 50, 60
Junior League, 50, 60

Kahn, Otto, 64, 95
Kaufman, Beatrice, 104, 108, 113, 127
Kaufman, George, 104, 108
Keating, Kenneth, 288, 289
Kefauver hearings, 233
Kempton, Murray, 274
Kennedy, Caroline, 291
Kennedy, Ethel, 290, 293
Kennedy, Jacqueline, 261, 279, 283, 290–98, 303, 313
Kennedy, Joan, 263

Kennedy, John F., 195, 259–62, 279–82, 289, 293, 294–95, 296, 297, 301, 304, 310, 331
Kennedy, John F., Jr., 291, 292, 293
Kennedy, Joseph P., 67, 158, 260–63, 290, 292, 296, 302, 303
Kennedy, Joseph, Jr., 262–63
Kennedy, Kathleen, 309–10
Kennedy, Kathy, 262
Kennedy, Robert F., 281, 288–90, 293, 294, 295, 296, 298–300, 301, 302, 304, 305, 306, 308–10, 313, 314, 330, 331
Kennedy, Rose, 263
Kennedy, Ted, 263, 311, 313, 314, 319, 320, 342
Kennedy Foundation, 290
Kent, Frank, 127
Kheel, Theodore, 268–71
Khruschev, Nikita, 265
Kibya, 239
King, Martin Luther, 298
Kipling, Rudyard, 107
Kishinev pogrom, 41
Kissinger, Henry, 311–12, 316, 317, 325–30, 331
Kissinger, Nancy. See Maginnes Kissinger, Nancy
KLAC radio, 200
Knox, Frank, 200
Knox, Mrs. Frank, 200
Kraft, Joe, 324, 341
Kramarsky, Sarah-Ann. See Backer Kramarsky, Sarah-Ann
Kramarsky, Werner, 174, 340–41
Kraus, Nathan, 76
Kubie, Lawrence, 242, 255
Kuhn, Loeb & Company, 11, 13, 17, 38, 40, 53, 56, 61, 64, 72, 75, 78, 95, 117, 120, 199
Ky, Nguyen Cao, 308

La Guardia, Fiorello, 149–50, 155
Lait, Jack, 229
Landis, Jessie Royce, 224
Lansky, Meyer, 331
Lash, Joseph P., 181, 222
Lasker, Mary, 285, 300
Lawford, Pat, 299
Lawson, Aery, 12
Lawson, Everette, 12–13, 16, 303, 332
Lazard Frères, 313
Lee, Dick, 259–60
LeHand, Marguerite "Missy," 139, 140, 141, 150–51, 158, 166
Lehman, Herbert, 343
Lehman, Mrs. Herbert, 141
Lehman, Robert, 101
Lerner, Max, 95, 184, 242, 293, 300, 342

Lewis, John L., 229, 230
Liberal Party, 304
Liebling, A. J., 230
Lincoln, Abraham, 233, 308
Lindbergh, Charles, 193
Lindbergh, Charles, Jr., 193
Lippmann, Walter, 305
Lindsay, John, 302, 303, 311, 314, 316, 317–19, 341
Loeb, Solomon (DS's great-grandfather), 22
London Daily Express, 81, 84, 91
Luce, Clare Boothe, 312
Lucey, Archbishop, 307, 308
Ludwig, Emil, 151
Lyons, Leonard, 230, 303, 338

Mackay, Ellin. See Berlin, Ellin
Mackay, Clarence, 36
Mackay family, 55
Mafia, 331
Maginnes Kissinger, Nancy, 312, 326, 327, 328
Mailer, Norman, 88
Manchester, William, 303
Mann, Harrington, 13
Marie Harriman Gallery, 80
Marjoribanks, Edward, 88, 92
Marlborough, Duchess of. See Vanderbilt, Consuelo
Marlborough, Duke of. See Churchill, Jack
Married Love (Stopes), 63–64
Marshall, George, 234
Marshall, Mrs. George, 234
Marshall Plan, 212
Marta, Princess, of Norway, 173
Marx, Harpo, 104, 147
Marx, Karl, 279
Maxwell, Elsa, 294
May, Rollo, 242
McCarthy, Eugene, 253, 309, 310, 314
McCarthy, Joseph, 229–30, 250, 261
McGovern, George, 313–14
McKissick, Floyd, 306
McLuhan, Marshall, 297
McNamara, Robert, 283
Meadow Club, 64
Meany, George, 304, 313
Meir, Golda, 201, 227
Mercer, Lucy, 144, 146, 173
Metternich, Clémens, Fürst von, 328
Meyer, André, 313
Meyer, Matt, 275–76
M. M. Warburg & Company, 23
Montague house (London), 23
Montefiore Hospital, 107
Morgan, J. P., 50, 72, 81, 141

Morgenthau, Henry, 140, 151
Mortimer, Lee, 229
Moses, Grandma, 80, 323
Moses, Robert, 150, 221–22
Moses, Mrs. Robert, 222
Mount Sinai Hospital, 106–7
Moyers, Bill, 304, 305
Murrow, Edward R., 109
Myerson, Bess, 315

Nasser, Gamal Abdul, 257
Nation, 161, 177
Nehru, Jawaharlal, 145, 240
Neustadt, Siegmund (DS's grandfather), 23, 24, 101
Newhouse, Samuel I., 200
New Republic, 177
Newsday, 231, 250, 256
Newspaper Guild, 162, 164, 198, 207, 211, 212, 230, 322
Newsweek, 308
Newton, Maurice, 101
New York, 278, 342
New York *American*, 37–39
New York *Daily News*, 12, 15, 17, 156, 178, 193, 200, 256, 259, 267, 270, 275–76, 342
New Yorker, 95, 230
New York *Herald Tribune*, 175, 217, 253, 256, 267, 270, 271, 273, 274; merger with *Journal-American*, *World-Telegram*, 274
New York *Herald Tribune* Forum, 339
New York *Journal*, 37
New York *Journal-American*, 11, 267, 274, 294; *World, Tribune* merger, 274
New York *Mirror*, 267
New York *News*, 256
New York *Post*, 9, 11–17, 37, 80, 153, 161, 181 ff., 193, 243–44, 290, 296, 300, 301, 303, 305, 307, 317–18, 321, 328, 343; advertising, 217–18, 266; automation in composing room, 273; under George Backer, 161–64, 168, 175, 177–80; Bronx *Home News* purchase, 197, 200; columnists, 198, 214, 265, 278, 293, 305–6, 315; competition, 273–75; editorial policies, 161, 218, 228–29; founding, 12; investigative reporting, 221–22; labor disputes, 270, 273; move to *WJT* building, 276–78; newspaper strike (1962–63), 267–72; and Nixon resignation call, 330–31; presidential campaign (1960), 260–63; radio interests, 199–200, 204; under Schiff-Thackrey, 175 ff., 187 ff., 195–204, 206–7, 209, 211–13; under Schiff as sole publisher and editor, 214–22, 227 ff., 239, 245, 249, 250 ff.,

342–44; Schiff's column, 230–36, 237, 240–41, 257–59; separation of news and editorial departments, 265–66; tabloid format, 178, 198, *199*; value, 17
New York Post Foundation, 17
New York *Social Register*, 18, 27, 36, 37, 52, 53
New York State Constitutional Convention, 302
New York *Sun*, 177
New York *Telegram*, 176
New York *Times*, 12, 15, 17, 177, 178, 193, 267, 273, 342, 343
New York University, 338
New York *World*, 10
New York *World Journal Tribune*, 274–77, 278
New York *World-Telegram and Sun*, 267, 273, 274, 275; merger with *Journal, Tribune*, 274, 305, 306
Nixon, Richard M., 222, 258, 260–61, 263–65, 284, 311, 316, 317, 325, 327, 330–31
Norman, Dorothy, *252*
Northcliffe, Lord, 84
Northwood mansion, 18, *28*, 31, *33*, 42, 45, 60, 100, 109, 112, 113, 172
Norton, Jean, 95, 97
Norton, Marie, 73
Norton, Richard, 95, 97
Nhu, Ngo Dinh, 281

Obolensky, Serge, 10, 11, 70–72, 139, 224
Ochs, Adolph, 193
O'Connor, Basil, 140
Oil Fields mansion, 119 ff., 159, 168, 171–72, 174, 188
Onassis, Aristotle, 131
Onassis, Jacqueline. *See* Kennedy, Jacqueline
Oxford Union, 89
Oyster Bay, L.I., 18, *28*, 31–32, 34, 59

Palestine, 201–2
Paley, William, 147, 179, 216, 312
Paley, Mrs. William "Babe," 147, 210
Palm Beach, 64–67, 99 ff.
Paris *Herald*, 198
Parker, Dorothy, 108, 132
Patterson, Alicia, (Mrs. Harry Guggenheim) 180, 181, 204, 207–8, 223, *224*, 225, 226, 231–32, 250–51, 252, 256
Patterson, Joseph, 193, 200
Payson, Joan, 222
Peale, Charles Willson, 283
Peck, Gregory, 287
Perkins, Frances, 128
Peter, Paul and Mary, 287

Philadelphia *Record*, 161
Pine Hollow Country Club, 119
Pinter, Harold, 148
Piping Rock Club, 18, *33*, 37, 39, 70, 100
PM, 197, 206–7, 211, 220, 228
Poston, Ted, 221
Powell, Adam Clayton, 298
Powers, Bert, 269, 270–71, 273, 274–75, 276, 277
Pratt, Trude, 181, 194
Publishers Association, 259, 267–71, 273

Radziwill, Lee, 299
Radziwill, Stanislas, 299
Rayburn, Sam, 284
Rebozo, Bebe, 331
Red House, *154*, 168, 171, 172–74, 188, 333
Reid, Mrs. Ogden, 217, 253
Reston, James, 265
Richman, Harry, 55
Rockefeller, Abby, 34
Rockefeller, Happy, 301–2, 311, 324–27, 328
Rockefeller, Jay, 311
Rockefeller, John D., III, 311
Rockefeller, Nelson, 31, 257–59, 260, 264, 284, 310–2, 304, 311, 312, 316–17, 319, 324–25, 326–27, 328, 331, 341
Rockefeller, Mrs. Nelson, 302
Rockefeller Brothers Fund, 327
Rockefeller Center, 324
Rogers, William, 317
Roosevelt, Anna, 159
Roosevelt, Betsy (later Mrs. Jock Whitney), 159
Roosevelt, Eleanor, 129–30, 135, 140, 141–42, 144, 146, 151, 157, 158, 160, 169, 171, 181, 191–92, 234, 254–56, 334–35
Roosevelt, Elliott, 190, 334
Roosevelt, Franklin D., 11, 128, 129, 133, 134–35, 137, 138, 139–47, 150–60, 161, 162, 164–71, 173–75, 181, 182–86, 191–*96*, 222, 235, 240, 253, 255, 256, 262, 264, 266–67, 279, 281, 292, 306, 320, 328, 333–35
Roosevelt, Franklin D., Jr., 94, 303, 304, 320, 333–35
Roosevelt, Mrs. Franklin D., Jr., 192
Roosevelt, James, 151, 159, 228
Roosevelt, John, 335
Roosevelt, Mrs. Kermit, 255
Roosevelt, Mrs. "Rosie," 192
Roosevelt, Mrs. Sara Delano, 130, 134, 139, 140, 141, *142*, 143, 144, 145, 146, 194

Roosevelt, Theodore, 42, 145, 173
Rosebery, Lord, 74–75
Rosenberg, Anna. See Hoffman, Anna Rosenberg
Rosenman, Sam, 151–52, 154, 157, 167, 173, 185–86, 191, 194, 335
Rothschild, Carola, 117, 244
Rothschild, Mrs. Walter N. *See* Warburg, Carola
Rousseau, Henri, 80
Rumson Road estate, 18, 25
Rusk, Dean, 264, 307, 329
Russell, Bertrand, 107

Saarinen, Aline, 311
San Francisco *Chronicle*, 200
Sanger, Margaret, 107
Sann, Paul, 15, 181–82, 198, 201, 203, 211–12, 216, 221, 265, 267–68
Sarnoff, Robert, 286, 287, 288
Schiff, Adele Neustadt (DS's mother), 18, 19, 20–22, 23, 25, 27, 30, 32, 35, 36, 37, 40–41, 42–45, 49, 51, 53–55, 58, 61, 63, 65, 66–7, 73, 74, 75, 76, 78–79, 84, 87, 94, 99–101, 104, 108, 118, 122, 127, 186, 244, 337–38; the Brandt case, 37–39; death, 111, 112–13; disapproval of Richard Hall, 58, 60; funeral, 112; illness, 84, 96, 99, 102–3, 105–7, 109–11; and Sidney Smith, 46–47, 54, 56, 99–100, 106; her will, 113–14
Schiff, David (DS's nephew), 338
Schiff, Dorothy: and George Backer, 101–8, 113, 115–24, 126, 132, 146–48, *150*, 168–69, 177–80; and Lord Beaverbrook, 80–92, 95–99, 105–6, 118, 119, 132, 331–32; her birth, 25; birth of Adele, 63; birth of Mortimer, 63; birth of Sarah-Ann, 121; on Board of Child Welfare, 149; at Bryn Mawr, 19, 47–49; childhood, 25–41, 42–45, 50, 244, 323; column in *Post*, 230–36, 237, 240–41, 257–59, 294; confirmation, 45; daily routine, 12–17, 321; debut, 48, 50–54; and Democratic Party, 129–30, 133; dependence on others, 321–22, 336; description of, 9–11; divorces George Backer, 179–80; divorces Dick Hall, 109, 112, 114–15; divorces Ted Thackrey, 216–17; early education, 27–29, 32, 34, 47; editorial policy, 228–29; and entertaining, 323–24; her family, 18–25, 34–35, 42–43, 337–39, 342; and her father, 40, 73–77; and Sebastien Foy, 85–87, 88, 104–5; financial compensation, 17; and Richard Hall, 51–53, 54–55, 56, 58–59, 60–61, 61 ff., 96; and

Averell Harriman, 72–73; inheritance, 79; in Israel, 226–27; her Jewishness, 21, 23, 34–35, 36–37, 45, 116–17, 129, 136, 141, 341, 343; maiden name, 212; and money, 80; as a mother, 93–95, 121, 123, 170–71, 336; on her mother, 20–22; on national leadership, 331–32, 333; newspaper strike, 267–72; and Serge Obolensky, 70–72; ownership of *Post*, 161–65, 175 ff.; political influence, 235, 298, 299, 302, 306; and politics, 95, 128–38, 250–65, 279–320, 326–31; psychotherapy, 124–27, 132–34, 136, 137–38, 242; as publisher and editor of *Post*, 214–22, 227 ff, 239, 245, 249, 342–44; and Franklin Roosevelt, 135, 138, 139–47, 150–60, 164–70, 173–75, 181, 182–86, 191–95, 204; and Rudolf Sonneborn, 223–27, 236–49; and Jacob Schiff, 20; and Ted Thackrey, 175–86, 187, 195–203, 219; *World Journal Telegram* merger, 274–77, and World War I, 43–45

Schiff, Frieda (Mrs. Felix M. Warburg), 22, 23, 24, 117 *128*, *165*

Schiff, Jacob H. (DS's grandfather), 13, 17–20, 22–23, 24, 25, 28, 35, 38, 40, 41, 42, 48, 62, 72, 78, 81, 83, 84, 95, 106–7, 112, 113, 165, 258, 337, 339, 342

Schiff, John M. (DS's brother), 11, 18, 25, 26, 27, *28*, 30, 31, 34, 42–46, 51, 59, 73, 74, 76, 78, *79*, 94–95, 100–1, 108–9, 112, 113–14, 116, 117–18, 120, *128*, 129, 146, 164, *165*, 172, 177, 191, 199, 212, 238, 323, 337–38, 339

Schiff, Mortimer L. (DS's father), 18, 22–24, 25, 30, 35, 37–38, 40, 42–45, 49, 51, 53–55, 56–58, 61–62, 63, 64, 73–77, 78–79, *81*, 85, 87, 90, 95, 99, 101, 102, 109, 110–11, 112, 113–14, 118, 165, 219, 244, 263, 337

Schiff, Tee Tee (DS's sister-in-law), 27, 78, *79*, 339

Schiff, Therese (DS's grandmother), 42, 75, 112, 117

Schlesinger, Arthur, 290, 303, 306
Schlesinger, James, 330
Schine, C. David, 229
Schneiderman, Rose, 130–31, 259
Scripps-Howard newspapers, 274
Schurz, Carl, 161
Seldes, Gilbert, 63
Sevareid, Eric, 319
Shanghai *Post*, 176
Sheen, Fulton J., 235, 307
Sheppard, Eugenia, 274
Sherwood, Robert, 148
Shinnecock Club, 64

Shipman, Herbert, 60
Shriver, Sargent, 283
Simon, John (Lord Horder), 88, 98
Smith, Al, 19, 147
Smith, Consuelo Vanderbilt. *See* Vanderbilt, Consuelo
Smith, Earl, 62
Smith, Howard K., 286
Smith, Mrs. Howard K., 286
Smith, Jean, 299
Smith Sidney, 40–41, 46–47, 54, 56, 99–100, 106
Smith, Stephen, 299, 300
Snow, C. P., 136
Sonneborn, Rudolf (DS's fourth husband), 11, 223–27, 236–39, 241, 243, 246–49, 279
Sorensen, Ted, 303, 313, 342
Sorin, Savely, 71
Spellman, Francis Cardinal, 234–35, 301, 307
Spitzler, Robert, 15
Spivack, Bob, 232
Spock, Benjamin, 132
Stalin, Joseph, 183, 194, 203
Steffens, Lincoln, 127, 315
Stern, J. David, 161–62, 163–64, 200
Stevenson, Adlai, 200, 235–36, 250–54, 260, 282, 283, 284, 289, 299, 310, 336
Stewart, Donald Ogden, 132
Stewart, Mrs. Donald Ogden, 132
Stewart, William Rhinelander, 208
Stopes, Marie, 63
Stralem, Casimir, 101
Strauss, Lewis, 53, 75, 328
Sullivan, Harry Stack, 124–27, 132–34, 136, 137–38, 181, 242–43, 244
Sulzberger, Arthur Ochs, 342–43
Sulzer, William, 39
Suzy (column), 274, 294
Sweet, Mrs. Robert. *See* Hall Sweet, Adele
Swope, Herbert Bayard, 10, 64, 101, 104, 108, 128, 139, 162, 222
Symington, Stuart, 229
Szekely, Susan, 188
Szold, Henrietta, 202

Talleyrand, Charles Maurice de, 328
Taylor, A. H. P., 83, 87, 90, 97
Taylor, Maxwell, 293–94
Temple Emanu-El, 19, 76
Thackrey, Theodore (DS's third husband), 11, 175–86, 187 ff., 195–203, 214, 215–16, 218, 219, 220–21, 227
Thaw, Harry K., 23
Thayer, Walter, 267, 270, 271, 274
Thieu, Nguyen Van, 308
This I Believe, 109

Thomas, Norman, 250
Thompson, Malvina, 192
Titanic, 34, 40
Toombs, Henry, 154–56, 159
Tree, Marietta, 282, 284
Troy, Matthew, 315
Truman, Harry, 202–3, 207, 233–34, 258, 284, 308
Tully, Grace, *140*, 166–67, 191–92

Ulysses (Joyce), 63
Union Pacific Railroad, 72
United Nations, 239–40, 253, 304–5
Unruh, Jesse, 310
U Thant, 285, 287, 304–5

Valenti, Jack, 284
Vanden Heuvel, William, 303
Vanderbilt, Alfred, 173
Vanderbilt, Consuelo, 55–56, 60, 62, 64, 171–72
Van Doren, Carl, 34
Van Doren, Irita, 253
Vidal, Gore, 260
Vietnam, 283, 301, 305, 306–9, 312, 314, 320
Village Voice, 342
Villard, Henry, 161
Villard, Oswald Garrison, 161
Vladeck, Charney, 148–49

Wagner, Robert, 236, 268, 311
Wald, Lillian, 202
Wallace, George, 314
Wallace, Henry, 203–4, 207, 220
Wall Street Journal, 15
Wanger, Walter, 44, 101
Warburg, Carola (Mrs. Walter N. Rothschild), 22, 24, 34, 40, 54–55, 62
Warburg, Eddie, 62
Warburg, Felix, *128*, 129
Warburg, Frieda. *See* Schiff, Frieda

Warburg, Mrs. Paul M., 141
Warren Report, 295
Washington, George, 307
Washington *Post*, 176, 287
Watergate, 229
Wechsler, James A., 15, 17, 211, 219–21, 228–30, 233, 241, 243, 246, 262, 265–67, 283, 293, 310
Wechsler, Nancy, 246
Weizmann, Chaim, 175, 201, 227
Weizmann, Vera, 227
Wells, H. G., 88, 107
Wheeler, Burton K., 171
White, Stanford, 23
Whitney, Barbara, 59
Whitney, Joan, 31
Whitney, Jock, 31, 206, 222, 267, 271, 272, 274, 312
Whitney, Mrs. Jock. *See* Roosevelt, Betsy
Whitney, Sonny, 59, 73
Wicker, Tom, 317
Wilhelmina, Queen, of the Netherlands, 193
Willkie, Wendell, 194, 236, 252–53
Wilson, Woodrow, 145, 308
Winant, John, 255
Winchell, Walter, 229, 298
Windsor, Duke of, 293
Wise, Jonah, 112, 117
WLIB radio, 199
WMCA radio, 257
Wolff, Addie, 95
Women's Trade Union League, 130
Woollcott, Alexander, 104, 107–8, 113, 123, 146, 147, 169
World War I, 43–45
Wyatt, Wilson, 235

Young, Whitney, 306–7
Young Communist League, 230

Zilboorg, Gregory, 127, 207
Zionist cause, 223, 226, 239–41